# Britain's
## Great waterways outdoors

Phillippa Greenwood & Martine O'Callaghan

"The canal boat is right up there with the postbox
as one of the iconic images of British life."

Tony Hales. Chairman of British Waterways

Afternoon tea with strawberries and cream, cricket on the green, a friendly policeman when you're lost, the Queen's speech on Christmas Day, Elton John in the news, fish and chips in the rain, the song of a blackbird, a pint of mild over a chat in the local boozer. All resolutely as British as a conversation about the weather.

We Brits are rarely immodest enough to over-blow our own trumpets, yet folk beyond our shores somehow still know a few of the things of which we're most proud: our precious NHS, our silent condemnation of queue jumpers, sausage and mash, Morris Men, Blue Peter...

Yet the nation magnificently hides its quietest secret, out of sight from fuss and crowds. Beneath bridges, across the land, there lies a water world. Canals, tucked in leafy dips, hold a hush that tells visitors they are venturing into a different space: a sort of wardrobe adventure to a green Narnia, with boats! A unique linear haven, quintessentially British, defiantly unspoilt by progress.

our inland waterways - where Britain and Britishness remain inseparable
*Britain's best treasures...*

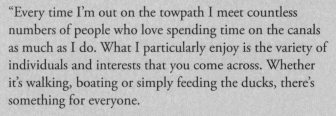

FOREWORD by

Tony Hales CBE
Chairman of
British Waterways

"Every time I'm out on the towpath I meet countless numbers of people who love spending time on the canals as much as I do. What I particularly enjoy is the variety of individuals and interests that you come across. Whether it's walking, boating or simply feeding the ducks, there's something for everyone.

In Cool Canals, Phillippa and Martine have managed to encapsulate all that is marvellous about our nation's canals. With modern life becoming increasingly hectic there's never been a better time to escape the rat race and grab a taste of the great outdoors. Luckily, you're never very far from a canal and even in the middle of London, Birmingham, Manchester or Glasgow, once you're by the water, life seems to slow down and an urge to gongoozle takes over!

I am constantly bowled over by the number of enthusiasts – from individuals to businesses and organisations - willing to give up their time and money to help keep them at their best. It was voluntary groups, led by the likes of the visionary Tom Rolt, that kick-started the renaissance of the UK's waterway network and it is these groups that provide the inspiration for the future.

In 2010 the Government announced its backing for British Waterways' proposal for its canals in England and Wales to be transferred from the public sector into a new 'national trust' for the waterways. The move, which will take place in 2012, will give a greater role for canal supporters and communities and create new opportunities to raise investment. The transfer will be the biggest shake up of the waterways since nationalisation in 1948 and we passionately believe it will transform the nation's canals, rivers and docks, and ensure they never again return to the decline and the dereliction of the last century.

Phillippa and Martine have summed up what millions of us have already discovered – the waterways are a national treasure. The more people we tell about it the better!"

**Dear all**

Since we first launched Coolcanals Guides, we've met so many people who share our passion for Britain's inland waterways. We've backpacked the canals from Cornwall to Scotland, and continue to seek out every tiny forgotten canal branch missed on the maps. Affectionately, we've been called waterways nomads, but that's not out of the ordinary since everyone who visits the water-road becomes an instant traveller. It's the nature of the place. And, once touched by waterways wanderlust, most people keep coming back.

On the water or along the towpaths, for a day, a week or longer, we are all pilgrims to a more peaceful pace of life. The waterways don't only belong to walkers, cyclists and boaters, they are a place for small businesses contained in narrowboats, pub landlords and ladies, traders and day trippers, charity organisations and rosy-cheeked volunteers. Our interests are diverse, yet the water-road binds us in a very special community with warm transient friendships and unaccountable camaraderie. Dissent and differences of opinion have their drums to beat of course, but the gentle culture of the waterways pervades with the common resolve to protect our precious waterways. In the current climate of government cuts, the waterways face testing times. But no matter what struggles present, with one voice we insist the future would be unimaginable without navigable routes and colourful narrowboats keeping Britain's priceless heritage alive.

We are all welcome, with just the polite request that the sacred 'slow' rule is never broken. Perhaps more than anything else, it's this simple slow mantra that makes the waterways community beat with one heart. A place where time matters, not for its race or deadlines, but for each moment to be savoured for nothing more than the splash of a duck, the glimpse of a kingfisher or the quiet nod from a passing stranger.

This guidebook arrives on a new tide for us all, as a new 'national trust' is forming to take care of our canals. And we are grateful to British Waterways, IWA, WWT, RSPB, SUSTRANS and all the people who care about our waterways who have contributed to this book. The enthusiasm of such diverse contribution is a monument to the immeasurable pleasure and pride that our nation's inland waterways bring to so many.

We hope this guide helps to spread the word about Britain's amazing inland waterways, our nation's priceless gem, and opens many doors to the first time visitor as well as uncovering some sweet surprises for old timers too!

Thank you all for your contributions.

This book belongs to everybody.
See you out there!

*Martine & Phillippa x*

There's a secret faraway place, close to home, where
life slows down and priorities reorder themselves.
People live here on boats and along the waterside,
others visit for a day, or a holiday, or a jog after work.
Together, it's a community that takes time to say hello
to each other and nod warmly to passing strangers.

There are over 2,000 linear miles of canals and rivers
meandering every contour of England, Wales and
Scotland. But these lazy country miles are more than
just water trails, they are an unhurried parallel world
hidden from the stress of urban life. Imagine a world
with no cars, without noise and chaos. Britain's inland
waterways are somewhere you can completely switch
off, ditch the daily grind and discover something
more peaceful and satisfying... seek out your own slow
adventures... unleash your inner tortoise.

There's plenty to be surprised by along these historic
water-roads, yet even simply getting outdoors by
water brings enforced balm, an escape, somewhere to
rediscover that the best things in life really are free.

A walk, a bike ride with the kids, a day out in the
open air or simply messing about in boats just for the
fun of it. It's easy to escape and find space to be alone,
with the comfort of knowing you can still find a warm
welcome at the waterside pub around the next bend in
the water.

Luckily the 9 to 5 world is too busy scurrying in a
craze to notice the canal peacefully ambling along.
The two worlds have different values, but don't need
Berlinesque walls – just a willingness from visitors to
enjoy the slow pace. The pleasure is immeasurable.
Foreheads un-crease as digital time loses its bearings
and folk turn to nature for the rhythm of the day.
Nothing needs to move faster than the morning flight
of geese... and woe betide any canal boater creating
shameful waves, or cyclist rudely speeding on the
towpath, for they trample the code that makes this
waterworld special.

So this guidebook is for you whether you fancy a spot
of sightseeing... wobbling away in a kayak for the first
time... letting your hair down at a waterside festival...
taking the family on that narrowboat holiday they'll
never forget... or simply finding a cosy waterside pub
where you can let the day slip away, unhassled by
time, chatting and sipping life to the full.

## ABOUT THIS BOOK

We hope you will enjoy reading and using this book whether you are visiting Britain's inland waterways for the first time or you are already a well-seasoned water traveller. Our guides are created for both the towpath tourist and the leisure boater... and the many of us who are both!

This is a practical guide to a fascinating destination, with handpicked highlights and hundreds of features to explore. And as everyone is having to tighten their purses, we've made sure there's loads of stuff to do that's absolutely free!

We went to the heart of the waterways to ask local people to share their favourite places in this book. The 'Great Waterways Outdoors' is a collaboration, with real-life stories from people who know the waterways best. We thank everyone who has been kind enough to contribute their amazing personal experiences.

# CONTENTS

# A brief history of the water-road
Britain is an island with water running through its history...

England, Wales and Scotland cohabit on this island... and the complete history of Britain can only be told by the water that flows full circle around them. At its most flamboyant, the seas and bold ships once drove the British Empire... and the coast still likes to shout about its old white-water tales. Yet quieter waters that reach inland hold the deep secrets of the nation. During the Industrial Revolution, inland waterways created vital trade routes for Britain's manufacturing business to dominate the world... And canals carried the 'Made in Britain' label to its highest peak.

Since time began, rivers and seas have aided and abetted invaders and defenders, and Britain has morphed into an island race.

As a nation, we once went outwards onto the seas to find new worlds. From the king's forests, Britain's great oaks made mighty royal ships that sailed arrogantly and adventurously to conquer the world and bring back rum, spices and stories. Trade routes romantically scurried the globe from sea to sea and then inland of our shores by river.

The importance of a city was once the size of its river. London had the Thames, Liverpool the Mersey and Bristol the Avon. But the arrival of the canals and the Industrial Revolution upset the status quo and a new urban geography changed the map. Factories erupted on the skyline wherever the canals linked raw materials and markets. Birmingham became England's second city, and the capital of the canals.

These new factories needed labourers and that led to the migration of people. Agricultural workers who belonged in Haywain landscapes were forced by poverty to climb into barges that would take them to new employment in the industrial towns of the Midlands and the North.

The brave new urbanism had its dark side, with Dickensian stories unfolding. The business boom was the entrepreneur's emancipation, yet the injustices of social and economic class often became the trials of life for the urban masses.

Canals cut deep cultural roots in their historic waters. They were built to function as a commercial transport system - and carved routes for salt, coal, iron, pottery, textiles and, revoltingly, even cargos of slaves in the early days. The outcome of their success changed the economics of the world forever.

Canals came before the motor engine, electricity, television and the internet... yet remarkably they have remained unspoilt by progress, unchanged in over two centuries, and still carry narrowboats uphill and downhill with unsurpassable, ingenious, jaw-dropping simplicity.

Before the great British tourist was invented, the nation's coastline was a place of undisturbed sands. The privy of fishermen and smugglers.

Holidaying as designated time 'away from home' was something the Victorians needed as an escape from the smog of their new urban lives. The 'factory fortnight' and 'Bank holidays' were going to stamp free time on the calendar.

Human nature is drawn to water, so it makes sense that an island's population would head for the coast. The railway era made the seaside accessible to the masses, and deckchairs and chip shops swamped the coastline, while the Victorians poked piers into the ocean and built promenades for seaside fun.

At the same time as the first trains carried holidaymakers to the seaside, commercial cargos were abandoning canal waters for speedier steam trains. Canal companies were being put out of business and the waterways were left to decay. Nobody seemed to care if they were lost forever. Victorians didn't see their disused water-motorways as a desirable place for leisure - it was too soon, just as if we closed the M6 today.

Generations later, no one missed those lost vulgar trade routes. That was, until 1939 when Tom Rolt took his narrowboat named Cressy on the now legendary journey that broke the rot. He cruised for pleasure, not haulage. His struggle to navigate neglected canals resulted in the foundation of the campaigning group now famously known as the Inland Waterways Association. The IWA gathered a voice through growing numbers of boaters who wanted to protect the canals and keep them navigable for boats. Rolt, a quiet but visionary man, had unwittingly become the founding father of tourism on Britain's canals.

Time away cruising the countryside by narrowboat, has now become a dream holiday. The canals have been heard and we love them again. The waterways no longer depend on the manufacturing trades of the Industrial Revolution - today its main industry is tourism.

With hindsight we can see that materialism had to be the prize and sacrifice of the Industrial Revolution. We measure national wealth by money and 'things', yet society and wellbeing are less quantifiable. We work hard and go shopping to anonymous malls for short-term gratification. But nature leaves us wanting respite. Holidays, days out, time off.

To escape from noise and distraction, we go to the waterways to find more satisfying stuff than money can buy. In an odd twist of fate, canals have become a retreat from the consumer mayhem they once helped create.

In sleepiest green England, Wales and Scotland, tourists willingly flock to the inland waterways - a haven away from it all. And even in unlikely parts of the Midlands and the North where mills and foundries once spewed over the skyline, relics of industry have transformed into tourist attractions too. From the water, industrial heritage is fascinatingly beautiful.

Now, when horse-pulled narrowboats nostalgically re-enact bygone scenes, British tourism shows its pride for the part canals played in Britain's history - and sightseers aren't shy to show their commitment to the waterways leisure we enjoy today... and the pledge for tomorrow.

# WATERWAYS TIMELINE

The history of an island is written by the waves that surround its shores... and the inland waterways that connect land to sea.

**CANALMANIA - THE ERA OF CANAL BUILDING**
The first fully manmade canal was the Bridgewater Canal, opened in 1761, and for the next half century the rivers Thames, Severn, Trent and Mersey were linked by narrow canals. At the height of Canalmania, there were over 6,000 miles of navigable rivers and canals scrambling across Britain's landscape - connecting mines and other raw materials, to factories, mills, and ports

**CAPTAIN COOK**
Born 1728 in Marton. His famous ocean-going vessel was the Endeavour

**THE INDUSTRIAL REVOLUTION**
Grips Britain and dominates world markets

**NAVIGABLE RIVERS**
During the 16th & 17th centuries, river navigation improvements began with the Thames locks and the River Wey Navigation. The River Wey was one of the first canalised rivers in England, built by Sir Richard Weston 1635-1653, allowing navigable waters for barges to transport goods to London

**THE DARK SATANIC MILLS**
Britain moved its workers from struggling agricultural labour into the new urbanism and its textile, pottery and iron-smelting industries

**THE MIDDLE AGES**
Estuarial rivers were used for transporting materials and goods

**THE GREAT ENTREPRENEURS PROSPER**
Josiah Wedgwood 1730-1795
Josiah Spode 1754-1827
Isambard Kingdom Brunel 1806-1859
Charles Rennie Mackintosh 1868-1928

**THE ROMANS**
The first to use inland waterways for linking routes from rivers

## 1500s 1700s 1800s

**WILLIAM SHAKESPEARE**
1564-1616

**BATTLE OF WATERLOO**
1815 Wellington victorious over Napoleon at Waterloo

**"LAND OF HOPE AND GLORY"**
1857-1934 Elgar's patriotic music marked an era of Canalmania, when the water routes had changed the fortunes of Britain and the lives of its population

**LUNAR SOCIETY**
Late 18C

**RAILMANIA**
The steam engine brings the arrival of the railways - making the slower canal systems old fashioned. Railmania took over and canals fell into commercial decline. 1829 George Stephenson's 'Rocket' made its first journey

**QUEEN ELIZABETH I**
1533-1603

**ABOLITION OF SLAVE TRADE**
1807

**QUEEN VICTORIA**
Came to the throne 1837

The humble navvy came armed only with his shovel and barrow; yet the cuts he made connected every corner of the land to the sea, and the world beyond. His labour drove The British Empire to peak in the early 1900s. Today the vestiges of empire creak apologetically at the edge of our island's history, yet remain glorious in the engineering heritage of Britain's canals.

**CANALS CLOSE**
Canals fall into disrepair and many are lost or become unnavigable

**THE RESTORATION YEARS**
Volunteers and organisations work together... building, campaigning, raising funds and protesting over DEFRA cuts

**2nd CANALMANIA**
Tourism on the canals booms. Narrowboat builders struggle to keep supply with record demand. The mod-con revolution of new fully-fitted boats with central heating, TVs and gadgets attracts a new era of boaters

**BRITAIN'S CANALS NATIONALISED**
1948 British Waterways became the governing body of the waterways

**BIRMINGHAM'S Brindley Place & LONDON'S** docklands were redeveloped mid 1980s

**WORLD WAR II IDLE WOMEN**
Women joined up to do their bit for the war effort working on canal boats carrying essential supplies along the nation's waterways. The women wore badges with the initials of the Inland Waterways, IW, which is how they got the nickname 'Idle Women'

**IWA**
Tom Rolt and Richard Aikman formed the Inland Waterways Association 1946

**NEW CHARITY STATUS**
British Waterways prepare to become a 'national trust' for the waterways

## 1900s

## 2000s

**RMS TITANIC SANK**
April 1912

**INTERNET REVOLUTION**
1980s-1990s

**FIRST WORLD WAR**
1914-1918

**FIRST MOTORWAY**
M1 opened 1959

**FIRST TV BROADCAST**
by BBC 1929

**SECOND WORLD WAR**
1939-1945

**QUEEN ELIZABETH II**
Came to the throne 1952

This book is a journey to uncover the best of every region in Britain where our inland waterways have shaped the landscape and people. Across the nation, each region has its own canal stories to tell. Tales about pots in Stoke-on-Trent, woolly sheep in Yorkshire, beer in Burton, World Heritage sites in Wales, and the Falkirk Wheel - one of Scotland's most visited tourist attractions.

Water is in Britain's psyche... an island where no one is ever more than 72 miles from the sea, and more than ½ of Britons live within 5 miles of an inland waterway.

End to end, our nation is a journey coloured by our love of different regions, and Pavlovian perceptions of social class and geography. The feistiness of brass bands from up North bellowing Corrie music over the rooftops of terraced houses, the deep-throated drum of Eastenders hovering over the map of London's river that can shout louder than Pat Butcher, the elbow-linking tum-te-tum-te-tum teum of straw hats and green wellies dancing around the maypole at Ambridge. Secretly, the canals are behind all these, as richly different as the regions through which they tread.

Britain is not a vast anonymous nation. It's intimate and bonded by the ability to travel coast to coast on a whim if you fancy. If you did, you'd notice how regions seem deliberately, or by coincidence, to take pride in local specialities that set them apart from the rest of Britain.

And not surprisingly, yet very quietly, the canals are behind much of that pride.

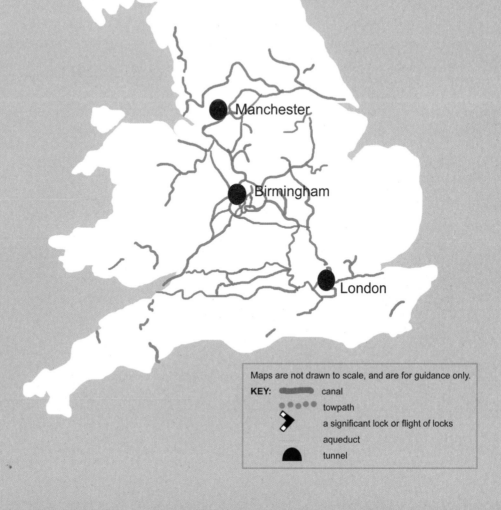

# Britain's canals
## HOW TO USE THIS BOOK

**USE THIS BOOK TO TRAVEL THE WATERWAYS. FOLLOW YOUR MOOD WHETHER IT TAKES YOU TO SOMEWHERE YOU'VE NEVER BEEN BEFORE, ON AN ADVENTURE TO THE HIGHLANDS OF SCOTLAND, THE FURTHEST EDGE OF ENGLAND OR JUST DOWN THE ROAD TO YOUR NEAREST LOCAL CANAL.**

There are over 2,000 miles of inland waterways, all with their own merits - and many canals we couldn't highlight in the space of this book. We've handpicked some of the best canals for their special qualities as a leisure destination.

Glasgow

Edinburgh

Manchester

Birmingham

London

Maps are not drawn to scale, and are for guidance only.

**KEY:**

canal

towpath

a significant lock or flight of locks

aqueduct

tunnel

# WEST COUNTRY

From sunny Somerset and its haystack landscapes, to Cornwall's craggiest coves, the West Country has got what it takes to be called 'chocolate-box' England. But no cliché is ample enough for this Celtic corner. Dorset, Devon, Somerset, Cornwall... the names speak for themselves, letting cream teas and visions of a wholesome lifestyle play in the tourist mind.

The weather savvy Brit knows the sun usually stays out longer in the South West than anywhere else on this island, so Britain's 'Riviera' reliably attracts holidaymakers in flocks. And the South West doesn't have to put on a fancy show for its visitors, it just has to be itself. The welcome is all the better for being effortless, with the ripe apples of Scrumpy land, barefoot beaches, mellow meadow walks and big brown-eyed dairy herds that stare at you.

This is the thin leg of England so, wherever you stray, you're never far from the coast. Yet the secret trick up the sleeve of the South West is that behind the great shouting miles of coast, there quietly lie hidden inland waterways too.

It's quietly pioneering to set off from the coast and head inland, following estuary trails and historic canals. Here, pleasure boats can potter on the safe waters of manmade canals, paying homage to the sea, just a breeze away from where ancient sailors met their fate travelling this beautiful and treacherous coastline.

The canal builders' plan was originally to create a safe inland waterway route linking coast to coast from north to south. But as money ran out before the complete trail was finished, fate left these short stretches of canal gloriously landlocked for us today.

So if the canal takes you by surprise as it spills onto a beach, take time to marvel over the meeting place between the mighty sea and passive inland water, with just a simple salt-battered lock gate. The forces of nature and the endeavour of man contain themselves in the moment.

# WATERWAYS
## of the West Country
boat, bike, boot

GLOUCESTER

BRISTOL

EXETER

## Highlights

GLOUCESTER DOCKS on the Gloucester
& Sharpness Canal - HORSE-DRAWN
BOAT TRIPS on the Grand Western Canal
- PURTON HULKS on the Gloucester &
Sharpness Canal - SEA LOCK on the Bude
Canal -TURF LOCK AND ESTUARY on the
Exeter Ship Canal

### Bridgwater & Taunton Canal

BRIDGWATER

TAUNTON

Taunton to Bridgwater
14 miles, 6 locks

Cut off from other canals, the Bridgwater &
Taunton Canal is a bit of a loner. Beyond its
resident boats, the only other boats here are those
that can be carried to the water. The absence
of slow convoys of narrowboats gives this canal
a different purpose and it finds novel ways to
intrigue visitors. There's the Space Walk, the
Mr Men Trail, and the West Country's long-
distance cycle trail keeping the towpaths alive.
And anyone who goes in late summer can vouch
for its thriving population of dragonflies. Small,
isolated, yet a dark horse often mistakenly
ignored by the crowd of canals elsewhere. If you
can, make the effort to find this one. (Don't miss
the prettiest bit in the middle).

### Bude Canal

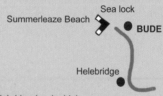

Sea lock

Summerleaze Beach        BUDE

Helebridge

Bude to Helebridge (navigable)
2 miles, 2 locks + sea lock

Sand in your toes and sea salt on your face.
This is the canal on the beach. Incongruously
positioned canal lock gates stretch over the
golden sands of a Cornish beach, allowing an
inland waterway to break the rules, tumbling
right into the sea. When the tide is out, the canal
lock gates are left stranded on the beach, and the
manmade canal has to wait for nature to bring
the sea to the canal. Come in seaside holiday
spirit, willing to hop in a paddle boat, slurp an

ice cream or just take a stroll along the little Cornish canal on the beach... oh, and bring your bucket and spade too!

## Exeter Ship Canal

EXETER

Double Locks

Topsham

TURF LOCK

Exeter Quay to Turf Lock, Exminster
6 miles, 2 locks inc. the double lock

The Exeter Ship Canal is detached from other canals, and stands alone with a lively Southern vibe. If you're after traditional canal boats and sleepy canals, you're going to be disappointed by this canal, but if you're ready for the real outdoors and an estuary-swept waterway, you're in for a treat. The wide straight water plays Pied Piper, picking up people in canoes, on bikes and in walking shoes. Everyone is heading to one place: the end of the canal and the Titanic experience it promises. The final sod of earth at the end of this short canal marks one of the most exhilarating points on England's canals. The Exeter Ship Canal and the estuary of the River Exe merge at an apex where the wind owns the distant sea and blows its story over a canal. Here, humdrum is flung to the wind and life is inhaled to the full, leaving canal pilgrims cleansed by the best of the waterways outdoors. English inhibitions loosen up visibly and, as the English would, we put a pub there!

A canal built to carry tall ships and, when it opened, it was the widest, deepest canal in the world. This bold, wide waterway is less quaint and less winding, yet more dramatic than most. What it lacks in traditional narrow canal charm, it resoundingly makes up for in its natural seduction. Slimbridge Wildfowl and Wetlands Trust, Purton Hulks boat graveyard, Gloucester's historic docks and the moon moods of the River Severn Bore all accompany this canal on its unforgettable journey. At Sharpness Docks the estuary slips gloriously into the horizon in a mournful, joyous moment of beauty that makes you want to spread out your arms and inhale history and nature.

## Grand Western Canal

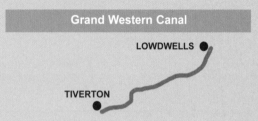

LOWDWELLS

TIVERTON

Tiverton to Lowdwells
11¼ miles, 0 locks

The entire canal is a designated Country Park and Local Nature Reserve. A linear treat stretching across Devonshire towards Somerset. Too short and landlocked to cater for canal boats on the mainstream cruising rings, but perfectly short and landlocked for the privileged few that cruise here. Anyone can hire a dayboat or take a trip on the horseboat, and the towpath tourist gets a taste of the best of the West Country's waterways.

## Gloucester & Sharpness Canal

GLOUCESTER

Saul Junction

Slimbridge

Purton Hulks

SHARPNESS DOCKS

Sharpness to Gloucester
16½ miles, 2 locks

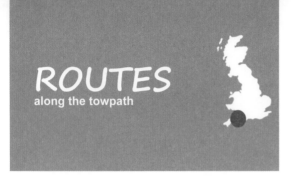

# ROUTES
### along the towpath

## SOME DESIGNATED TOWPATH ROUTES

### Bridgwater & Taunton Canal

**RIVER PARRETT TRAIL**
3½ miles (total trail 50 miles)
Follows the canal towpath from Fordgate Swing Bridge to Bridgwater Docks, before re-joining the river trail.

**SOMERSET SPACE WALK**
6 miles
Not just a canal walk, it's a tour of galactic dimension. There are models of the sun, its planets and our nearest other star in their proportionally correct sizes and distances apart.

**WEST COUNTRY WAY**
National Cycle Network (NCN) Route 3
Land's End to Bristol
Follows the canal towpath most of the way from Taunton through to Bridgwater.

### Bude Canal

**PLANEKEEPERS' PATH**
10 miles circular
Follows the canal from the sea inland to Helebridge, then continues along the line of the former tub-boat canal up two inclined planes before turning back across country to Bude.

**WEST COUNTRY WAY**
National Cycle Network (NCN) Route 3
Land's End to Bristol
Follows the canal towpath from Bude to Marhamchurch.

### Exeter Ship Canal

**EXE CYCLE ROUTE**
National Cycle Network (NCN) Route 2
Exeter to Exminster
Through Riverside Valley Park, Devon Wildlife Trust Nature Reserve, Exminster Marshes & the RSPB Nature Reserve.

**EXE VALLEY WAY**
6 miles (total trail 50 miles)
Follows the canal the whole way from Turf to Exeter before carrying on inland towards the source of the river.

**EXETER WOOLLEN TRAIL**
2 miles
A trail around Exeter discovering the importance of the woollen trade, which includes the quayside and canal.

**SOUTH COAST CYCLE ROUTE**
National Cycle Network (NCN) Route 2
Will run from St Austell to Dover (once fully open)
Follows the canal towpath all the way from Exeter to the Turf.

**THE TWO COUNTIES WAY**
6 miles (total trail 56 miles)
Follows the canal towpath all the way from Exeter to the Turf.

## Gloucester & Sharpness Canal

**SEVERN & THAMES CYCLE ROUTE**
National Cycle Network (NCN) Route 41
Will run from Bristol to Rugby (once fully open)
Follows the canal towpath much of the way from Slimbridge to Gloucester (though it is possible from Sharpness).

### Grand Western Canal

**THE TWO COUNTIES WAY**
11 miles (total trail 56 miles)
Follows the canal all the way from Lowdwells to Tiverton.

**WEST COUNTRY WAY**
National Cycle Network (NCN) Route 3
Land's End to Bristol
Follows the canal towpath all the way from Tiverton to Sampford Peverell. NB Please dismount to walk under bridges. Always give way to horses pulling the trip boat.

### More info

For more detailed information and maps of all National Cycle Network Routes, go to www.sustrans.org.uk

For more walks and trails, go to www.ramblers.org.uk

sustrans
JOIN THE MOVEMENT

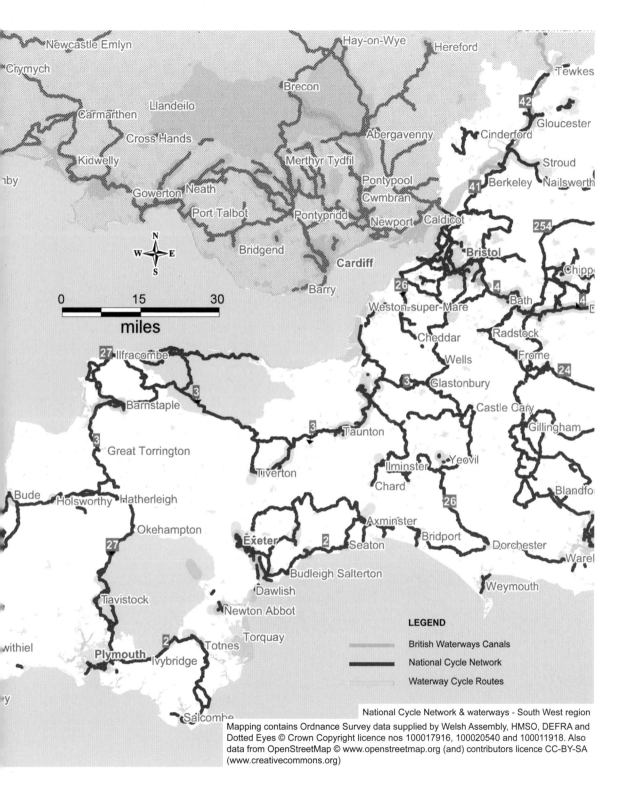

LEGEND

British Waterways Canals

National Cycle Network

Waterway Cycle Routes

National Cycle Network & waterways - South West region

Mapping contains Ordnance Survey data supplied by Welsh Assembly, HMSO, DEFRA and Dotted Eyes © Crown Copyright licence nos 100017916, 100020540 and 100011918. Also data from OpenStreetMap © www.openstreetmap.org (and) contributors licence CC-BY-SA (www.creativecommons.org)

# Routes
along the towpath

**JOIN THE MOVEMENT**

Jan Gannaway
Sustrans Volunteer Ranger

## My favourite bike ride
Bridgwater & Taunton Canal

"The Bridgwater & Taunton Canal is one of my favourite places to cycle. The path is level and mostly well-surfaced so the cycling is relaxing, giving me a chance to look around and enjoy the beautiful and tranquil surroundings.

On weekdays, the canal is usually quiet and undisturbed but at the weekends, especially in the summer, the canal is busy and I love to see families out on the towpath on their bikes having fun and enjoying the easy, safe cycling.
I look out for wildlife as I cycle or walk along and I try to log all my observations as part of a project to build up a picture of bio-diversity along the canal corridor.

I regularly call in at the Canal Centre and Café at Maunsel, about halfway along the canal, to talk to visitors and find out what they have recorded on the Wildlife Information Board - large numbers and great variety of dragonflies and damselflies, kingfishers, swallows and martins, birds of prey, otters and water voles, roe deer and many other species, all suggest that the canal is a healthy ecosystem as well as a lovely place to walk or cycle."

## Factfile

Start: Bridgwater OS ST298376
Finish: Taunton OS ST230253
National Cycle Network (NCN) Route 3
14 miles, 6 locks

### Highlights
Maunsel Lock Canal Centre

### Bike hire
**KING'S CYCLES** Short walk from the canal. Taunton.
T:01823 352272 www.kingscycles.co.uk

### More info
For more detailed information and maps of all National
Cycle Network Routes, go to www.sustrans.org.uk

l Near Maunsel Lock - From Coxhill
Bridge - Higher Maunsel Lock l

# Routes
## along the towpath

JOIN THE MOVEMENT

**Peter Grainger**
**Sustrans Area Manager**

## My favourite bike ride
**Exeter Ship Canal**

"I work as an area manager for Sustrans and have the job of extending the National Cycle Network and getting more people out on it by bike and on foot. Over the last few years we have worked with Devon County Council and the owners of this canal (Exeter City Council) to create a good wide path along its entire length. What better for families and others than a leisurely 12-mile round trip on a flat path with good pubs at each end?

The Exeter Ship Canal in Devon runs from a basin in Exeter, downstream alongside the River Exe for 6 miles to Turf Lock where it joins the tidal Exe Estuary. It was built from 1563 and extended over several centuries to enable large

sailing vessels to reach the heart of the city at any time, bypassing weirs and shallow tidal waters in the river. Like all canals it has a towpath, in fact two, one each side, as it is deep enough to take large boats that needed extra towing horsepower.

This route is part of National Cycle Route 2 along the south coast of England and locally will go right round the Exe Estuary.

The area is an internationally renowned wetland for birdlife all year round too, and attracts all types of boating on the canal and river.

On the other side of the Exe Estuary is the small historic town (they say they are not a village or part of the city) of Topsham. As long as it is not Tuesday or all weekdays in winter, you can break your ride down the canal with a small ferry crossing to sample the many eating and drinking opportunities there. Also the old lockkeeper's cottage there is just being opened up as a café and lodging. The pub at the Turf Lock end of the canal and Double Locks pub nearer Exeter are highly recommended.

At certain times of year, beware of swans nesting right by the path."

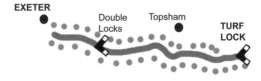

EXETER

Double
Locks

Topsham

TURF
LOCK

| Topsham - Topsham Lock
(disused) - The Turf |

## Factfile

Start: Exeter OS SX920920
Finish: Turf Lock OS SX963860
National Cycle Network (NCN) Route 2
12 miles return, 2 locks (inc. the double lock)

### Highlights
Double Lock + Double Locks pub
Turf Lock + The Turf pub
Topsham, across the estuary

### Bike hire
**SADDLES & PADDLES** On the quayside.
Exeter.
T:01392 424241 www.sadpad.com

### More info
For more detailed information and maps of all
National Cycle Network Routes, go to
www.sustrans.org.uk

# Routes
## along the towpath

**Phillippa & Martine**
Some of the highlights of our epic canal walk from Cornwall to Scotland

## Our favourite walks

The canals in the South West are mostly isolated from the main canal networks of England, so there are no busy cruising rings for long backpacking holidays. But the canals here are dreamily short, allowing nothing to cloud the basic pleasure of walking.

This region is perfect for daylong ambles under innocent skies that are a comfortable country mile away from traffic jams and urban nonsense.

Whenever we walk the waterways of the West Country, we go armed with a picnic, and our own permission to dawdle if the mood takes.

### A walk along the Bude Canal

The sound of seagulls overhead tells you the Bude Canal is different from other canals. It's the inland waterway that tumbles onto the beach. Mighty lock gates, with outstretched arms, hold the canal and the sea apart, shockingly, right on golden Cornish sands. When the tide is out, the canal is stranded, leaving the lock gates dry on one side. An incongruous non-meeting of two waters. Then, when the sea rides in over the beach, the Bude Canal can function again... until the moon decides to pull the sea back with the non-negotiable rhythm of time.

Starting a canal walk with your back to the sea is a novel experience. You set off stepping over lobster pots and dodging the temptation of ice-cream parlours. It's a seaside mood with the acoustic accompaniment of breaking waves and cool surfers screaming with fun. Heading inland, the canal retreats into greenery and calm.

The Bude Canal was built to carry mainly sand, limestone, coal and farm manures and, by 1825, 35½ miles of canal ran from the barge canal near the beach to the tub-boat canals inland. The railways reached Bude in 1898 and, within a couple of years, the waterways closed with most sections being sold back to the landowners.

Nature reclaimed the waterway, making it a haven for rare species of flora and fauna. The two miles from Bude to Helebridge have remained open and, over recent years, the Bude Canal Regeneration Project has drummed a battle to revitalise the canal. Now, oars, paddles and Cornish cream teas rest more in mind than narrowboats - and the towpath has been laid with easy-walking surfaces.

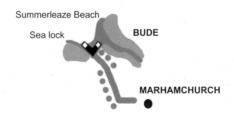

| Sea lock - Bude Wharf |

### Sea Lock

Bude Canal's sea lock is one of only two in the UK opening directly out to the sea and it's a Scheduled Ancient Monument. It was built to allow sea vessels into the wharf for trading and still operates today. The lock was set in a huge breakwater to protect and enhance the wharf area and has had to be refurbished and repaired many times, the most recent being in 2008 when a storm wrenched one of the gates off its hinges.

### Historic tub boats

Bude was the first canal in the UK (second in the world) to use water-powered tub boats. The canal was also the first in the world to use tub boats with permanent iron wheels. The boats needed the wheels so that they could be pulled on rails up the canal's six inclined planes (the most on any one canal). The boats were hauled up the inclined plane to the next level by chains driven by huge underground water wheels (all except one which used the gravity of huge water buckets). At the top of the inclined plane, the boats were refloated to carry on their way.

### Inland locks

At Rodd's Bridge, the towpath crosses over to the right side of the canal and continues towards the canal's only other locks, Rodd's Bridge and Whalesborough, with open views of the Cornish countryside. The two locks have been restored making this stretch navigable again.

### Wier

Just before Helebridge, where the River Neet and the canal merge, a weir off to the left is used to control the flow of water to the canal. At Helebridge, continue under the A39 and walk the last few hundred tree-lined yards to the site of the canal's first inclined plane to Marhamchurch.

### Low bridge

Watch out for the low bridge near the wharf. It was a brutish addition during the canal's redundant years to let cars cross the water, and since then has rudely restricted access to only low-lying boats.

## Factfile

### Bude
Start: Summerleaze Beach OS SS203064
Finish: Marhamchurch OS SS221036
2 miles, 3 locks

### Highlights
Bude's sea lock

### Did you know?
Summerleaze Beach is dog-friendly, although all dogs must be on a lead during daytime in the summer months.

# Routes
## along the towpath

### A walk along the Gloucester & Sharpness

We didn't immediately fall in love with the Gloucester & Sharpness Canal the first time we walked its wide grassy towpath. It strides with a Spartan-straight course, never narrow and cosy nor teasing with bends like some other canals. But the dynamics of this canal catch you unawares and, once smitten, it becomes a firm favourite.

Every way you turn, if you look twice, the water is sending clues about the past. But it's not only heritage that makes this walk fascinating. The canal is bursting with wildlife and birds making their way to the adjacent Slimbridge Wetland Centre. The River Severn Estuary clings to one side of the canal and changes the view with its tides. This is an ancient waterscape riddled with English history. The Gloucester & Sharpness Canal was built during troubled times when Horatio Nelson was fighting the Battle of Trafalgar, and Napoleon was losing at Waterloo.

When it opened in 1827, it was the world's broadest, deepest canal. Under the guidance of Thomas Telford, it was built as a bypass from the treacherous waters of the river Severn as far as Gloucester. Since Roman times, Gloucester had been an important port, but seafaring vessels that ventured inland too often met their end with the unpredictable sands and tides of the Severn. With the canal's help, Gloucester became Britain's furthest inland port where sea vessels could venture incongruously inland flagging high sails through the rural landscape. Cargoes from around the globe arrived by sailing ship, barge, narrowboat, tanker and steamship. During the Industrial Revolution, it carried grains imported to feed the hungry towns of the Midlands. And

in the 20th century, it carried cocoa beans to Cadbury's factory at Frampton on Severn where they were made into chocolate crumb and then sent on narrowboats to Bournville. The canal also played an important role in the economy of the Midlands carrying coal from Forest of Dean.

Sharpness Docks is the start of the Severn Way. The docks are blunt and not meant for tourists, which adds to the fascination. Old tram rails hide in the grass, chunky chains coil and rust, and what's not functional is ignored. But the estuary looks out to sea and softens the heart of the place.

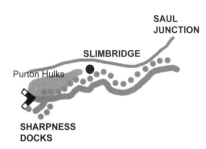

**SAUL JUNCTION**

**SLIMBRIDGE**

Purton Hulks

**SHARPNESS DOCKS**

### Severn Railway Bridge

The plaque by a round stone tower tells the story of the fate of the old Severn Railway Bridge. The bridge was built in the 1870s to carry coal from the Forest of Dean to Sharpness but in 1960 two tankers, blinded by fog, collided with one of its piers. The bridge was later demolished and the remains of the columns and the unfortunate tankers can be spotted on the river bed at low tide.

### Swing bridges

These are a feature of this canal as they allowed the passage of ships with tall sails. On the towpath, you pass the Rapunzelesque tower that once housed the steam engine which created power to open the swing bridge.

### Purton Hulks

A sand-dusted graveyard for boats, between the River Severn and the canal. Thought to be one of the largest clusters of historic wooden boats in the world (Days Out page 50-51).

### Shepherds Patch

Shepherds Patch offers a chance for a cuppa or a pint, or a visit to Slimbridge Wetland Centre (Days Out page 42-47).

### Frampton on Severn

To detour through the pretty village of Frampton on Severn, take the road or cross the field by Splatt Bridge.

### Saul Junction

Follow the towpath towards the busy hub of Saul Junction where the on-going restoration of the Cotswold Canals will one day reopen a link to the Thames.

The inland waterway rolls into the estuary at a huge lock where the scale of the untamed sea spreads out beyond. If you wanted, you could arrive by car, park in British Waterway's car park and do no more than watch the tide come in and go back out again here. The best viewpoint is on the edge of the estuary, where herds of lone souls gather to watch the tides. The waiting is wistful, and when tides come in the drama is quick. It's a Turneresque skyline with flat sand swirling in a wash of water and the Severn Bridge faintly in the distance. If you time your walk with the tides, you might see ships making their skilful approach from the river into Sharpness Docks.

## Factfile

**Gloucester & Sharpness Canal**

Start: Sharpness Docks OS SO667020
Finish: Saul Junction OS SO756093
8 miles, Sharpness Lock

### Highlights
Purton Hulks
Slimbridge Wetland Centre
Saul Junction

### Did you know?
To time your walk with ships coming into the docks from the Severn, find out the ship movements and tides from:
www.gloucesterharbourtrustees.org.uk

I Near Frampton on Severn - Site of
Railway Bridge - Saul Junction I

# ROUTES
## boating

## Some favourite boating routes

The deeper you wander into the West Country, the more tranquil it becomes. Narrowboats aren't always the most common canal boats in this region. The land-locked canals are perfect for small boats, and the Bude Canal even has rowing boats and pedaloes. The Exeter has its regular ferries too and the Grand Western is famous for its Horse Boat trips (Days Out). Although the Gloucester & Sharpness Canal is connected to England's main canal networks and does see some narrowboats cruising its water, it is most spectacular when it hosts the annual Tall Ships Festival (Days Out page 54).

The joy of the West Country's land-locked canals is that they can't get overcrowded. So if you can carry a boat to the canal, you're guaranteed a relaxing day messing about on the water... Perfect canoeing country. And it doesn't matter if you're a novice with paddles - canals never attack you with an unwanted white-water experience.

This is gentle paddling - and without an engine to spoil your fun, canoeing along the canals leaves you free to listen to the sounds of nature and the real peace of the waterways. Pack a picnic, or stop at the pub for lunch.

### Our favourite route for a pub lunch

The Exeter Canal, from the Quay to the end of the canal at the estuary of the river Exe - stopping at either (or both!) of the fabulous pubs on route. The Double Locks and the Turf are two of our favourite canalside pubs anywhere in Britain. Bank holidays and weekends throughout the summer can get quite busy with canoes, bikes and walkers on this canal... but the ambience is good-spirited and the wide-armed outdoor sociability is part of the fun.

### A great lock-free route to get away from it all

The Grand Western is an idyllic canal stealing its way from Somerset into Devonshire with the hush you'd expect. The route takes you through the country park and is completely lock-free (for safety reasons, never canoe through a lock). A good route for uninterrupted paddling... but watch out for the horse boat!

### Go on a canoe-camping break

After a full day's paddling, pitching a tent for a night under the stars has to be the cherry on top of the cake. The next morning, after a cuppa and a camp-stove full English, set off again to explore more slow waterways miles. The Gloucester & Sharpness Canal has a handy campsite along its route - with a pub next door.

---

## Factfile

**Grand Western Canal**

**PERMITS**
Boat users must obtain a permit before launching their boat or canoe. These are available from the Ranger Service, and from other outlets including Minnows Touring Park and Tiverton Canal Company.

Ranger Service T:01884 254072
Minnows Touring Park T:01884 821770
Tiverton Canal Company T:01884 253345
You can also download a form at www.devon.gov.uk

**Gloucester & Sharpness Canal**

**TUDOR CARAVAN PARK 4-PENNANT**
(David Bellamy Conservation Award - Gold)
Shepherds Patch. Canalside by Patch Bridge.
T:01453 890483 www.tudorcaravanpark.co.uk

# Boats
## in the West Country

**EXETER CRUISES**
Trip boat to Double Locks pub. Private charter also available.
Exeter. T:07984 368442
www.exetercruises.com

**SADDLES & PADDLES**
Single and double kayaks, open Canadian canoes. Also bike hire.
Exeter. T:01392 424241
www.saddlepaddle.co.uk

**SEA DREAM II**
Ferry from Topsham to Turf. Private charter also available.
Topsham. T:07778 370582
www.topshamtoturfferry.co.uk

**STUART LINE CRUISES**
Estuary cruises from Topsham and limited special cruises along the Exeter Ship Canal.
Exmouth. T:01395 222144
www.stuartlinecruises.co.uk

**TOPSHAM FERRY**
Ferry across the estuary from Topsham to the canal.
Topsham. T:07801 203338

**WHITE HEATHER**
Ferry from Double Lock to Turf.
Exeter. T:07806 554093

## Gloucester & Sharpness

**ENGLISH HOLIDAY CRUISES**
Hotel boat cruising the canal and the river Severn.
Gloucester. T:01452 410411
www.englishholidaycruises.co.uk

**GLEVUM BOAT HIRE**
Day boat hire.
Slimbridge. T:01453 899190

**GLOUCESTER WATERWAYS MUSEUM**
45-min boat trips run from the Waterways Museum along the canal. Private charter also available.
Gloucester. T:01452 318200 www. gloucesterwaterwaysmuseum.org.uk

**'PERSEVERANCE'**
Cotswold Canals Trust Trip boat.
Saul Junction. T:01285 643440
www.cotswoldcanals.com

## Grand Western Canal

**TIVERTON CANAL COMPANY**
Horse-drawn boat trips. Motor boat day hire, rowing boats and Canadian canoes. Teas & gift shop
Tiverton. T:01884 253345
www.tivertoncanal.co.uk

## Bridgwater & Taunton

**MAUNSEL LADY**
Trip boat. Charter trips available.
Maunsel Lock. T:01278 663160
www.maunsellock.co.uk

## Bude Canal

**BUDE CANAL BOAT HIRE**
Rowing boats and pedalos for hire from the wharf, near the sea lock.
Bude.
www.visitbude.info

**SHORELINE EXTREME SPORTS**
Canoe & kayak beginners' courses & Adventure sessions on the canal
Bude. T:01288 354039
www.shorelineactivities.co.uk

## Exeter Ship Canal

**ESSENTIAL ADVENTURE**
Full or half day canoe trips along the canal including some basic bush craft lessons.
Based at Totnes. T:01395 200522
www.essential-adventure.co.uk

**British Waterways**

The big canals on the cruising rings often steal all the attention whilst small canals cut off from the main networks can be overlooked.

Ian Powdrill lives on a boat and is passionate about his little canal that is so often overlooked or forgotten!

"I'm a waterway operative on the beautiful Bridgwater & Taunton Canal, where I live and work. We aren't linked to the rest of the waterway network, but our 14 miles of canal are still home to a great community of boats, a whole host of wildlife, walking, cycling and angling groups; we've even got our own canal Wardens and Volunteer scheme. The Bridgwater & Taunton Canal has a bit of everything - it passes through towns and countryside, it has quiet sections and busy bits, it has waterside pubs and trip boats, and it's home to the Somerset Space Walk."

Ian's enthusiasm proves size isn't any measure of a canal's credentials, and the waterways community in the South West definitely agree with him.

"One of my best days here on the B&T was when I received a customer award for helping at the Bridgwater Docks water festival. This was so well attended and I look forward to many more festivals here on the B&T."

# WILDLIFE & NATURE

## Wildfowl & Wetlands Trust – Slimbridge

**A great day out**

Forget neon lights, plastic hoo-hah and fake noise? Go to Slimbridge for a 'real' day out with the sort of living experience that doesn't leave you and the kids hollow after the event.

Slimbridge Wetland Centre is set within 325 hectares against a spectacular Severn Estuary backdrop. You can unravel in the satisfying fun of interacting with nature.

Go on a Land Rover safari or paddle along the canoe trail. Let the kids go wild in wellies, splashing through the centre's wet play area. Discover the world of ponds through a range of interactive activities, or just enjoy feeding the birds.

The site looks after endangered and rare species and has permanent residents, as well as welcoming all sorts of feathered passers-by. Spectacularly, it is home to the world's largest collection of swans, geese and ducks. There's something different happening all year round... Go once, and you'll want to keep going back.

## Factfile

**Gloucester & Sharpness Canal**

Slimbridge OS SO721047
Between the canal and the river Severn at Patch Bridge. On National Cycle Network (NCN) Route 41

Open daily all year (only closes on Christmas Day)
Nov-Mar 0930-1700 (Christmas Eve to 1530)
Apr-Oct to 1730. Last admission an hour before closing (Christmas Eve ½ hr)

Restaurant and gift shop.
Admission charge. Wheelchair access.

T:01453 891900
www.wwt.org.uk

**WWT**

## Bewick's swan

These elegant wild swans fly thousands of miles from their breeding grounds in Arctic Russia every year to Slimbridge Wetland Centre to spend their winter months here.

The founder of the Wildfowl & Wetlands Trust, Sir Peter Scott was the first to realise that each swan had a unique bill pattern and to recognise that this could be used to help protect the vulnerable species by recording their movements and number. He sketched and recorded the 300 or so swans which came each year to Slimbridge and this process is still used today for research purposes at the Centre.

Bewick's swans are smaller than the more common Mute swan and have yellow and black patterned bills. You can see the ones at Slimbridge being fed at one of the daily swan feeds at the Centre (4pm November to February).

## White-fronted Geese

The presence of white-fronted geese grazing by the banks of the River Severn first alerted Sir Peter Scott to the potential of Slimbridge as a place to showcase and protect the rich wildlife that thrived there.

Then there were 8,000 wintering on the site, now because of climate change less need to seek shelter here each year so numbers generally reach 500.

This bird will always hold importance for us at Slimbridge Wetland Centre as it led to this spot being chosen for the headquarters of the Wildfowl & Wetlands Trust, which now has nine sites in the UK and works globally to protect wetlands.

## Lapwing

This bird is as distinctive in flight as it is up close. With its crested head and striking plumage it is easily identifiable on the ground and perhaps even more so in the sky with its irregular flight. The lapwing is commonly associated with farmland and in many parts of the UK numbers have been in decline through lack of suitable habitat. The Reserve at Slimbridge Wetland Centre is carefully managed to create an ideal habitat for birds like the lapwing. The site can be bustling with up to 10,000 wintering there - and also about 30 breeding pairs there in the summer.

# Wildlife & Nature

Dave Paynter
Reserve Manager
WWT Slimbridge

Dave Paynter has been working at WWT's reserve at Slimbridge for nearly 28 years. He's seen much change at the centre and has observed the subtle changes that have developed in its relationship with both the River Severn and the Gloucester & Sharpness Canal.

He is responsible for 750 sq. acres of wild area bordered by river and canal, and has daily contact with both waterways which provide a positive impact on the life of the centre.

Slimbridge has a particularly close relationship with the Severn Estuary. The huge tidal range of the river encourages growth of Atlantic Salt Pasture which provides ideal grazing grounds for geese. Dave's work also brings him into close contact with the canal. The vast majority of the water used by the reserve is drawn from the canal so it's a vital part of daily life of the wetland habitat.

The history of the canal is an example of habitat regeneration - when the canal was built in the late 18th century, it created a barrier between the rivers flowing off the Cotswold Escarpment and the River Severn with an effect of draining the natural wetland habitat. Nowadays the regenerated wetland relies heavily on the canal to survive and flourish.

The centre has close ties with the canal. Of course, as all who visit this marvellous place will testify, the swing bridge across the canal is not always immediately accessible as narrowboats make their steady way up and down the canal, requiring the opening of the bridge for them to pass through. The canal, once the widest and deepest in the world, also acts as a settling tank for silt, so the quality of water leaving the canal and entering the wetland habitat is very high. The health of the canal has improved greatly since Dave has been at Slimbridge. This is reflected not only in the cleanliness and clarity of the water but also in the species that now populate the waterway. Arrowhead, a broad-leaved plant to which ducks are particularly

## Wigeon

The most common duck at Slimbridge Wetland Centre, the wigeon arrives in great numbers for the winter months. When numbers peak in mid-winter, there can be as many as 7,000 of the dabbling duck on the Reserve. This species is a high arctic breeder nesting alongside the Bewick's swans and white-fronted geese in Arctic Russia. Its favourite food at Slimbridge is grass and areas of grassland adjacent to open water are carefully managed as wigeon lawns to maximise grazing.

partial, is now widespread on the canal and is a very good indicator of a healthy habitat.

Wildfowl and small mammal populations have also grown in numbers over the past few years and Dave is particularly pleased to see water voles flourishing and smew and scaup (two species of duck) occasionally in the area.

The canal has proved itself as an ideal winter refuge in recent years. With cold spells freezing the lakes at Slimbridge, birds have used the nearby canal to shelter and to feed in its deep water, which rarely freezes. Kingfishers in particular, feed on the canal but nest on the reserve, demonstrating how the canal is integrated into the landscape.

Dave sees these positive developments as encouraging indicators for the future of the waterways local to Slimbridge. He sees education

and conservation as vital to the development of the area as a sustainable habitat in which the canal is an integral feature. It is both a leisure facility and a flourishing ecosystem. He also welcomes the recent cancellation of the Severn Barrage consultation. A full barrage would have changed the nature of the reserve forever with the disappearance of the Atlantic Salt Pasture and a return to cattle pasture right up to the estuary. He is quietly pleased that the full barrage is no longer on the agenda.

### Which part of Dave's job has given him the most fulfilment?

Without hesitation Dave points to the transformation of farmland into a wetland habitat of great variety and richness. Habitat re-creation that encompasses the great river to the west, the canal to the east and his wetland workplace in the centre.

# Wildlife & Nature

### Grand Western Canal

The entire canal, a Country Park, is also a designated County Wildlife Site and Local Nature Reserve. Some of the common species enjoying the habitat include moorhens, kingfishers, reed warblers, badgers and otters. The Canal Ranger Service also runs several 'bat walks' each year.

T:01884 254072
www.devon.gov.uk/grandwesterncanal

### Exeter Ship Canal

**The Old Sludge Beds, between the canal and the river Exe just outside Exeter, used to be the final process for treated sewage sediment but the former settling lagoons were dug out to create ponds and reedbeds which have now become a haven for wetland birds.**

www.devonwildlifetrust.org

## Bude Canal

**Bude Marshes Local Nature Reserve**
Alongside the canal, Bude Marshes is the fourth largest area
of reed in Cornwall and was the first area in the county to be
declared a Nature Reserve. Apart from acting as a natural
flood defence, it's also an important habitat for breeding birds
such as reed warblers and migrating birds such as bitterns.
Otters also love this combination of canal, river and marsh.

# DAYS OUT

in the West Country

## PURTON HULKS

A whispering graveyard of boats, thought to be one of the largest clusters of historic wooden boats in the world. The first boat was dumped at Purton in 1909 after a landslip between the river Severn and the canal near Purton caused the canal to empty its water. To slow down further erosion, retired vessels were towed to the banks of the river and beached for over half a century. They've wallowed there ever since, in the smells of wet sand and grass. Years of tides have taken their toll on the beached wrecks, and the landscape has grown in and out of the bones of the boats. Tufts of grass sway in silence over still boat carcasses that stand like statues of soldiers in an empty battlefield. Visitors catch an unmistakable spirit that sweeps the landscape. Whatever the weather, the wind always blows.

## Factfile

**Purton Hulks**
Between the river Severn and the Gloucester & Sharpness Canal.
OS SO687044

Park or moor near Purton Lower Bridge. Walk towards Sharpness and leave the towpath at any point from there.

There are no barriers or admission charges - simply visit and respect the environment.

www.friendsofpurton.org.uk

# Days out
in the West Country

## CREAM TEA

The West Country is Mother Nature's patch for scrumptious good produce. Fertile and sunny, it's where the grass grows greener and the cows are creamier.

Spring arrives notoriously early in the South West and so do the visitors, all drooling for the promised treat of a Devon Cream Tea. A dollop of clotted cream, a pot of jam, a freshly cut scone and a pot of hot tea of course.

Britain being Britain, there's etiquette involved in the real cream tea. Strawberry jam, not raspberry. A split scone with clotted cream and no butter. Served with a well-brewed pot of tea and never hurried. Oh, and strictly speaking, afternoon tea is between 3 and 5pm.

Devon's cream teas have a long tradition and local historians claim the whole ritual began with the monks of Tavistock's Benedictine Abbey. It's

said that when workers graciously helped them by repairing their building, the monks chivvied them with a platter of clotted cream, scones and preserves. When the monks saw how popular their offerings were, they decided to treat passing travellers to the feast too. The Devon Cream Tea had been born... and passing travellers have been coming in eager droves ever since.

### Ducks' Ditty at Tiverton Wharf

A floating cream tea on Devon's own waters is even more special. Expect more than a quick cuppa with the ducks when you climb aboard the Ducks' Ditty, a barge café-bar. A Tivertonian Cream Tea is to drool for: 'One freshly baked Scone, halved and topped with Clotted Cream and Strawberry Jam, with a wedge of home-baked Sponge Cake and a cup of tea.'

Tables spread out across the grassy towpath, and there's plenty of waterside activity to watch as the horse-drawn boat comes and goes. There are day boats, rowing boats and Canadian canoes for hire and a tiny canalia shop just along the towpath.

### Horse-drawn boat trips

Step back in time - go on the Tivertonian, a horse-drawn boat, and glide peacefully along the water with genuine horsepower.

### Factfile
**Grand Western Canal**
Tiverton Wharf SS963123

Tiverton Canal Company & Ducks' Ditty Floating Café Bar
Day/rowing boats May-Sep when ticket office is open.
Horse-drawn boat Apr-Sep. Trips and timings vary.
T:01884 253345 www.tivertoncanal.co.uk

# Days out
## in the West Country

## Bridgwater & Taunton Canal

### MAUNSEL LOCK CANAL CENTRE
Displays about the history of the Bridgwater & Taunton Canal. Boat trips on the Maunsel Lady, and a Tearoom with views over the canal. A good starting point for the Somerset Space Walk, with Mars right next to the lock.

Maunsel. OS ST307297

Wheelchair access to the building.

T:01278 663160 www.maunsellock.co.uk

### SOMERSET BRICK AND TILE MUSEUM
Explores the history of the brick and tile industry in Somerset, which had such influence on the look of the county's buildings today. Demonstrations of the skills involved.

Bridgwater. OS ST300375

Open Tue-Thu 1000-1600 (opens other days for groups by arrangement). FREE admission.

T:01278 426088 www.somerset.gov.uk

## Bude Canal

### CASTLE HERITAGE CENTRE
Exhibitions, archive library, shop & restaurant.

Bude. OS SS203064

Open daily Easter-Oct 1000-1700, rest of year to 1600. Admission charge. Wheelchair access.

T:01288 357300 www.bude-stratton.gov.uk

### THE BUDE LIGHT 2000
A celebration of both the Millennium and the discovery of the 'Bude light' by Sir Goldsworth Gurney. The 30ft-high concrete cone is coloured in sections to represent sand, sea and sky, including planets and constellations. Lit by fibre-optic cables from within (the first large-scale public sculptiure of its kind to do so), the cone comes alive at night.

Bude. OS SS203064 (In the grounds of the Castle)

## Exeter Ship Canal

### QUAY HOUSE VISITOR CENTRE
An exhibition with audiovisual displays of the history of Exeter's woollen industry and the canal. The Visitor Centre is in a former warehouse built in the 1680.

Exeter. OS SX920920

Open daily Apr-Oct 1000-1700, Nov-Mar Sat-Sun 1100-1600. FREE admission. Gift Shop.

T:01392 271611 www.exeter.gov.uk

## Gloucester & Sharpness Canal

### GLOUCESTER WATERWAYS MUSEUM
Find out all about the heritage of Britain's waterways and Gloucester Docks. The museum is in a Grade I-listed former warehouse with exhibits on wildlife, boating, touch-screen and interactive displays, and floating boats to explore. The National Waterways Archive is also housed here and can be visited by prior appointment only.

Gloucester Docks. OS SO827183

Open daily all year 1100-1600 (Jul-Aug 1030-1700). Closed Christmas Day, Boxing Day and New Year's Day. Admission charge. Café next door to the museum. Gift shop. Wheelchair access (except to floating exhibits).

T:01452 318200 www.gloucesterwaterwaysmuseum.org.uk

### TALL SHIPS FESTIVAL
Brings a taste of maritime history back to Gloucester Docks. Tall ships, family entertainment, shopping and food.

Gloucester Docks. OS SO827183

Held mid August in the heart of the Docks.

T:01452 396572 www.thecityofgloucester.co.uk/tallships

### PURTON HULKS
(Days Out page 50-51)

### SLIMBRIDGE
(Wildlife page 42-47)

## Grand Western Canal

### TIVERTON CANAL COMPANY & DUCKS' DITTY FLOATING CAFÉ BAR
(Days Out page 52-53)

# FOOD & DRINK

## Pubs

in the West Country

### Bridgwater & Taunton Canal

**BELL INN**
Short walk from the canal in typical Somerset village.
Creech St Michael.
T:01823 443703

### Bude Canal

**BRENDON ARMS**

Canalside by Falcon Bridge. Run by same family since 1872. Free House with West Country ales and a warm welcome.
Bude. T:01288 354542
www.brendonarms.co.uk

**FALCON INN**
Grandiose setting in Falcon Hotel, canalside by the bridge.
Bude. T:01288 352005
www.falconhotel.com

### Exeter Ship Canal

**DOUBLE LOCKS**
Canalside by the Double Lock. Cosy scrubbed wood, real fires, real ales and fab food. Huge garden with BBQs in summer. Dogs welcome.
One not to miss
Exeter. T:01392 256947
www.doublelocks.com

**ON THE WATERFRONT**
It's all in the name! Bar restaurant in a converted warehouse on the quayside. Known for their huge pizzas.
Exeter. T:01392 210590
www.waterfrontexeter.co.uk

**THE TURF**

Fantastic setting that can only be reached by boat, bike or boot, as this is one of only a few pubs in UK which you can't drive to (parking ½ mile). Local real ales, great food, dogs welcome. Another not to miss!
By Turf Lock. T:01392 833128
www.turfpub.net

### Gloucester & Sharpness

**THE BELL INN**
Worth the short walk from Fretherne Bridge. On the edge of the longest village green in the UK. Earthy finesse & good ambience with 4-star rooms.
Frampton on Severn.
T:01452 740346
www.thebellatframpton.co.uk

**TUDOR ARMS**
Canalside by Patch Bridge and perfectly placed for visiting Slimbridge Wildfowl & Wetlands Trust. 3-star rooms and award-winning campsite next door.
Shepherds Patch. T:01453 890306
www.thetudorarms.co.uk

### Grand Western Canal

**THE GLOBE INN**
Short walk from canal. Guest rooms available.
Sampford Peverell. T:01884 821214
www.the-globeinn.co.uk

# Teashops
## in the West Country

### Bridgwater & Taunton Canal

**MAUNSEL LOCK TEA SHOP**

Canalside by Maunsel Lock. The teashop is part of the Canal Centre with canal info and boat trips. Cream teas, sandwiches & homemade cakes Large outside area overlooking the canal. North Newton. T:01278 663160
www.maunsellock.co.uk

### Bude Canal

**THE BRASSERIE**

Canalside at the wharf. Restaurant and café. Sells ice creams too.
Bude. T:01288 355275

**CASTLE RESTAURANT/TEAROOM**
In the Castle Heritage Centre, at the wharf. Museum & gift shop.
Bude. T:01288 350543
www.thecastlerestaurantbude.co.uk

**LIFE'S A BEACH**
Café/restaurant overlooking Summerleaze Beach.
Bude. T:01288 355222
www.lifesabeach.info

**WOODLANDS TEA ROOMS**
Short walk from the canal.
Helebridge. T:01288 361317

### Exeter Ship Canal

**THE COFFEE CELLAR**
In a former warehouse right on the quayside.
Exeter. T:01392 410000
www.coffeecellar.co.uk

### Gloucester & Sharpness Canal

**CASTLE RESTAURANT**
Canalside near Parkend Bridge.
Parkend. T:01452 720328

**SLIMBRIDGE BOAT STATION
(THE BLACK SHED)**

Canalside near Patch Bridge. Homemade cakes and lunches. Large patio for watching boats go by. Boat & bike hire and shop.
Nr.Slimbridge. T:01453 899190

**THE STABLES CAFÉ**
Canalside near Sandfield Bridge. Large terrace overlooking the canal.
Saul Junction. T:01452 741965
www.thestablescafe.co.uk

### Grand Western Canal

**CANAL TEA ROOMS**
Canalside in the wharf.
Tiverton. T:01884 252291

**DUCKS' DITTY**

Floating Café Bar in the wharf. Tivertonian cream teas, snacks and drinks served by staff in 19th-century costume. Horse-drawn boat trips, boat hire & gift shop.
Tiverton. T:01884 253345
www.tivertoncanal.co.uk

For listings of waterside pubs & teashops in the UK, visit our website:
www.greatwaterwaysoutdoors.com

# WATERWAYS LIFE
## The story of tea

**"A nice cup of tea?"**

Office workers, nurses, road diggers, factory folk, shop assistants, clergy, builders, housewives, househusbands, the Prime Minister and all Britain grinds to an instant halt at the kettle-call. Everything stops for tea!

The immaculate break. "Cup of tea?" "Another one?"

Tea is the miraculous cure, the celebration, and the traditional displacement activity to gather ourselves, as we pop the kettle on when visitors drop by. It has seen us through wars, comforted us at funerals, slurped solidarity into group meetings and bonded us in front of the telly in our slippers. The simplicity of 'putting the kettle on' peculiarly binds us as a nation.

## Factfile

### The ships that brought tea to Britain

The Cutty Sark is the last surviving and most famous Tea Clipper in the world. The ship is preserved at Greenwich.

The Cutty Sark was launched from the Clyde in 1869 and set off on her first voyage in 1870 on a journey from London to Shanghai via the Cape of Good Hope.

www.cuttysark.org.uk

### Take a cruise along the Thames

www.thamesclippers.com
www.thamesriverservices.co.uk

In the 17th century, gin and ale were the most popular drinks. Clean piped water was the masterpiece of the Victorians. Before that ale and gin were safer to drink than impure water. When the canals brought chests of tea inland to the people, water was boiled, and the era of tea drinking began.

### When did tea first arrive in Britain?

A Portugeuse Jesuit, Father Jasper de Cruz introduced tea to Europe in 1560. China has been drinking tea for over 5,000 years, but the first reference to tea in Britain was recorded in 1658 in a London newspaper, Mercurius Politicus, when an advert announced that a 'China drink' was on sale at a coffee house in the city. Coffee houses were established in the city around 1652, but tea didn't become popular until King Charles II married a Portuguese princess who happened to have a passion for tea. She introduced tea to royal circles, and inevitably the well-off concentric was bound to fashionably follow suit.

Boatloads of tea started to arrive in the ports of Bristol and Gloucester, transported inland by canal boats and, by the mid-1800s, afternoon tea had become mandatory etiquette. Tea was expensive and desirable, and brought all the way from China to be poured elegantly from China tea pots. Tea was the bastion of rigid social class (a fat mug of tea for the workers would have been obscenely unthinkable!) In 1851 Anne Corbett wrote in the publication 'The English Housekeeper' that "tea, like sugar and wine, should be kept locked up to remove temptation from the servants".

Yet tea grew to be obligatory for wellbeing, whatever a person's social class. The poor would brew their cuppa from the cheapest blends, often with reused leaves and even bulked up with leaves from British trees. Things improved for the poorer folk when in the 1870s teas began to arrive from India and Ceylon which were less expensive. The next chapter in the story of tea is stamped in the British way of life.

Today Britain wants its tea in tea bags that come round, square, triangular, in family-sized boxes, with Fair Trade symbols... then there's Earl Grey, black teas, green teas, white teas, herbal teas and fruit teas. Supermarkets allot shelves full of choice today, and daily life without the punctuation of a cup of tea would be an uncomfortable affair for most of us Brits.

**THE OLDEST TEASHOP**
Twinings' tea shop 'The Golden Lyon' is the oldest in Britain, opened in 1706, on the Strand, London. It now has a small museum at the rear.

www.twinings.co.uk

I Festival teapots - Kizzie's, Lower Heyford, Oxford Canal - Gloucester Museum I

# SOUTH

The south shouts loudest about its city, London, the nation's number one tourist destination. It's where the Queen lives and where English history is still in the making. Buckingham Palace is the place where the public squashed their noses on the railings to grieve Diana's death, celebrate Her Majesty's birthday, catch a glimpse of the princes, protest with anti-fox hunting banners, and watch the changing of the guard.

The first city is renowned for cosmopolitan buzz and ranked amongst the best cities in the world for its energy, and the lure of the South Bank and the water always pulls the crowds. The River Thames bows through the city with a waterside show of iconic sightseeing from the Houses of Parliament, Big Ben and the London Eye to Tate Modern, the Globe and St Paul's Cathedral.

Then there's Camden's markets and the famous canal lock where London glows with colourful street cred, and further on its way to little Venice, the Regent's Canal can show off more regally. Since Roman times, London has been a vital port and in 1802 the West India Company built the first dock on the Isle of Dogs to allow ships to bring rum, sugar and coffee to a country ready for new pleasures and riches. The docklands today have been transformed for the leisure industry and businesses far removed from the seas. But Canary Wharf keeps history alive in its name.

London might be the big cheese, but it is not the only flavour of the south. There's the South Downs, the New Forest, Brighton, all brazen with tourist appeal. Yet constantly, water is the linking feature of the south. Where the Thames runs out, the canals take over. The Oxford Canal leads to the seat of learning, the Grand Union Canal connects London with Birmingham, and the Kennet & Avon Canal heads to the big apple of Bristol, magical Wiltshire and the indomitably touristy Cotswolds. The lost Cotswold Canals are under ambitious restoration, with the determined hopes of many wanting to see the waterway link between the Thames and the Severn again... to complete the story of the south.

# WATERWAYS
## of the South
boat, bike, boot

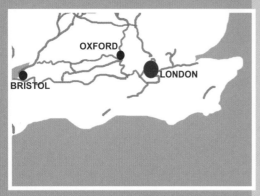

OXFORD

LONDON

BRISTOL

## Highlights

BRAUNSTON village on the Grand Union
Canal - CAEN HILL LOCKS on the Kennet
& Avon Canal - DUNDAS AQUEDUCT
on the Kennet & Avon Canal - HATTON
LOCKS on the Grand Union Canal -
LITTLE VENICE, LONDON on the Regent's
Canal - STOKE BRUERNE village on the
Grand Union Canal - VALE OF PEWSEY on
the Kennet & Avon Canal

### Basingstoke Canal

WOODHAM
JUNCTION

Mychett

WOKING

GREYWELL
TUNNEL

Greywell Tunnel to Woodham Junction
31 miles, 29 locks

A lush green canal that has become a haven
for wildlife. And among its peaceful features
are a large number of concrete bunkers used in
World War II to defend against invaders. Due to
the partial collapse of Greywell Tunnel and its
subsequent abandonment, it is now home to the
largest colony of bats of any known location in
Britain.

### Grand Union Canal

BIRMINGHAM

Shrewley
Tunnel

Stockon Locks

Hatton Locks

Blisworth Tunnel

Braunston Tunnel

MILTON
KEYNES

LONDON

London to Birmingham
137 miles, 166 locks

The waterway that links London to Birmingham,
with a few adventures along the way. A bold
route that was built to travel from the capital of
England to the capital of the canals. Arguably,
not the quaintest lock gates or winding
backwaters, but definitely some magnificent
places of interest along the way (such as Stoke
Bruerne, Hatton and Braunston). The Grand

Union Canal never lets you forget that the purpose of its water is the route it takes. Luckily, the M1 is out of sight and mind for most of the way - the Ugly Sister left to stomp with road rage, too brutal to understand the sparkly-slippered waterway going its own quiet route.

## Kennet & Avon Canal

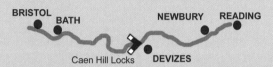

BRISTOL
BATH
NEWBURY
READING
Caen Hill Locks
DEVIZES

Reading to Bristol
93 miles, 104 locks

A canal that has everything. From Bristol to Bath, sweeping through Wiltshire and eventually meeting the River Thames. A buzzing beauty almost every step of the way. This generous canal shares its gifts in uncontrived flamboyance, as the White Horse of Wiltshire wafts magic over a superior waterscape. The Kennet & Avon Canal is even home to the mighty Caen Hill lock flight, one of the 7 wonders of the canals.

## Oxford Canal

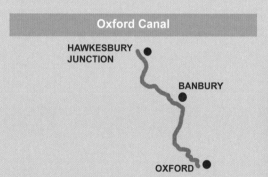

HAWKESBURY JUNCTION
BANBURY
OXFORD

Oxford to Hawkesbury Junction
77 miles, 43 locks

The Oxford Canal willingly performs the role of fair daughter to old father Thames, as she branches beautifully from the big river at her namesake city. Full of Oxford grace, this canal enjoys a rural amble, heading northwards from Oxford until it reaches the Coventry Canal.

The northern section is arguably less appealing, but in the lower stretches, the canal swirls a narrow dance through leafiest England, stopping off at irresistible real ale pubs and idyllic villages that city-folk would die to live in. One highlight of the canal is the quintessentially English village of Cropredy - adored by boaters, frequented by tourists and infused with gentle acoustic souls every August when hoards turn up for Fairport Convention's annual reunion.

## Regent's Canal

Islington Tunnel
LITTLE VENICE
Camden Lock
LIMEHOUSE

Little Venice to Limehouse Basin
8½ miles, 13 locks

A secret tour of the big city sneaking unnoticed through charismatic Little Venice, quirky Camden, Regent's Park and regal London by the back door. This is London in its slippers, extraordinarily peaceful and fascinating.

# Waterways
## of the South
boat, bike, boot

## The Thames Ring

BRAUNSTON
NORTHAMPTON
LEIGHTON BUZZARD
OXFORD
LONDON
READING
WINDSOR

252 miles, 175 locks

by boat - a muscle-flexing cruise that takes a full 2 weeks
by bike - a leisurely slow ride takes around one week
by boot - a walk with time to sightsee takes around 2½ weeks

River Thames, Oxford Canal and Grand Union Canal

Sometimes called the Grand Ring, this is the route for adventurers. An exhilarating challenge that takes you through some stunning countryside and English landmarks like Henley, Windsor, Oxford and Banbury.

## River Thames

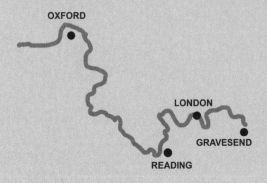

OXFORD
LONDON
GRAVESEND
READING

215 miles from source to sea
146 miles from Inglesham Junction in the Cotswolds to Limehouse Basin in London, 45 locks

The big one. Old Father Thames. The river that our Houses of Parliament sit obediently alongside. The Thames famously flows through Windsor, Henley, Oxford, the power and pleasure, classroom and playground of a nation. And it plays host to trip boats, party boats, taxi boats, police boats, trading boats, naval boats, live-aboard boats, motor and paddle boats and every shape in between.

## The Warwickshire Ring

FAZELEY
BIRMINGHAM
COVENTRY
RUGBY
KINGSWOOD
WARWICK
BRAUNSTON

100 miles, 94 locks

by boat - a relaxing cruise takes 10 days
by bike - a leisurely slow ride takes around 3 days
by boot - a walk with time to sightsee takes around one week

Grand Union Canal, Birmingham & Fazeley Canal, Oxford Canal and Coventry Canal

A deliciously rural ring with real treats along the way that include Warwick Castle, Braunston village and Gas Street Basin in Birmingham.

# ROUTES
## along the towpath

## SOME DESIGNATED TOWPATH ROUTES

### Basingstoke Canal

**THE SATURN TRAIL**
National Cycle Network (NCN) Route 221
Brookwood to West Byfleet
Follows the canal towpath from Pirbright Bridge through to the canal's junction with the Wey Navigation.

### Grand Union Canal

**GRAND UNION CANAL WALK**
137 miles
Follows the canal towpath all the way from London to Birmingham.

**NATIONAL CYCLE NETWORK (NCN) ROUTE 6**
Will run from London to Keswick (once fully open)
Follows the canal towpath from Leighton Buzzard through to Milton Keynes.

### Kennet & Avon Canal

**KENNET & AVON CYCLE ROUTE**
National Cycle Network (NCN) Route 4
Bristol to Reading
Follows the canal towpath all the way from Bristol to Reading.

### Oxford Canal

**NATIONAL CYCLE NETWORK (NCN) ROUTE 5**
Reading to Holyhead
Follows the canal towpath for a short while out of Oxford, before heading across country towards Woodstock.

**OXFORD CANAL WALK**
77 miles
Follows the canal towpath all the way from its start in Oxford to Hawkesbury Junction, where you can continue along the Coventry Canal into Coventry.

### Regent's Canal

**GRAND UNION CANAL WALK**
8½ miles
Follows the canal all the way from Little Venice to Limehouse Basin. The full walk follows the Grand Union to Birmingham.

### More info

For more detailed information and maps of all National Cycle Network Routes, go to www.sustrans.org.uk

For more walks and trails, go to www.ramblers.org.uk

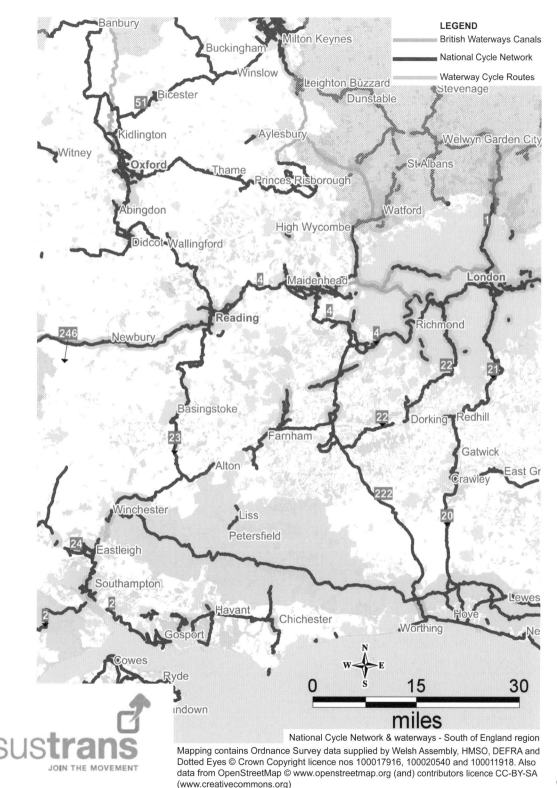

LEGEND
British Waterways Canals
National Cycle Network
Waterway Cycle Routes

Banbury
Buckingham
Milton Keynes
Winslow
Leighton Buzzard
Dunstable
Stevenage
51 Bicester
Kidlington
Aylesbury
Welwyn Garden City
Witney
Oxford
Thame
St Albans
Princes Risborough
Abingdon
Watford
Didcot Wallingford
High Wycombe
1
4 Maidenhead
London
4
246 Newbury
Reading
4
Richmond
Basingstoke
22
21
23
Farnham
22 Dorking Redhill
Alton
Gatwick
222
Crawley
East Gr
Winchester
Liss
20
24 Eastleigh
Petersfield
Southampton
2
Lewes
2
Havant
Chichester
Hove
Gosport
Worthing
Ne
Cowes
Ryde
ndown

N
W E
S

0          15          30
miles

National Cycle Network & waterways - South of England region

Mapping contains Ordnance Survey data supplied by Welsh Assembly, HMSO, DEFRA and Dotted Eyes © Crown Copyright licence nos 100017916, 100020540 and 100011918. Also data from OpenStreetMap © www.openstreetmap.org (and) contributors licence CC-BY-SA (www.creativecommons.org)

sustrans
JOIN THE MOVEMENT

# Routes
## along the towpath

Along with hundreds of other people, I regularly cycle and walk along the canal path. It's a great leisure route and a flat 9-mile ride into the lovely city of Bath.

At weekends the canal is really busy with walkers, cyclists, anglers, dogs, runners, boaters and canoeists. But, on weekdays and in the evenings, it is much more peaceful and you are more likely to see kingfishers and herons.

It's a fantastic section of the NCN to be a Ranger. The canal is alive with activity – there is an increasing number of hire boats, but also many boaters for whom the canal is their home. And for some it's their place of work. There is a metalworker who tows his own workshop and forge behind him, a cheese and ice cream seller, 'The Dawdling Dairy', a fender maker and even a floating hairdressing salon."

Richard Craft
Sustrans Volunteer Ranger

## My favourite bike ride
### Kennet & Avon Canal

"I'm a very lucky person. I live in the beautiful town of Bradford on Avon, in Wiltshire, through which runs the Kennet & Avon Canal - also Route 4 of the National Cycle Network.

I'm also a Sustrans Volunteer Ranger for the canal path either side of the town, and can often be seen trying to keep the path litter and bramble free, as well as talking to path users. It's a great job to do and really satisfying when people thank you as they go by.

## Factfile

Start: Bradford on Avon OS ST825602
Finish: Bath OS ST754643
National Cycle Network (NCN) Route 4
9 miles, 7 locks, 1 tunnel

### Highlights
Dundas Aqueduct
Avoncliff Aqueduct
Somersetshire Coal Canal
Claverton Pumping Station

### More info
For more detailed information and maps of all National Cycle Network Routes, go to www.sustrans.org.uk

# Routes
### along the towpath

JOIN THE MOVEMENT

Simon Pratt
Sustrans Regional Director
South East of England

## My favourite bike rides

"We have many excellent waterside paths around the region, including canals, rivers and seaside promenades. Whenever I get the opportunity, you'll find me cycling or walking beside water, because it's away from traffic, paths are level and there is always something to see. Above all, water has a calming effect and it's a great way to relax and recharge.

### A bike ride along the Basingstoke Canal

This is a very pleasant and easy to follow walking or cycling route along eight miles of surfaced, wide towpath between Brookwood in the west and the Wey Navigation in the east. The route is well used, especially at weekends, by walkers, anglers and cyclists. Along its whole length, the canal is lined with verdant banks and mature, often overhanging, trees through which can be seen vast stretches of woodland and fascinating views into suburban gardens. The many bends create tableaux of new vistas opening out as you proceed. The flights of locks add much interest as do the water lilies and birds, along with the deep reflections in the water on a bright day. The many bridges also offer shelter from rain showers.

The great thing about this canal is that it runs through the heart of the town, but you feel as though you are in the countryside. For many everyday journeys, it is the quickest route as it avoids busy roads and is level. It is possible to continue the waterside journey along the Wey Navigation to Weybridge, then beside the River Thames all the way into London.

## Factfile

Start: Brookwood OS SU955575
Finish: Woodham Junction OS TQ054620
National Cycle Network (NCN) Route 221
8 miles, 14 locks

### Highlights
Horsell Common
Pirbright Common
Brookwood Locks

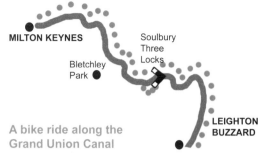

## Factfile

Start: Reading OS SU724734
Finish: Newbury OS SU472672
National Cycle Network (NCN) Route 4
19 miles, 22 locks, 11 swing bridges

### Highlights
Nature reserves and gravel pits outside Reading
Monkey Marsh Lock - a listed monument
Newbury Wharf - info centre, shop and boat trips

### A bike ride along the Kennet & Avon Canal

With its gentle gradients and the close-up view of canalside life, this route is a wonderful way to explore this corner of Berkshire. From the modern centre of Reading, the route follows the canal towpath for 19 miles into Newbury.

The surface is variable, generally well-compacted stone, but with some unimproved sections. There is usually something moving on the Kennet & Avon, either the waterfowl or one of the many narrowboats that navigate its waters. Either way, a cyclist pedalling at a leisurely pace will probably be the fastest thing on the move.

You can't rush along a canal towpath, especially if it's popular with anglers, so allow enough time to enjoy the slower pace of life here.

With several railway stations along the route, there are numerous options for shorter trips or there-and-back combined with a rail journey.

### A bike ride along the Grand Union Canal

The Grand Union Canal came into being in the 1920s, when the marriage of numerous small historic waterways created a trunk route from London to Birmingham. These days it is mostly used as a leisure facility, but with existing and future sections of the National Cycle Network using its towpath, it is once again becoming a vital part of local and national transport infrastructure. As the route is narrow in places, and is shared with walkers and anglers, it has a 10mph limit - ideal for a leisurely cycle ride. Take this opportunity to slow down to the gentler pace of life on the towpath and see if you can spot a kingfisher.

The canal has as its companion, the River Ouzel, which meanders away for a while, and then returns, repeating this pattern for the rest of your journey. If you need a break, there are pubs at Linslade and at Three Locks. The towpath has a good surface, but is a little narrow in places. Much of the towpath through the new city of Milton Keynes has been widened as a tree-lined avenue and you can travel for several miles without seeing a car."

## Factfile

Start: Leighton Buzzard OS SP915250
Finish: Milton Keynes OS SP870383
National Cycle Network (NCN) Route 6
16 miles, 6 locks

### Highlights
Valley views out of Leighton Buzzard
Soulbury Three Locks
Nature reserve by Cosgrove Lock

### More info
For more detailed information and maps of all National Cycle Network Routes, go to www.sustrans.org.uk

# Routes
### along the towpath

**Phillippa & Martine**
**Some of the highlights of our epic canal walk from Cornwall to Scotland**

## Our favourite walks

Canals were pragmatically built to haul goods from A to B, with little regard for the joys of the journey. But the joys are ample for the canal walker in the south of England. This is the zone of the long-haul marathon canals - Bristol to London along the Kennet & Avon Canal, Birmingham to London along the Grand Union Canal, and the ever popular Thames Path too.

### A walk along the Oxford Canal

Big skies, green fields, water and a windmill on top of the hill in the distance - this is England at its best.

We love the Oxford Canal, and this walk through the countryside is full of all the sounds and smells you'd expect from a lush location. This stretch along Napton Locks is 2½ miles of unspoilt pleasures for the walker. The water bends and turns making the route trickier for the tillersman than the towpath tourist. Brindley built the canal in his typical winding fashion, flowing around contours rather than bulldozing a straight course. When the much straighter Grand Union Canal was built, it stole much of the Oxford Canal's commercial traffic - but the Oxford Canal fought back by charging extortionate tolls to use its water in the London to Birmingham link between Napton and Braunston.

The windmill which has been at Napton since 1543 dominates the landscape, and would have been a useful landmark for traditional boatmen in the commercial carrying days. The church, adjacent on the hill, is worth a detour. When we have visited, it has been joyously open, and a dose of soothing silence is always a great way to start a walk. Along the hill path from the church you pass a cluster of wooden seats. They perch under a rowan tree which was planted to mark the spot where local people sat during the Second World War to watch the miserable blitz over Coventry in the distance. A plaque

over the seating asks us to reflect, and cherish the freedoms of today. Even on a breezy day the windmill's sails don't turn, but the grass sways and a panorama sings enough to make up for the stillness of the retired mill. From a bird's eye view on top of the hill, the Oxford Canal meanders in and out of sight, with dots of miniature boats.

When you head down the road to bridge 111 to get to the canal towpath, you meet an idyllic towpath with the grace of olde England. For much of the way we couldn't hear the revolting noise of cars and that is all too rare, even on the canals. This is a buttercup-yellow place where the bumble bees seem bigger and wild forget-me-nots peep from the water's edge. The canal is bordered with glorious oaks, elders, willow, clover and grass that isn't trodden bare.

To make a perfect day of it, be sure you leave enough time to browse around the canal shop and then pop next door to the pub (dogs are welcome too).

## Factfile

**Oxford Canal**
Start: Napton OS SP456619
Finish: Marston Doles OS SP465585
3 miles, 9 locks

**Highlights**
Napton Locks
The views from Napton Windmill & Church

**Did you know?**
This stretch of the Oxford Canal forms part of the Millenium Way, a 100-mile walk from Middleton Cheney in South Northamptonshire to Pershore in Worcestershire.

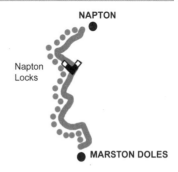

# Routes
along the towpath

### A walk along the Kennet & Avon Canal

A canal walk in the Vale of Pewsey from aptly named Honeystreet to Pewsey Wharf simply sings, heads up, with Wiltshire magic. Some of our favourite canals from our end-to-end routes have won us over with their engineering marvels, but this stretch of the Kennet & Avon Canal lets nature do the work. A towpath that really is a breath of fresh air, striding wide open with Englishness, exploring the region's swirling green landscape.

It follows the White Horse Trail with chalk-carved mysteries and suspense around the corner. Crop circle mysteries and ley lines keep canal explorers wide-eyed in wonder, travelling under big skies that keep the secrets to themselves. The scene lies flat with interruptions of hills and burial mounds... and the White Horse peeps in and out of view. (The white horse was cut into the hill in 1812, tracing the famous one at Cherhill).

This prolific walk speaks for itself as it made the front cover of this book - it would win the rosette in our handpicked top 10 canal spots for no reason other than its knack of uplifting and grounding at the same time.

### Pewsey Wharf

A mini-hub with a good community buzz, a bar-bistro/café where you can eat outside or in, and a beer garden.

### The Barge Inn

This is more than a dog-friendly pub with a good atmosphere, good food and good ales. Its bare floors overhear the ramblings of boaters who pull up outside and moor here overnight... and, when the moon is right, croppie-folk turn up from across the globe in the hope of witnessing crop circle magic. The pub is alive with music and chat, books and maps. There's a mural on the ceiling over the pool table that is surrounded by newspaper cuttings and magic crop circle stories to believe or not.

The pub has a small campsite in a grassy field with virtually nothing, and everything you need.

### Wilcot

Wilcot is a thatched village with an ancient 12th-century church. The village green has been the scene of the annual carnival since 1898 (starts on the third Saturday in September and lasts for two weeks).

### Lady's Bridge

Just as Great Missenden is objecting to the proposed high-speed London link railway today, and the battle of Newbury climbed into trees to object to the road builders of the 1990s... so the canal builders faced fierce resistance from landowners to the new water-motorway of the 'canal mania' era. In 1793 Lady Susannah Wroughton was bound to moan about the transport route cutting through her land and she had to be calmed by £500 and the commissioning of a bridge with Rennie's ornate stamp (built 1808), and an attractive widening of the water set in a marshy landscape.

### Pickled Hill

Celtic and medieval cultivation has beautifully scarred the terraced landscape with Pickled Hill rising dramatically from the flat landscape.

**HONEYSTREET**

Pewsey Wharf

Lady's Bridge    Wide Water    **PEWSEY**

### Factfile

#### Kennet & Avon Canal
Start: Honeystreet OS SU099615
Finish: Pewsey Wharf OS SU157610
4½ miles, 0 locks

#### Highlights
The White Horse on the hill opposite the Barge Inn
Lady's Bridge and Wide Water
Pewsey Wharf

# ROUTES
boating

The McCubbin family - Fran, Angus and children Ellen, Finlay, Henry. This was their second holiday on a narrowboat.

They shared a short break together with another family - Inger and Tony and their 3 children Cormac, Cody and Erin, who had never been on a boat before.

## Our favourite route
### A cruise along the Kennet & Avon Canal

For an easy 3-night trip, we started from the boat base at Hilperton and cruised leisurely along the Kennet & Avon Canal, stopping off to explore along the way.

### DAY ONE
Hilperton to the medieval town of Bradford on Avon with its Tithe Barn, pubs, teashops and irresistible shops with oodles of character.

### DAY TWO
Bradford on Avon to the glorious Dundas Aqueduct designed by Rennie. Canals are narrow, so turning round isn't that simple in a 69ft boat. You have to find a special turning point called a winding hole and keep a sense of humour! We survived the manoeuvre and returned to Bradford on Avon to moor for the night.

### DAY THREE
Bradford on Avon to the foot of the spectacular Caen Hill lock flight. The flight looked like hard work to us, so we were quite pleased we were turning back to Hilperton. After a cosy night at Semington, we returned our boat to Hilperton the next morning.

"I got to drive the boat! It's more difficult than it looks."
Finlay (12)

"I liked it when I saw the heron!"
Erin (5)

"I liked sitting on top of the boat having my lunch & my fave bit was the exciting locks with all the water gushing."
Cody (8)

"It was much better than I expected! My fave bit was going through the locks 'cos I felt really involved and part of it all helping."
Cormac (13)

"I liked all the different boats, and the herons, swans and moorhens I saw."
Henry (9)

"It was exciting to have a holiday over a short space of time. It was like luxury camping, but on water."
Ellen (15)

"It's a really relaxing pace of life in beautiful scenery. And I enjoyed doing the locks - they keep you fit!"
Fran (Mum)

"I loved sitting at the front of the boat with my cup of tea, watching the world go by".
Inger (Mum)

"As a group, it's good to have someone to share the jobs with. I can do a bit on the tiller and then do some ropework or just walk alongside on the towpath if I want to."
Angus (Dad)

Crewing a boat is teamwork, with something for everyone to do. The freedom of an enforced outdoor experience really can bring families together in a special way. Working the locks is fun, even though it can be exhausting on heavily-locked canal routes. If you prefer a lazy time, ask your hireboat company which route they suggest. Your hireboat company will also give you all necessary instructions to cruise safely.

Good food is an important part of most holidays. If you want to, you can shop locally along the way for fresh produce. Food on a narrowboat always tastes good whether you do full foodie-feasts with condiments, or you dish up one-pot meals. And if you don't want to cook or wash up at all, there's a waterside pub platter around almost every corner.

## Factfile

Hilperton Marina OS ST859600
25 miles, 16 locks

**Highlights**
Caen Hill lock flight
Dundas Aqueduct
Avoncliff Aqueduct

**More info**
69ft boat. 'Goose' class. Sleeps up to 8
UK Boat Hire
www.ukboathire.com

# Boats
## in the South

## Basingstoke Canal

**GALLEON MARINE**
Narrowboat holiday & day hire. Rowing boats, canoes & kayaks.
Odiham. T:01256 703691
www.galleonmarine.co.uk

**JOHN CALE CANAL CRUISES**
Trip boat, charter & day boat hire.
Mychett. T:01252 837165
www.jccanalcruises.co.uk

## Grand Union Canal

**INDIAN CHIEF**
Trip boat run by the Boat Inn.
Stoke Bruerne. T:01604 862428
www.boatinn.co.uk

**OXFORDSHIRE NARROWBOATS**
Narrowboat holiday hire.
Stowe Hill. T:01869 340348
www.oxfordshire-narrowboats.co.uk

**STOKE BRUERNE BOAT CO.**
Trip boat, charter & day boats.
Stoke Bruerne. T:07966 503609
www.stokebruerneboats.co.uk

**WYVERN SHIPPING CO.**
Narrowboat holiday hire.
Leighton Buzzard. T:01525372355
www.canalholidays.co.uk

## Kennet & Avon Canal

**ANGLO WELSH**
Narrowboat holiday & day hire.
Bath, Bradford on Avon & Monkton Combe. T:0117 3041122
www.anglowelsh.co.uk

**BATH & DUNDAS CANAL CO.**
Day boat & Canadian canoe hire.
Monkton Combe. T:01225 722292
www.bathcanal.com

**BATH CANAL BOAT COMPANY**
Widebeam holiday boat hire.
Bath. T:01225 312935
www.bathcanalboats.co.uk

**BATH NARROWBOATS**
Trip boat and day boat hire.
Bath. T:01225 447276
www.bath-narrowboats.co.uk

**FOXHANGERS CANAL HOLS**
Narrowboat holiday hire.
Rowde, Devizes. T:01380 828795
www.foxhangers.co.uk

**KENNET & AVON CANAL TRUST**
Trip boats.
Bradford on Avon, Brassknocker Basin, Devize & Hungerford. T:01380 721279
www.katrust.co.uk

**KENNET HORSE BOAT CO**
Horsedrawn boat & day hire.
Kintbury. T:01488 658866
www.kennet-horse-boat.co.uk

**MOONRAKER CANALBOATS**
Widebeam holiday boat hire.
Bradford on Avon. T:07973 876891
www.moonboats.co.uk

**OXFORDSHIRE NARROWBOATS**
Narrowboat holiday & day hire.
Bradford on Avon. T:01869 340348
www.oxfordshire-narrowboats.co.uk

**SALLY NARROWBOATS**
Narrowboat holiday & day hire.
Bradford on Avon. T:01225 864923
www.sallyboats.ltd.uk

**UK BOAT HIRE**
Narrowboat holiday & day hire.
Aldermaston Wharf & Hilperton.
T:0845 1264098
www.ukboathire.com

**WHITE HORSE BOATS**
Narrowboat holiday hire.
Devizes. T:01380 728504
www.whitehorseboats.co.uk

## Oxford Canal

**BLACK PRINCE**
Narrowboat holiday hire.
Napton. T:01527 575115
www.black-prince.com

**CANALBREAKS**
Narrowboat holiday hire.
Hillmorton Locks.
T:01788 578661
www.canalbreaks.com

**CLIFTON CRUISERS**
Narrowboat holiday hire.
Clifton upon Dunsmore.
T:01788 543570
www.cliftoncruisers.com

**COLLEGE CRUISERS**
Narrowboat holiday hire.
Oxford. T:01865 554343
www.collegecruisers.com

**NAPTON NARROWBOATS**
Narrowboat holiday hire.
Napton. T:01926 813644
www.napton-marina.co.uk

**OXFORDSHIRE NARROWBOATS**
Narrowboat holiday & day hire.
Lower Heyford & Thrupp.
T:01869 340348
www.oxfordshire-narrowboats.co.uk

**ROSE NARROWBOATS**
Narrowboat holiday & day hire.
Nr Rugby. T:01788 832449
www.rose-narrowboats.co.uk

**WILLOW WREN**
Narrowboat holiday hire.
Rugby. T:01788 562183
www.willowwren.co.uk

## Regent's Canal

**JASON'S TRIP**
Trip boat between Little Venice & Camden. April to October.
London. T:0207 2863428
www.jasons.co.uk

**LONDON WATERBUS CO.**
Trip boat between Little Venice & Camden, plus special day trips.
London. T:020 7482 2660 / 2550
www.londonwaterbus.com

# waterway recovery group

Being originally from Scotland most of my early waterway experiences relate to crossing swollen rivers whilst out hill walking, or maybe walking up the Union Canal on my way home from school… that was until I joined the Inland Waterways Association in 2004 as a project officer.

Since then I have slowly got more and more 'outdoors and dirty' with the Waterway Recovery Group. In 2005 I had my first 'WRGie' experience on the Herefordshire & Gloucestershire Canal which involved clearing vegetation, learning how to brick-lay and of course standing knee deep in mud. It was a great week and I met loads of fantastic people from all over the country.

After that I've not looked back and have definitely got the WRGie bug (and lots of canal camp T-shirts.) This year I've already spent two weeks and several weekends working on the Cotswold Canals helping to restore Eisey Lock and Gough's Orchard Lock, along with lots of other 21st century navvies.

With over 2,500 miles of waterways still derelict I am sure I will be involved in waterway restoration for many years to come … and one day I hope to enjoy a boating holiday on a canal that I have helped to restore.

# Waterways people
Joseph Young, Towpath Ranger
London's canals and rivers

British Waterways

"I work for British Waterways and Transport for London on a joint project called Two Tings, which encourages the thousands of people who use the capital's canals to share the towpath amicably."

"My role means I get to be out and about a lot, especially on the Regent's Canal. It's great seeing people as they discover the canals, and how they provide a car-free route through the city. The canal is a space to get away from the bustle of the city. There's a different feel to London by the water, you can slow down, take in the sights of the city from a new perspective and appreciate the wildlife that exists alongside the houses, offices, warehouses, boats and businesses that line the canals. You can normally spot me out on the canal during the commuter hours, early in the morning, or at the end of the day. I manage a series of events to remind cyclists that pedestrians have the right of way, encourage people to slow down and ring their bell if they are riding a bike on the towpath, and also remind pedestrians to listen out for considerate cyclists who are tinging to try and pass by."

"I frequently meet people who are new to the waterways, having just discovered their local canal. The sight of children walking to school along the towpath is wonderful. I recently met a lady in her sixties who hadn't cycled since she was a child and was nervous about doing so, but after encouraging her to try her new bike on the towpath she fell in love with cycling and now cycles all over London."

"Meeting people that love the waterways is an inspiring part of the job. There are some real characters and on certain stretches of the canal there is a genuine sense of community. For example, at one of the events I coordinate on the towpath in Islington to encourage considerate shared use of the towpath, I'm often joined by parents from the local school, who care deeply about making the towpath a nicer, more amicable place to be for their children."

Canals are an amicable place by nature, but speeding cyclists are a menace to everyone along the waterways who loves walking, boating and deliciously slow cycling. Find out about the Two Tings campaign: www.waterscape.com

ting your bell twice.
two tings 2
pass slowly, be nice!

# WILDLIFE & NATURE

## Wildfowl & Wetlands Trust – London

### A great day out

London is the big beautiful city, and right in the heart of it is London Wetland Centre doing beautifully big things. This is city-water and wildlife living together magnificently.

The site has 105 acres to touch, smell and revel in the marvels of nature. Wander around the lakes, explore the adventure playground, go hunting with your eyes for rare birds, or crouch quietly in one of the hides and scarcely dare to breathe in the thrill of coming so close to wildlife.

The centre gained its SSSI status due to the number of overwintering birds they have such as the shoveler and gadwall. Lapwings breed at the centre and their gorgeous petrol coloured plumage makes them popular with visitors. It is also the closest place to central London to have bitterns. The Main Reedbed is managed in 3 distinct beds of varying wetness, with pools dug to attract bitterns to feed - they are best seen from the Wildside Hide.

London Wetland Centre is an urban wildlife centre next to the Thames and a world away from the city. A wildlife day out that reaches deeply, to humble the human.

## Factfile

### The Thames

London OS TQ229770
Beside the River Thames in Barnes, London.
On National Cycle Network (NCN) Route 4

Open daily all year (only closes on Christmas Day)
Nov-Mar 0930-1700 (Christmas Eve to 1500)
Apr-Oct to 1800. Last admission an hour before closing.

Café and gift shop.
Admission charge. Wheelchair access.

T:0208 4094400 www.wwt.org.uk

**WWT**

### The Gadwall

The gadwall is no ordinary duck. It is slightly smaller than the mallard with a smaller, squarer head. Its grey colouring doesn't dazzle from afar, but, up close, its colouring is made up of fine speckling. A stunner in its own right.

Gadwalls feed at the surface in shallow water then, in autumn and winter often flock on reservoirs and flooded pits. They often associate with coots in order to benefit from the food the coots stir up from the bottom when they dive. They are renowned thieves, often snatching food from other ducks and coots.

They nest in nettle clumps and, during courtship, indulge in spectacular aerial displays in which pairs can sometimes collide.

Populations of the duck in Britain and Europe have been boosted in recent years by deliberate introduction. The gadwall spends summers in the prairies of North America, British Columbia, Alaska, Europe, eastern Russia, Japan and China and winters in southern USA, Mexico, Cuba, northern Africa and India, and the Middle East.

### The Bittern

The population of bitterns in Britain was in serious decline, but the creation of large and wet reed beds has successfully changed that in recent years. London Wetland Centre regularly has five bitterns on site each winter now, so is a fantastic place to see these elusive birds.

This secretive bird doesn't flaunt in public, yet you may hear its call even when it is out of sight. The territorial male lets everybody know he's around by 'booming' with his ludicrously loud voice that is said to travel up to 2 kilometres in a good wind! Males are polygamous, with up to five females, and in spring the volume pumps up.

The nest is built in the previous year's dead reed stems and consists of a small platform. In lean times, chicks may turn to their smaller siblings and eat them. Bitterns are big birds that hunt fish, amphibians, reptiles and invertebrates. They wade effortlessly through reed beds grasping reeds with their huge toes.

When startled, bitterns adopt a camouflage posture, with the neck stretched vertically and bill pointing straight up, making them blend in with the reeds... Catching a glimpse of this bird is a rare joy.

# CANAL HEDGEROWS

The humble hedgerow is an icon of the British countryside.

A hedge is more than a hedge - it is a boundary mark, screaming silently with living history and often telling the most revealing story of man's relationship with the landscape.

Hedges have shaped England's green and pleasant lands and, as far back as 1,000BC, folk have used hedges as boundaries. Bronze Age farmers cleared wild woods to farm the land, and often left strips of woodland at the edges to mark the boundary. Romans typically used thorny hedges, and Anglo Saxons used full hedges to enclose their fields.

After the Second World War, Britain's government was encouraging the nation to become self-sufficient, asking farmers to rip out hedgerows to use bigger machinery in bigger fields. The loss to the environment from mass removal of hedges is now recognised, and farmers are being encouraged to plant and protect hedgerows.

Thankfully, the canals have protected their hedgerows, providing a natural habitat for countless plant species and creatures. A walk down the canal usually promises the treat of a rustling boundary bursting with elder, hawthorn, hazel, and edges that may contain our most darling woodland plant of all - the bluebell.

# DAYS OUT
## in the South

## London
## River Thames
## & the Canals

London is the big city built over Roman ruins, the stage to evolving thrones of power, maritime history and the docks of the British Empire, where a canal network linked England to the world.

London's relationship with the big river is no coincidence. The city was conceived when the Romans set up camp on the banks of the Thames in 43AD. They called the place Londinium and used its strategic river position to trade wines and other Romanesque priorities.

Trade is the key word in London. Across our small island, all roads lead to the capital and London has grown up on the strength of its position in global trade. Linked by its river to the sea and then the world beyond... Paris, New York, Tokyo.

The British Empire was orchestrated from inside the great Georgian and Victorian architecture of London's streets. And outside, on the Thames of the 18th century, boats were furiously laden with exotic cargoes carried from all around the world: rum, tomatoes, sugar, cocoa, citrus fruits, coffee and (the nation's favourite) tea. Canary Wharf even gets its name from the fresh fruit that once arrived from the Canary Islands.

The Thames played its part in the fortunes of the British Empire - a primary gateway to and from the world, it is Britain's waterline for defence and rule. In the 16th century, naval ships were made in the royal dockyards that boomed on the Thames. And Britain's warships continued to be built along the banks of the Thames until 1869.

But for trade to work efficiently across the country, Britain had to build a network of trade routes. A manmade water road was Britain's answer. London's canals were built to link the docks to the new industrial Midlands.

## Greenwich - A World Heritage Site

A place with maritime history inseparable from the Thames. Birthplace of Henry VIII and Elizabeth I and home to the National Maritime Museum. But Greenwich is best known for Greenwich Mean Time (GMT). England ran on local time until, in 1880, the government decided there was a need for one standard time.

In 1833 a bright red 'time ball' had been installed on the roof of Flamsteed House, and it was dropped every day at 1pm - ships in London's Dockyard and the public beyond could set their clocks on the ball.

The Royal Observatory led to Greenwich being declared the Prime Meridian of the world in 1884 - you can now stand with one foot either side of the invisible line marking Longitude 0° 0' 0''. In 1884 GMT was announced as the standard time for the world and by 1924 the legendary BBC pips had set the tune for good.

Now the railways that took over from the canals could run on time, wherever you were in the country! And generations later, if the waterways have their way, time remains a quality to savour rather than a quantity to measure.

National Maritime Museum & Royal Observatory
Open daily 1000-1700. FREE admission.
T:0208 8584422 www.nmm.ac.uk

## London Canal Museum - Regent's Canal

Housed in a Victorian former ice warehouse (built for famous ice cream maker Carlo Gatti) where Norwegian ice was stored after being brought by ship and canal boats to London.
Open Tues-Sun & Bank Hols 1000-1630 (to 1930 first Thurs every month). Last admission ½hr before closing. Small admission charge. Wheelchair access.
T:0207 7130836 www.canalmuseum.org.uk

## London Museum Docklands - Thames

Based in a Grade I-listed Georgian warehouse, the museum tells the story of the social and economic importance of London's Docklands. The museum includes the only permanent collection on London's involvement in the slave trade.
Open Daily 1000-1800. FREE admission.
Wheelchair access.
T:0207 0019844 www.museumindocklands.org.uk

## Thames Barrier

The Thames can flood and the city is understandably twitchy. Even way before global warming and climate change were hashed into the public mind, the Thames behaved badly on occasions. Samuel Pepys mentions in his Diary,1663, "all Whitehall having been drowned" after floods on the Thames.

## Little Venice

A great spot for a waterside coffee in the city, with the calm of the countryside. A walk from Little Venice along the towpath through Regent's Park to Camden is the perfect city escape.

# Days out
## in the South

## CAEN HILL FLIGHT
### One of the 7 Wonders of the Waterways

On the Kennet & Avon Canal, a silent fanfare awaits as the 16-lock Caen Hill flight cascades the landscape with outstretched black and white arms. The flight is part of a longer stretch of 29 locks, spread over 2¼ miles leading to Devizes. Under the engineer John Rennie, the 29 locks made it possible for boats to climb a 237ft hill. You can arrive by boat, bike or boot along the canal, or just find your way along country lanes and leave your car in the leafy car park half way up the flight. For the perfect, no-fuss day out, bring a picnic (or go to the teashop) and spend the day watching the water world go by.

There are several locks up the flight named after volunteers from the Kennet & Avon Canal Trust who worked so hard to achieve the successful restoration of this canal. The Trust, based in Devizes with other branches along the canal, has worked tirelessly for over 40 years. Initially formed to bring about the restoration of the Kennet & Avon, its main objectives now are to continue to protect, enhance and promote it.

### Devizes Canal Museum, Shop & Boat Trip

Run and staffed by the K&A Canal Trust, the small museum is above the well-stocked shop in Devizes Wharf, and gives an insight into the Kennet & Avon Canal from inception to restoration. The Trust also runs a trip boat from the wharf from April to October.

### Wadworth Brewery Visitor Centre & Shop

Wadworth's, founded in 1875 in Devizes, is still run as a family business by the family of Wadworth's business partner. The Victorian brewery is well known not only for its beer but also for its shire horses, whose stables are open to the public. The Visitor Centre has an interesting small exhibition and shop, and guided tours of the brewery are available.

## Factfile

**Kennet & Avon Canal**
Caen Hill, Devizes OS ST988615

**DEVIZES TOURIST INFORMATION CENTRE**
T:01380 734669 www.visitwiltshire.co.uk

**KENNET & AVON CANAL TRUST**
T:01380 721279 www.katrust.org.uk

**DEVIZES WHARF CANAL MUSEUM & GIFT SHOP**
Open daily 1000-1600. Small admission charge to the museum. T:01380 729489 www.katrust.co.uk

**WADWORTH BREWERY**
Open Summer Mon-Fri 1000-1730, Sat 1000-1630. Winter Mon-Sat 1000-1600. Bank Hols, Christmas & Easter can vary. Free admission. Guided tours of the brewery twice daily (Charge for the tours). T:01380 732277 www.wadworthvisitorcentre.co.uk

# Stoke Bruerne

The perfect canal village to visit for a day out. Everyone here joins in with shameless gongoozling and nothing spoils the lazy ambience along the canal. Stoke Bruerne Top Lock conveniently creates a lively focus in the hub of the village.

### Pubs

The Boat Inn sits right on the waterside, overlooking the top lock. It is a thatched pub, that creaks with old stone-flagged floors and planked seats tucked into corners, and the tiny front bar chatters with waterways charm. The Woodward family have been running the pub for four generations since 1877. Real fires, real ale and really good food make lunch at the pub a must - and dogs are welcome too. There is also the historic Navigation pub alongside the canal just below the lock.

### The Toll House

See the 18th-century toll house that used to collect tariffs from canal boats carrying cargo.

### Sister Mary Ward

One of the canalside cottages at Stoke Bruerne was once the home of Sister Mary Ward. Despite having no official training, she became the acting nurse and doctor to traditional boat families. Proud and independent boat people trusted her, and would wait until they could get to Stoke Bruerne to be treated.

### Blisworth Tunnel

It's only a short stroll along the towpath to the entrance of Blisworth Tunnel, the third longest on the canal networks. Look out for the old stables along the way that once gave rest to the working boat-horses.

### Boat trips

The Boat Inn has its own narrowboat, the 'Indian Chief', and runs 25-minute trips from the pub to the tunnel and back. The boat is available for private parties with extended cruises beyond the tunnel. Stoke Bruerne Boat Company also runs a selection of day trips and chartered cruises. They offer day boat hire and skippered evening cruises.

### The Canal Museum

The museum is housed in an old rustic corn mill and has displays telling the story of the canals, and collections of fascinating canal artefacts. This is a living museum, with a jam-packed diary of events throughout the year for children & adults.

---

## Factfile

**Grand Union Canal**
Stoke Bruerne OS SP743498

**THE CANAL MUSEUM**
Open daily Apr-Oct 1000-1700
Nov-Mar Wed-Fri 1100-1500, Sat-Sun 1100-1600
Closed Christmas Day & Boxing Day.

Café and gift shop. Admission charge. No wheelchair access to museum galleries (short film of the collection).

T:01604 862229 www.stokebruernecanalmuseum.org.uk

**STOKE BRUERNE BOAT COMPANY**
T:07966 503609 www.stokebruerneboats.co.uk

**THE BOAT INN**
T:01604 862428 www.boatinn.co.uk

**THE NAVIGATION**
T:01604 864988 www.navigationpubtowcester.co.uk

---

# Days out
## in the South

## Grand Union Canal

### IWA CANALWAY CAVALCADE
Each year London's Little Venice hosts a big water event. Usually over 100 boats gather with pageants of decorated boats, illuminated processions on the water, boat-handling activities, boat trips, trade stalls, music, theatre and always plenty to interest the kids. Organised and run by the Inland Waterways Association (IWA).

Little Venice, London. OS TQ262818

Held on Bank Holiday weekend beginning of May

T:01494 783453 www.waterways.org.uk

### STOKE BRUERNE & CANAL MUSEUM
The village of Stoke Bruerne (Days Out page 96-97)

## Kennet & Avon Canal

### CLAVERTON PUMPING STATION
Built in 1810 by John Rennie to pump water from the River Avon into the Kennet & Avon Canal. The water wheel which drives the pump is the largest of its kind in the world. Special 'Pumping Days' throughout the season. Run by the Kennet & Avon Canal Trust.

Crofton. OS SU263626

Open from end April to end Sept Wed, Sat-Sun & Bank Hols 1000-1700 (1600 Wed). Admission charge. Severely restricted wheelchair access.

T:01225 483001 www.claverton.org

### CROFTON PUMPING STATION
Grade I-listed building containing the oldest working beam engine in the world. Special 'Steaming Weekends' throughout the season. Run by the Kennet & Avon Canal Trust.

Crofton. OS SU263626

Open daily from end April to end Sept 1030-1700, except Wed. Admission charge. Tea room. Severely restricted wheelchair access.

T:01672 870300 www.croftonbeamengines.org

### KENNET & AVON CANAL MUSEUM & SHOP
Run and staffed by the Kennet & Avon Canal Trust, the small museum is above the well-stocked shop, and gives an insight into the Kennet & Avon Canal from inception to restoration.

Devizes. OS SU004617

Open daily all year 1000-1600. Small admission charge to the museum.

T:01380 721279 www.katrust.co.uk

### CAEN HILL LOCK FLIGHT
One of the 7 Wonders of the Waterways (Days Out page 94-95)

### BRISTOL HARBOUR FESTIVAL
Bristol's biggest cultural festival and one of the largest FREE festivals in the UK. Dragon boat races, music, entertainment, market and the SS Great Britain.

Bristol. OS ST577724

Held on the last weekend in July. FREE admission (with some ticketed events at venues around the harbour).

www.bristolharbourfestival.co.uk

# FOOD & DRINK

## Pubs
### in the South

## Grand Union Canal

### BOAT INN

Canalside by the lock. Traditional stone-floored pub with restaurant and shop. Very busy in summer.
Stoke Bruerne. T:01604 862428
www.boatinn.co.uk

### THE GROVE LOCK
By lock 28. Large garden.
Leighton Buzzard. T:01525 380940
www.fullers.co.uk

### THE NAVIGATION INN
Canalside by bridge 65. Voted one of the UK's Top 10 waterside pubs by the Sunday Telegraph.
Cosgrove. T:01908 543156
www.navigationinn.net

## Kennet & Avon Canal

### BRIDGE INN
Canalside by Horton Bridge (134), the pub has been voted one of the Top 10 Waterside pubs. Large garden, and rooms too. Dogs and muddy boots welcome.
Horton. T:01380 860273
www.wadworth.co.uk

### BARGE INN

Canalside by lock 19. Busy foodie pub with large canalside garden and log fires for winter.
Seend Cleeve. T:01380 828230
www.bargeinnseend.co.uk

### BARGE INN

Canalside pub with 'white horse' views & its own campsite. Hive of activity and HQ of international crop circle enthusiasts - dedicated room with maps of sightings.
Pewsey. T:01672 851705
www.the-barge-inn.com

### GEORGE INN

Canalside near bridge 183. Rambling pub with real fires, cosy corners & outdoor ambience.
Bathampton. T:01225 425079
www.thespiritgroup.com

### THE THREE TUNS
In the heart of the village, a short walk from the canal. Traditional pub with

nteresting fresh menu.
Great Bedwyn. T:01672 870280
www.threetunsbedwyn.co.uk

### WHEELWRIGHTS ARMS
Short walk from Dundas Wharf. Voted one of 50 Best Gastro-pubs by the Independent. 4-star rooms.
Monkton Combe. T:01225 722287
www.wheelwrightsarms.co.uk

## Oxford Canal

### BOAT INN
Traditional stone-built pub close to the canal.
Thrupp. T:01865 374279
www.theboatinnthrupp.co.uk

### BRIDGE AT NAPTON
Traditional pub with large canalside garden by bridge 111.
Napton. T:01926 812 466
www.thebridgeatnapton.co.uk

### FOLLY INN
Traditional pub with huge garden. Canalside by bridge 113. Holiday cottages and gift shop next door.
Napton. T:01926 815185

### GREAT WESTERN ARMS
Interesting foodie pub with Hook Norton Ales, real fire and rooms.
Aynhno. T:01869 338 288
www.great-westernarms.co.uk

### JOLLY BOATMAN

Recently refurbished pub, with plenty of outside seating, canalside by bridge 223.
Thrupp. T:01865 377800

### RED LION

A few yards from the canal. Olde England thatched pub in folkie hub of Oxfordshire.
Cropredy. T:01295 750224
www.redlioncropredy.co.uk

# Teashops
## in the South

## Basingstoke Canal

### BASINGSTOKE CANAL CENTRE
Canalside. Canal info and gift shop. The centre runs boat trips and day boat hire, and there's even a large canalside campsite.
Mytchett. T:01252 370073
www.basingstoke-canal.co.uk

## Grand Union Canal

### GONGOOZLERS' REST CAFÉ

Narrowboat moored by the Marina, with a garden to spill over into on sunny days.
Braunston. T:07730 125849

### HATTON LOCKS CAFÉ

Canalside by Hatton Top Lock. Large garden alongside the canal and an interactive canal features play area for children.
Hatton. T:01926 409432

### BLUEBELLS TEAROOMS
Canalside by lock 39. Large gardens overlooking the canal and plenty of room indoors. Homemade cakes, snacks & full meals with hefty portions.
Tring. T:01442 891708

## Kennet & Avon Canal

### CAEN HILL CAFÉ
Canalside by lock 44. Small inside but with large garden and terrace overlooking Caen Hill lock flight and the countryside views beyond. Dog-friendly.
Devizes. T:01452 318000

### GRANNY MO'S TEA ROOM
Jutting out into the canal with outdoor tables overlooking the activity at Bradford Lock.
Bradford on Avon. T:01225 867515
www.grannymos.co.uk

### LOCK INN CAFÉ
Canalside just below Bradford Lock. Cosy interior, covered terrace and hearty meals.
Bradford on Avon. T:01225 868068
www.thelockinn.co.uk

### RAFT CAFÉ BOAT

Moored By bridge 183. Homemade cakes in a modern interior. There's room to sit out on the back deck or sprawl on the generous grassy towpath.
Bathampton. T:07733 336989

### TROUGHS
By Avoncliff Aqueduct. Café open daily 0900-2000. Huge garden.
Avoncliff. T:01225 868123
www.troughsatavoncliff.co.uk

### WHARF COTTAGE TEAROOM
Canalside by Bradford Lock. Run by the Kennet & Avon Canal Trust, they also operate boat trips from here.
Bradford on Avon. T:01225 868683

## Oxford Canal

### ANNIE'S TEA ROOM
Courtyard by Thrupp Lift Bridge.
Thrupp. T:07590 296672

### BADSEY'S CAFÉ BISTRO
Canalside opposite Hillmorton Locks. Busy inside with canal pictures and memorabilia. Large garden and

former Grand Union Canal Carrying Co working boat, Badsey, is moored outside.
Hillmorton. T:01788 553562
www.badseys.co.uk

### JANE'S TEAS
Farm Shop & Tea rooms, canalside by Pigeon Lock. Jane lives in a narrowboat alongside the sprawling smallholding with teas, homemade cakes and snacks. Home-made jams and chutneys. Open on Sundays only,
Kirtlington. T:07837 362683

### KIZZIE'S

Waterside Bar & Bistro, canalside in the wharf. Bright and spacious inside, and a garden right by the hireboats. Delicious homemade cakes and snacks.
Lower Heyford. T:01869 340348
www.oxfordshire-narrowboats.co.uk

## Regent's Canal

### CORE GRILL
Canalside in the canal basin. Scrubbed wood tables, organic deli-style meals, snacks & cakes.
Nr Paddington. T:0207 7244945
www.coregrill.co.uk

### TOWPATH CAFÉ
Tiny canalside café, so small the tables are on a floating jetty alongside. Interesting food.
Hackney. T:0207 2547606

### WATERSIDE CAFÉ

Boat moored in Little Venice, covered in flowers and with tables spilling out along the towpath.
T:0207 2661066

For listings of waterside pubs & teashops in the UK, visit our website:
www.greatwaterwaysoutdoors.com

# WATERWAYS LIFE
## Britain's secret village

Britain is proud of its thatched cottages and black and white villages that nestle deep in the countryside. But what is it that makes village life special and different from towns and cities?

Wisteria is optional, yet the post office, a church, a pub, the corner shop are essentials. These are the things villagers cherish. And these are the things that nurture community wellbeing.

Canals have all those credentials in one long linear village, and those who visit sense the secret instantly - the canal is a narrow floating village, rambling wherever, and singing with community spirit.

Canal people have ways that are uniquely different from their 'landlubbed' neighbours.

Somehow the slow culture has held time at bay and kept a special place steeped in good old-fashioned manners and cap-touching Britishness.

For visitors, that's part of the attraction and intrigue. Something undeniably special happens under the spell of friendliness. It's contagious. Water does its bit to balm, but perhaps it's also the marvels of wildlife, the outdoor air, the absence of class barriers and the unique spirit of a transient floating community that allows folk to commune better. The community is as precious as the canals themselves, both keep a forgotten Britain alive.

## Go to a canal pub

The Great British pub. A sing song, a good old natter, a cracking joke, a shoulder to cry on. The pub community is legendary and anyone who joins in is as British as the British.

No village across the land would be complete without its corner shop, church, and welcoming pub. Luckily, the linear water village has them all, and there's especially no shortage of the latter. Pub stops are the stuff of canal travel. It's where the boater tells his best stories and cyclists, walkers and car drivers crane to listen.

Of course any of the best British pubs can be lauded for roaring fires and real ale, summer beer gardens with cool cider and apple blossom... But traditional canal pubs go the extra mile with waterside character, dazzling heritage, nautical charisma and the ultimate addiction of gongoozling. Whether you arrive by boat, bike, boot or road, the best canalside pubs are a bubble of comfort that won't burst until you have to leave.

## Village life

Just like any destination that attracts holidaymakers, waterways villager see distinct changes of mood through every season. Some boats are year-round homes for travelling live-aboards, other boats are second homes for urban escapees. And in summer when gangs of hire boats wake up, the water wakes up with sun lotion and holidaymakers.

But it's not just boaters who inhabit the water village. Like any good village, there are many who shape the community - small local shopkeepers, pub landlords, the crew on the hotel boats, the nice couple who do the rounds on the coal-boat, the artists and craft makers who make a humble living in tourist hotspots, 'landlubbed' locals who come to chat to the ducks whenever they can, lock keepers, towpath wardens, volunteers and people who look after the canals.

I Braunston - Oxford Canal - Foxton - Napton Locks I

# HEART OF ENGLAND

The Heart of England surely earns its title for more than just a geographical position in the middle of the nation. Visit the region and you will be thrust two ways in a ruthless affair: a romance with the rhythm of a Tango sweeps one moment into an underworld of manmade urban heritage and then, in an unexpected turn, flings the visitor cheek to cheek into nature's green virgin countryside.

It's the birthplace of the Industrial Revolution and the homeland of the English meadow too. Shakespeare, Elgar, Mr Cadbury, Mr Wedgwood, Lady Godiva... entrepreneurs, artists and the boldest souls have left a tourist trail for the intrepid to discover.

England's glossiest holiday brochures tell us to go South to meet the Queen or to go North where the countryside is wild and the folk talk in dialect that hugs straight from the mouth. But the wise traveller won't overlook the bit that is neither up-north nor down-south. The Midlands.

Birmingham, the Potteries and the Black Country grew up on the canals and boomed during the heyday of the Victorian entrepreneurial stampede.

It is the industrial hub in the middle of England, but beyond the perceived grubby façade lies an unyielding spaghetti of charismatic inland waterways - the so-called 'green corridors'. The Midlands has enough water-miles to explore, you could fill every day of the year and still need to go back for more. A leisure destination of contrasts not to be missed.

Midland's travel talk is often shy of Britain's industrial truth and steers us to visit more conventionally palatable Stratford-upon-Avon or the nearest accessible chunk of the Peak District. But waterways folk know that the canals take the tourist to the aorta of interest. A bend in the water-road can carry the traveller through the backdoor of our industrial past, with a different view than from the polluted hard roads above. Heritage trails that uncover the people as well as the places. Truly fascinating, and frankly beautiful.

# WATERWAYS
## of the Heart of England
### boat, bike, boot

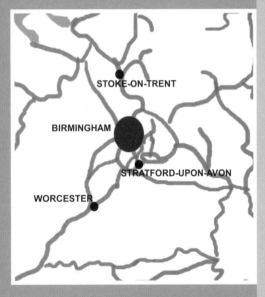

## Highlights

NATIONAL WATERWAYS MUSEUM on the
Shropshire Union Canal - TARDEBIGGE
LOCK FLIGHT on the Worcester &
Birmingham Canal - ANDERTON LIFT on
the Trent & Mersey Canal - HARECASTLE
TUNNEL on the Trent & Mersey Canal
- BANCROFT BASIN, Stratford on the
Stratford Canal - BRINDLEY PLACE,
Birmingham on the BCN

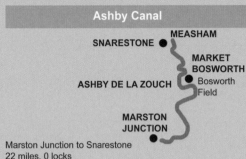

### Ashby Canal

Marston Junction to Snarestone
22 miles, 0 locks

This lockless, lazy water road must be the best
way to tour Leicestershire's countryside. Boaters
can put their windlasses away and uncork the
wine to cruise this uninterrupted short canal.
Only history contradicts the tranquillity, as the
canal skims the site of the bloodiest battle of the
War of the Roses. Richard III fell to a gruesome
death here at the Battle of Bosworth Field in
1485. A day out at the Heritage Centre is a must.

### Birmingham Canal Navigations (BCN)

Birmingham
(A network of canals, canal arms and branches)
100 miles (approx)

Down-staging its European rival, Birmingham
claims to own an even more outrageous spaghetti
of canals than Venice. The BCN canal network
knits across the Black Country and Birmingham,
colliding in a hub at Gas Street Basin - right in
the centre of England's second city. The basin
is as it should be, bustling with cool calm. But
follow the canal out of the city in a north easterly
direction, and a remote urban wilderness unfolds.
A tourist-free zone for the discerning adventurer.

### Caldon Canal

Etruria to Froghall
17 miles, 17 locks

A canal that begins in the fascinating, if unglamorous, territory of Stoke-on-Trent, made famous by its Potteries. But this down-to-earth start is deceptive, since the canal soon blusters away into unspoilt countryside, blossoming into a stunner. The deep greens of the Churnet Valley give the canal all it needs, and the Churnet Valley Steam Railway adds muscle to the attraction.

## Droitwich Canals

**RIVER SEVERN**     **HANBURY WHARF**
**DROITWICH**

River Severn to Hanbury Wharf
7¼ miles, 16 locks

A recent restoration success, creating a new link between the Worcester & Birmingham Canal and the River Severn. The opening of the Droitwich Canals completes a ring for boaters, walkers and cyclists. But these canals are more than a cog in a bigger ring, they stand boldly in their own right as a glorious unspoilt picture of green England. Ancient farm buildings quietly spice a rural route riddled with pleasure.

## River Severn

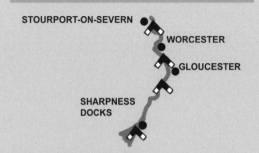

**STOURPORT-ON-SEVERN**
      **WORCESTER**
      **GLOUCESTER**
**SHARPNESS DOCKS**

Stourport to Gloucester (navigable)
42 miles (220 from source), 5 locks

Without the manmade ease of canals, a river's high banks often block the traveller's all important views, but the unpredictability of nature's waterways does give rivers a different energy from canals. The largest river in Britain starts life as an unnoticed trickle in Wales and then gathers muscle for its rite of passage into the sea at Sharpness in Gloucestershire. The River Severn isn't just a local star, it's a national phenomenon. The Severn Bore has entertained and challenged folk throughout history. Man has always used the river as a transport route, and sometimes tried to tame her, but never completely won over her wilfulness. This ancient river has claimed countless lives and drowned the ships of past kings and queens galore. The Gloucester & Sharpness Canal was built to bypass the treacherous tidal stretch as far as Gloucester, and northwards from there the river forms a vital link to the canal cruising ring between Worcester and Stourport.

## Shropshire Union Canal

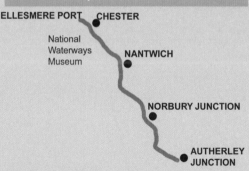

**ELLESMERE PORT**    **CHESTER**

National Waterways Museum     **NANTWICH**

**NORBURY JUNCTION**

**AUTHERLEY JUNCTION**

Autherley Junction to Ellesmere Port
66½ miles, 47 locks

The trademark of this route is its brutishly gentle journey. The canal carves its way through deep cuttings and strides along straight embankments as if it were in a hurry. Long stretches are lock free and boats can throttle away at 4mph without a care in the world. This isn't a big city hopper, it's more solitary and professes to do no more than gambol through villages of no notoriety other than their village appeal. The National Waterways Museum is the crowning glory at the end of the trail. Here, the canal (and anyone in a boat who dares) tumbles into Liverpool's intrepid River Mersey.

# Waterways
## of the Heart of England
boat, bike, boot

## Staffordshire & Worcestershire Canal

**STAFFORD**

**GREAT HAYWOOD JUNCTION**

**STOURPORT-ON-SEVERN**

Stourport-on-Severn to Great Haywood Junction
46 miles, 43 locks

One of the busiest and one of the best. The Staffs & Worcs Canal is outrageously rural for a canal that clings to the edges of the Black Country. It defies the rules of the urban map as it follows its winding course, pearling secret leafy trails in the Midlands. Fiery red sandstone rocks overhang the breathtakingly narrow water route. A canal that is a soft adventure by boat and an undiluted treat by towpath.

## Stratford-on-Avon Canal

**KING'S NORTON JUNCTION**

Lapworth Locks

**STRATFORD-UPON-AVON**

Kings Norton Junction to Stratford-upon-Avon
25½ miles, 54 locks

You get everything you'd expect from an English canal that tiptoes through Shakespeare's patch. A narrow floral route marked distinctively with ironwork bridges painted black and white, unusual aqueducts, and willow trees boughing over the river Avon where the canal and river meet at the basin in Stratford. On the doorstep of the bardic town, yet far away from the coachloads of souvenir shoppers, this waterway composes its own sonnets.

## Trent & Mersey Canal

Anderton Boat Lift

Harecastle Tunnel

**STOKE-ON-TRENT**

**BURTON UPON TRENT**

**GREAT HAYWOOD**

**DERWENT MOUTH**

Derwent Mouth to Preston Brook
93½ miles, 76 locks

Boaters must submit to slog up Heartbreak Hill, endure the dark passage through Harecastle Tunnel and the iron labyrinth of the Anderton Boat Lift. Enough to fluster any helmsman, yet the Trent & Mersey Canal has an unaccountable character that makes it lovable. The canal's features of interest are never in short supply. Notoriously it served the Potteries in Stoke-on-Trent, and by no coincidence the canal cuts through Burton, the historic brewery capital of Britain, and at Great Haywood it hobnobs with the upper class at Shugborough Hall Estate. Never a dull moment, yet remarkably tranquil and green in most parts.

## Worcester & Birmingham Canal

**BIRMINGHAM**

Wast Hills Tunnel

Shortwood Tunnel

**ALVECHURCH**

Tardebigge Locks

Tardebigge Tunnel

**WORCESTER**

Worcester to Birmingham
30 miles, 58 locks

A journey from Birmingham to Worcester by road doesn't compare to this. The Worcester & Birmingham Canal leaves the second city behind and steals into Elgar countryside with handsome locks on a homely narrow waterway. Treats include tunnels reputedly inhabited by ghosts and the legendary Tardebigge, the longest lock flight anywhere on Britain's entire canal system. Dreaded and adored.

## The Avon Ring

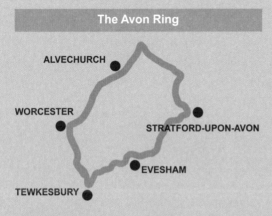

109 miles, 131 locks

by boat - a relaxing cruise takes 10/11 days
by bike - a leisurely slow ride takes around 3-4 days
by boot - a walk with time to sightsee takes around one week

River Avon, River Severn, Worcester & Birmingham Canal and Stratford-on-Avon Canal

This is the real full English! The Avon Ring travels through the heart of England on canals and the rivers Avon and Severn, weaving through some of the prettiest countryside and best tourist sites in England. You'll visit Stratford-upon-Avon, pass through idyllic English villages, cross the Edstone Aqueduct, and meander through Tewkesbury, Evesham and Pershore (reputed to be Borchester in the Archers, BBC Radio 4).

## The Black Country Ring

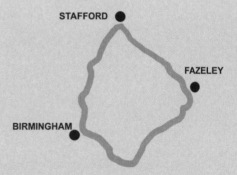

80 miles, 79 locks

by boat - an energetic cruise takes one week
by bike - a leisurely slow ride takes around 3 days
by boot - a walk with time to sightsee takes around 5 days

Birmingham & Fazeley Canal, Coventry Canal, Trent & Mersey Canal, Staffs & Worcs Canal & BCN

An energetic route, with the fascinating Black Country Living Museum, Fradley Junction, the sprawling green territory of Cannock Chase and the historic canal basin in Birmingham city centre.

## The Stourport Ring

84 miles, 118 locks

by boat - an energetic cruise takes one week
by bike - a leisurely slow ride takes around 3 days
by boot - a walk with time to sightsee takes around 5-6 days

Worcester & Birmingham Canal, Dudley Canal, Stourbridge Canal, Staffs & Worcs Canal, River Severn & BCN

A popular ring for holiday hire boats. The ring is the chameleon that includes canals and rivers that amble through secret countryside, industrial heritage, the Tardebigge Flight, the Black Country and the canal capital of Birmingham.

# ROUTES
## along the towpath

## SOME DESIGNATED TOWPATH ROUTES

### Coventry Canal

**NATIONAL CYCLE NETWORK (NCN) ROUTE 52**
Will run from Warwick to Route 6 near Loughborough
Follows the canal towpath all the way from Coventry to
Hawkesbury, and from Bedworth to Nuneaton.

### Grand Union Canal (Midlands)

**GRAND UNION CANAL WALK**
137 miles
Follows the canal towpath all the way from London to
Birmingham.

**LIAS LINE CYCLEWAY**
National Cycle Network (NCN) Route 41
Will run from Bristol to Rugby (once fully open)
Follows the canal towpath much of the way from Long
Itchington to Leamington Spa.

### Grantham Canal

**NATIONAL CYCLE NETWORK (NCN) ROUTE 15**
Will run from Castle Donington to Route 1 near Tattershall
(once fully open)
Follows the canal towpath all the way from Grantham to
Muston.

### Staffordshire & Worcestershire Canal

**NATIONAL CYCLE NETWORK (NCN) ROUTE 54**
Will run from Stourport to Derby (once fully open)
Follows the canal towpath all the way from Stourport to
Kidderminster.

### Trent & Mersey Canal

**CHESHIRE RING CANAL WALK**
29 miles (total trail 97 miles)
Follows the canal towpath all the way from Kidsgrove to
Preston Brook.

**NATIONAL CYCLE NETWORK (NCN) ROUTE 5**
Will run from Reading to Holyhead (once fully open)
Follows the canal towpath all the way from Barlaston to
Kidsgrove.

### Worcester & Birmingham Canal

**THE MERCIAN WAY**
National Cycle Network (NCN) Route 45
Will run from Salisbury to Chester (once fully open)
Follows the canal towpath all the way from Worcester to
Offerton.

### More info

For more detailed information and maps of all National Cycle
Network Routes, go to www.sustrans.org.uk.

For more walks and trails, go to www.ramblers.org.uk

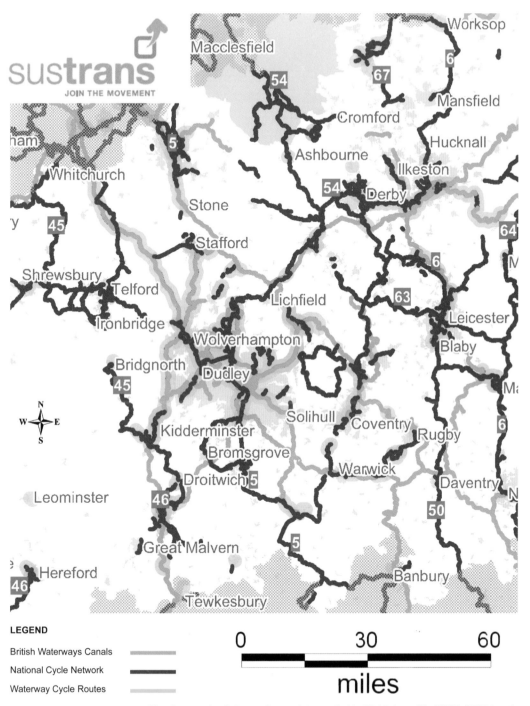

**sustrans**
JOIN THE MOVEMENT

Worksop
Macclesfield
54
67
6
Mansfield
Cromford
Ashbourne
Hucknall
ham
5
Ilkeston
54
Whitchurch
Derby
Stone
y
45
Stafford
64
Shrewsbury
6
Telford
Lichfield
63
Ironbridge
Leicester
Wolverhampton
Blaby
Bridgnorth
Dudley
45
Solihull
Coventry
6
N
Kidderminster
Rugby
W    E
Bromsgrove
Warwick
S
Droitwich 5
Daventry
Leominster
46
50
Great Malvern
5
Hereford
Banbury
46
Tewkesbury

**LEGEND**

British Waterways Canals ————

National Cycle Network ————

Waterway Cycle Routes ————

0       30       60

**miles**

Mapping contains Ordnance Survey data supplied by Welsh Assembly, HMSO, DEFRA and Dotted Eyes © Crown Copyright licence nos 100017916, 100020540 and 100011918. Also data from OpenStreetMap © www.openstreetmap.org (and) contributors licence CC-BY-SA (www.creativecommons.org)

# Routes
along the towpath

JOIN THE MOVEMENT

Richard Fairhurst
Sustrans Volunteer Ranger
for North Oxfordshire
& Editor, Waterways World magazine

## My favourite bike rides

"I've always been a boater. In my childhood years it was a cabin cruiser on Leicestershire's River Soar - in my 20s, an old Grand Union wooden carrying craft optimistically described as a 'project boat' - now, a 40ft narrowboat in which I've explored pretty much all the Midland canals. (Still working on restoring the wooden boat...)

I've always been a cyclist, too. But somehow the idea of cycling along towpaths had never really occurred to me until I first started working as a waterway journalist in 1998 - and realised you can get much better photos of the canals if you're not always steering a boat. Better still, you can shove the bike on the train, and go and explore a canal it would take you a month to reach by boat.

### A bike ride along the Bimingham Canal Network (BCN)

Birmingham's canal system is fascinating to explore whether by boat or bike. The towpath from Birmingham city centre to Wolverhampton forms part of National Routes 5 and 81 - make sure you stop at Wolverhampton, or you'll end up in Aberystwyth (with a short spell on the Montgomery Canal towpath). It's a unique ride. The canal was straightened out by Thomas Telford in the 1840s, cutting off the bends of the old line - but with so many canalside factories, there was no question of abandoning the original canal. So they were retained as 'loops'. Some survive today: others have closed, but you can still see the bridges, in brick or cast iron, where they crossed the new line. Look out, too, for the islands where boatmen paid their tolls.

Birmingham has over 100 miles of canals, most with cyclable towpaths (the Tame Valley Canal is one exception). So take a good map, and lots of photos.

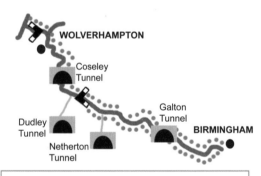

## Factfile

Start: Birmingham OS SP063864
Finish: Wolverhampton OS SJ902011
National Cycle Network (NCN) Routes 5 & 81
13 miles, 3 locks (+Wolverhampton 21), 2 tunnels (The mightly Dudley and Netherton Tunnels are off the route)

### Highlights
Gas Street Basin & Brindley Place - Birmingham
Cast-iron bridges along the route
Wolverhampton's flight of 21 locks leading down to the Staffordshire & Worcestershire Canal

### More info
For more detailed information and maps of all National Cycle Network Routes, go to www.sustrans.org.uk

# Routes
along the towpath

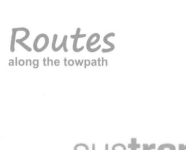

## sustrans
### JOIN THE MOVEMENT

**A bike ride along the Worcester & Birmingham and Droitwich Canals**

There are two National Cycle Network routes between Worcester and Droitwich (45 and 46), making for an enjoyable afternoon's cycling with plenty of waterway interest. Start at Diglis Basin or Shrub Hill station in Worcester, and cycle along the newly upgraded towpath of the Worcester & Birmingham Canal. After Offerton's picture perfect locks, you dive off onto country lanes (and a terrific downhill bridleway) for the approach to Droitwich.

But the canal tour isn't over yet. Far from it. Droitwich's canals, closed in the 1930s, have been restored and reopened to bring boats back to this historic salt town; and as you thread your way through the town streets to join National Route 46, you'll encounter the Droitwich Barge Canal, where, unusually, boats were once pulled by donkeys. Take an hour or two to explore the newly rebuilt canal, before following the Route 46 signs back to Worcester on country lanes criss-crossing the canal here and there.

Eventually you'll arrive at magnificent Worcester Cathedral, on the banks of the Severn. Continue beside the river for a mile more, to Diglis Locks and Sustrans' shiny new pedestrian and cycle bridge (part of the Lottery-funded Connect2 project). Diglis is where the canal and river meet, completing the loop.

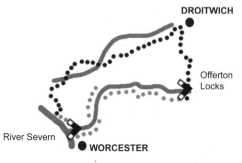

## Factfile

Start: Diglis Basin, Worcester OS SO848538
Finish: Diglis Basin, Worcester OS SO848538
National Cycle Network (NCN) Routes 45 & 46
18 miles, 16 locks

### Highlights
Diglis Basin
Offerton Locks
The newly restored Droitwich Canal

### More info
For more detailed information and maps of all National Cycle Network Routes, go to www.sustrans.org.uk

### A bike ride along the Trent & Mersey Canal and Derby Canal

And for the real enthusiast, head to Derbyshire for a grand waterway tour.

Starting at the pretty little town of Melbourne, in the south of the county, take National Route 6 north on the fine railway viaduct over the River Trent - navigable here until the Trent & Mersey Canal stole its trade.

After a pretty spell on the towpath beside the T&M, it follows the old Derby Canal more or less all the way through Derby - and who knows, this restoration project might be the next Droitwich - to Long Eaton and the broad, quiet Erewash Canal. From here Route 67 takes you to the almost forgotten Nutbrook Canal. Like the Derby Canal, it's been many years since a boat passed along here - so why not cycle it instead?"

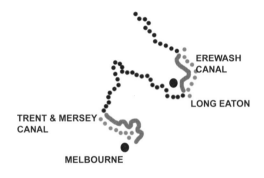

EREWASH CANAL

LONG EATON

TRENT & MERSEY CANAL

MELBOURNE

## Factfile

Start: Melbourne OS SK394260
Finish: Ilkeston OS SK471425
National Cycle Network (NCN) Route 6
23 miles, 4 locks

### Highlights
Swarkestone Lock & the bridge over the River Trent

### More info
For more detailed information and maps of all National Cycle Network Routes, go to www.sustrans.org.uk

| New bridge at Diglis - Hanbury Locks, Droitwich Canal |

# Routes
along the towpath

**Phillippa & Martine**
Some of the highlights of our epic canal walk from Cornwall to Scotland

## Our favourite walks

We have walked every extreme canal, skipping along sunny canals in Cornwall, and hiking in all-weather boots over Scotland's heather-speckled waterways - and yet the unassuming canals of the Midlands have burned the soles of our feet with some of the most pleasurable miles we could dare to tread. Every canal in this region has its own character, and we never get bored of revisiting some of our favourite towpaths. The narrow winding routes bursting with engineering features are always fascinating to walk.

We like to set off early in the morning, especially in winter when the days are shorter. As dawn breaks, nothing beats the call of the wild over the Midlands' tranquil waterways. Often only a hedgerow away from the urban world, the morning air smells of water. You can sense the wildlife huddled in the hedgerows, on the water's edge, in the trees and on the water - all waiting for us to pass before they come out to play. There's nowhere on earth quite like the canals in the Heart of Britain.

**A walk along the Worcester & Birmingham**

This is a journey that climbs the Tardebigge, the longest lock flight in Britain - 30 locks with the audacity to carry narrowboats 220 feet uphill and downhill in still water. A staggering route with scenery dominated by outstretched black and white lock arms.

Despite being one of Britain's most lock-ridden waterways, the Worcester & Birmingham Canal is remarkably popular with holidaying boaters. A hilly journey is more of a physical workout for boaters than walkers, and the Tardebigge takes hours longer by boat than on foot. To make matters worse for the Tardebigge boater, there's no overnight mooring allowed midway through the flight, so it's a gruelling, non-stop challenge - each narrow lock takes around 10 to 15 minutes to work through.

The boater's challenge makes the walker's journey even more exhilarating, and everyone shares the flight with 'we're in it together' camaraderie.

On summer towpaths, walkers mingle with gongoozlers and everyone gets whisked into the boating experience. In winter, there are fewer boats and the lone towpath walker is left with emptier views. Don't be put off by winter though - we've walked this stretch of canal in all seasons and whether the flight is snow-covered or sun-scorched, it's uplifting territory.

Halfway through the flight, views span as far as Worcestershire, Gloucestershire and Shropshire. This is Elgar's patch and his Malvern Hills peep from the distance, stringing music over the water.

An uplifting walk any time of year.

## Factfile

### Worcester and Birmingham Canal
Start: Stoke Prior OS SP022721
Finish: Tardebigge OS SO951670
3 miles, 36 locks

### Highlights
Tardebigge Lock Flight
Stoke Lock Flight
Tardebigge Reservoir, near the top of the flight

### Did you know?

The entire Worcester & Birmingham Canal is part of the Stourport Ring - one of the most popular boating routes on the canal network. The ring also includes the Staffordshire & Worcestershire Canal, the Birmingham Canal Navigations (BCN) and the River Severn. The canal is always busy with boats being picked up and dropped off at the home bases of three major boat hire operators.

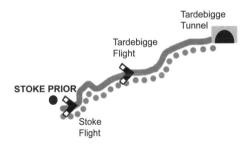

### The Tardebigge Flight

The longest flight of locks in the UK, with 30 locks raising the canal 220 feet in just over 2 miles. Tardebigge Top Lock is one of the deepest in Britain, with a rise of over 11 feet. Originally a boat lift was built on the site but it was replaced by an extra deep lock for technical reasons and to save money for the company building the canal.

### Historic boat

The Birmingham, a tug built in 1912, is on display in the boat yard at Tardebigge. The tug's primary purpose was to pull working horse boats through the canal's tunnels.

### IWA plaque

At the top of the flight, a plaque commemorates the famous meeting between Tom Rolt and Robert Aickman which took place aboard narrowboat Cressy, near Tardebigge Top Lock. Rolt and Aickman were behind the founding of the IWA (Inland Waterways Association) in 1946.

# Routes
## along the towpath

### A walk along the Staffs & Worcs Canal

The Staffs & Worcs Canal is a stunner, and the towpath walk from Wolverley to Stourton can rival anywhere along the canals of Britain for sheer appeal. It's a leafy slice of tranquillity and a retreat from the treacherously nearby urban mass.

Amongst boaters it's famous for its narrow winding route and roaring-red sandstone rocks that perilously overhang the water. The canal is a boater's favourite for its distinctive beauty, and always popular (despite the menace of foxy rocks waiting to scratch the precious paintwork of narrowboats). The walker's secret amusement is to watch pale-faced helmsmen navigating with bated breath and scrunched eyes.

This fascinating route leads over the boundary from Worcestershire to Staffordshire. The towpath takes you past mysterious caves carved into the red sandstone, a historic toll house, wildlife and flora, canopies of trees and sheep-filled fields. The canal was built to carry cargoes of coal, steel, carpets and all kinds of materials that scarcely fit its delicious green ambience. Now it has become one of the busiest and best in Britain for leisure boating (and gongoozling). The whole walk is leafy and uplifting, but the highlight is from Hyde Lock to Stourton.

### Factfile

**Staffordshire & Worcestershire Canal**
Start: Wolverley OS SO831791
Finish: Stourton Junction OS SO861848
6½ miles, 6 locks

**Highlights**
Hyde Lock
Crossing the county border
Stourton Junction

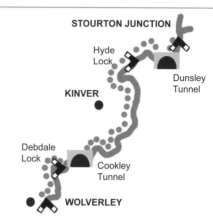

Hyde Lock is one of England's most idyllic canal locks. Perched above the village of Kinver, it looks down from a green woodland oasis. From here to Stourton is as good as walking gets. We come in April to see the bluebells, again in summer when the trees are green, return in autumn to see the leaves turn golden, and we can't resist winter, the most peaceful season of all.

### Border stone

Between bridges 26 and 27, a large stone was erected by the Staffs & Worcs Canal Society in 1999 to mark the border between Worcestershire and Staffordshire. The survival of the canal as a leisure destination is thanks to the tireless hard work of the Society

### Caves

A small cave is cut into the red sandstone by Debdale Lock. This was formerly used as overnight stabling for the working boat horses.

### Brindley's bends

The Staffordshire & Worcestershire Canal, opened in 1772, was one of the earliest canals built by the great canal engineer, James Brindley. This winding walk from Wolverley to Stourton dramatically highlights his preferred engineering method of following the contours of the land rather than climbing over and through obstacles.

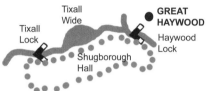

**A walk along the Trent & Mersey and Staffordshire & Worcestershire Canal**

This north Staffordshire walk keeps stories blowing in the wind at every turn of the canal. A map will tell you that Great Haywood is the T-junction where the Staffs & Worcs meets the Trent & Mersey, but more quintessentially it is where the North teeters on the Midlands and dialects mingle amongst boaters. In the boating season it's a popular spot, almost guaranteed to be stem-to-stern mooring with plenty of canal life for the walker to soak up. From the water, boaters' kettles boil, Sunday papers sprawl the decks and it's the sort of place where boaty paraphernalia and Brasso come out with pride.

There's something inexplicably graceful about this circular canal walk around Shugborough Hall, the ancestral home of the Earls of Lichfield. The mansion dates back to 1693, exuding panache and royal connections over the landscape. Patrick, the photographer, was its most famous guardian, until his death in 2005. The towpath heads south along the canal, briefly curving into an unusually wide swell of water. The canal tries to fool you that it has become a lake - and the illusion is deliberate. The story goes that in the 18th century, when the canal was being built, Clifford Thomas who occupied the once nearby Tixall Hall was unimpressed by the idea of a water-motorway ruining his views. He grumbled enough to force the canal company to widen the bit of canal he could see from his home. Although it seems odd to walkers today that our idyllic narrow canals were once perceived as ugly, the disguise at Tixall Wide is still a treat.

The whole walk is a haven for wildlife as the canal winds through a conservation area. If you're lucky, you might spot a heron or even the blue flash of a kingfisher. It's probably true that gaggles of geese don't usually get the cooing 'aahs and oohs' that glamorous birds and swans do, but if you catch the air display they put on around dawn and dusk, you'll understand how goose bumps got their name. Great Haywood is a popular daytime spot for geese, so there's a chance to witness the hullabaloo of mass landing or take off and an arrow-shaped flight of geese flapping and honking in the sky. One of the natural wonders of the waterways. Not to miss.

**Watch out for cameras!**

It's rumoured that the listed bridge at Great Haywood Junction is the most photographed bridge on the canals. It's a popular mooring spot for narrowboats and home to one of Anglo Welsh's hireboat bases.

**Scheduled Ancient Monuments**

Essex Bridge and the bridge at Great Haywood Junction are both Scheduled Ancient Monuments, and the gardens and landscape around Shugborough Hall are Grade I registered. Great Haywood, Tixall and Shugborough are also all designated Conservation Areas.

## Factfile

**Staffordshire & Worcestershire Canal**
Start & Finish: Great Haywood Junction OS SJ994229
4 miles (circular), 1 lock

**Highlights**
Essex Bridge
Tixall Wide

**Did you know?**
Legend has it that the ladies of Shugborough Hall in the 18th century didn't relish the uncouth idea of riding their own horses across Essex Bridge, a narrow packhorse bridge over the River Trent. So a new wider bridge was built to carry them in carriages, in all their finery, over the river to church in the village - yards away!

# Routes
## along the towpath

### A walk along the Droitwich Canal

IN 1651 when King Charles II was defeated in the Battle of Worcester, he made his escape along the route now known as the Monarch's Way. This way-marked footpath follows part of the route of the Droitwich Canal today.

Long after King Charles' antics, Droitwich Canal faced its own battle for survival. Abandoned, forgotten and doomed to dereliction, few cared about the canal as it crumbled from neglect after its commercial carrying days were over. But Droitwich has always been a feisty place. Romans settled here, in about 47AD, knowing the value of salt. They called the town Salinae (salt) and Roman soldiers even received part of their pay (salary) in salt. The Domesday Book repeatedly mentions Droitwich and its natural asset of salt, and medieval Droitwich kept its meat fresh with local salt long before electric fridges existed.

Later, the leisure-seeking Victorians lavished their Spa town with love. The arrival of canals helped the salt industry prosper in Droitwich and boats carrying salty cargoes kept the canal busy until the canal officially closed in 1939. There was no turning back for the fortunes of the canal and if there had been a glimmer of hope, it would have been doused when WWII swamped Britain. The water-route was lost, unnavigable for boats and overgrown for walkers. But it wasn't

### Barge Canal and Junction Canal

Strictly speaking, the Droitwich Canal is two canals. The Barge Canal, engineered by James Brindley, was opened in 1771 to allow river barges (trows) to travel from the River Severn as far as Droitwich. The narrower Junction Canal was built later, in 1854, to connect Droitwich to the Worcester & Birmingham Canal at Hanbury.

### The Monarch's Way

This long-distance trail, 615 miles, follows the route taken by Charles II during his escape after the battle of Worcester in 1651. It joins the Droitwich Canal for a short way before heading off cross-country to the Stourbridge. www.monarchsway.50megs.com

## Factfile

**Droitwich Canal**
Start: Hanbury Wharf OS SO922629
Finish: River Severn OS SO842599
7¼ miles, 16 locks

**Highlights**
Salwarpe's medieval church and Tudor manor house
Ladywood Locks

**Did you know?**
Italian prisoners of war were put to work during the Second World War to fill in one of the bridges in order to strengthen the road above (now the A449) for troop and tank movements. During the canal's restoration, a new tunnel was built next to the original one.

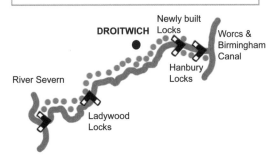

lost forever. The now legendary enthusiasm of intrepid leisure boaters in the early 1970s meant a new movement was growing. The Droitwich Canal whispered for help and the triumph of its restoration has come from the co-operation and collaboration of many voices, and the sweat and stalwart vision of 'mere' volunteers.

We've walked this canal many times and watched its progress. Where there were once dry armies of reeds, there is now a water trail to follow. New red bricks cobble with the old and a lost route has come back to life. Don't forget to admire the new lock arms and the welcome sight of wildlife on the water. The canal briefly nips through the outskirts of the Spa town. Beyond town, the views open out and the canal is at its rural best heading towards the river. Untouched blankets of green are scattered with ancient farm buildings that haven't been visually spoilt by corrugations of concrete extensions. If you allow your mind, it will hear a canal still whispering back to 1770s.

| Hanbury Locks |

# ROUTES
boating

**Two families from Sussex shared a narrowboat holiday.**
**The Saunders family - Tony, Julie and Jack - with their friends Simon and Karen Harris and Emily.**

## Our favourite route
### A cruise along Birmingham's Canals

Ask anyone who has just been on a narrowboat holiday how far they've travelled and they'll reply in lock numbers not miles. "We've done 72 locks" say the Harris and Saunders families on their return from their first ever hireboat holiday on the canals. Karen and Julie grin as they tell us, "Tony and Simon did all the driving and left us women to do the hard work at the locks. We discovered muscles we never knew we had!"

On the canals this is not a real gender war - it's the mandatory good banter boaters share, because when we throw out the question, "What was the highlight of your holiday?" everyone chants together, "The locks!"

"Our hire boat had all the mod cons from central heating and hairdryers to a proper TV. But none

of us, not even the children, bothered to waste time watching TV," says Karen.

"...and we had a real break from cooking and ate at a canalside pub every night. Except for the day we'd done 46 locks and we were too exhausted to leave the boat."

**Would you do it again?**
"YES!"

"...the holiday was a good mix. It's the sort of holiday for people who don't want to sit by a pool. An adventure!"

**What's the best thing?**
"One of the best things I've discovered - it's sunset at 8.30."
Karen

**What's the wierdest thing?**
"When we stood in the pub at night, we felt like the floor was still rocking after being afloat all day."
Julie

**A confession?**
"We crashed a few times (but don't tell Alvechurch Boats)."
Simon

**But what do the kids say?**
"We slept on bunk beds"
Emily (with an ear-to-ear smile)

"I liked doing the ropes best when we moored up at night."
Jack

## Factfile

Alvechurch Marina OS SP020720

**More info**
66ft boat. 'Gull' class. Sleeps up to 6
UK Boat Hire
www.ukboathire.com

**Route for a short break**
The **BIRMINGHAM MINI RING** is a good route for a short cruise. From Alvechurch, the route follows the Worcester & Birmingham Canal, the Grand Union Canal and then the Stratford Canal. You can spend a night in the city, moored in the heart of Birmingham centre and cruise through fascinating industrial architecture as well as quiet Warwickshire villages.

Slow travel at its best. A narrowboat holiday reaches the psyche in ways other holidays can't. From the minute you climb aboard your boat, you're in charge of your own tiller and nothing can rush you. There are enough challenges to levy adrenalin, and learning new boat-handling skills is all part of the fun, but cruising Britain's inland waterways has to be the ultimate break away from the stress-ridden clutter of everyday life.

Push off from the water's edge and leave any cares behind, stopping when you choose, enjoying lazy sightseeing from the water and a good waterside pub at the end of the day.

Everyone on the waterways becomes part of the unique community spirit. No one is exempt from a friendly nod or helping hand over a tight boating manoeuvre. Towpath tourists and fellow boaters unite in compulsory gongoozling, yet no one gloats over the misfortune of a badly steered bend or helmsman's hair-raising brush with overhanging branches. The water-road is laid-back, still nurturing blissfully old-fashioned manners and camaraderie that hard-surfaced roads have forgotten.

# ROUTES
boating

Two families, sharing a narrowboat holiday.

**Andrew and Ruth Davies and teenagers Emily and Grace, with friends Mike and Nia Donnelly and Bethan.**

## Our favourite route
**A cruise along the Worcester & Birmingham Canal**

Andrew has experience of sailing boats on the sea, but this was his first time in charge of a tiller on the canals. "It's harder than being at sea!" Andrew laughs, "There's more room for mistakes on the ocean, but on the canals you crash into the banks if you take your eye off the task." It doesn't matter if you've never been on a narrowboat before - learning how to steer with a tiller and handle ropes is all part of the fun. Steer right to go left, and left to go right. Simple (and hilarious till you get the hang of it!)

Holiday hireboats come with every mod con from a measuring jug to an umbrella, and a cold fridge to a hot shower. Just turn up with your personal belongings and cruise away into the sunset.

**Did you have a good time?**
"Really good. Really relaxing."

**Best holiday memory?**
"Birmingham and the fascinating industrial heritage along the canal, as well as the lovely countryside."

**Wierdest thing?**
"We all got on so well in such a narrow space."

**Funniest thing?**
"We met a family on another boat who hated the whole boating thing. They moaned nonstop about how much hard work it was."

**Would you do it again?**
"Yes, absolutely. We're booking again next year."

## Factfile
Alvechurch Marina OS SP020720

**More info**
69ft boat. 'Goose' class. Sleeps up to 8
UK Boat Hire
www.ukboathire.com

**Route for a short break**
The **MID-WORCESTERSHIRE RING** is the 'newest' ring on the canal networks. The recently restored Droitwich Canals link the Worcester & Birmingham Canal with the River Severn at Hawford, creating a mini cruising ring. The opening of the ring (2011) is cause for celebration for canal enthusiasts, and this scenic route will also be a joy for boaters looking for a short cut from the Stourport Ring that joins the river further south at Worcester.

# Boats
## in the Heart of England

## Ashby Canal

**ASHBY BOAT COMPANY**
Narrowboat holiday & day hire.
Stoke Golding. T:01455 212671
www.ashbyboats.co.uk

## Caldon Canal

**COUNTRYSIDE CRUISING HOLS**
Narrowboat holiday hire.
Endon. T:01538 381690
www.countrysidecruising.co.uk

## Coventry Canal

**VALLEY CRUISES**
Narrowboat holiday hire.
Nuneaton. T:02476 393333
www.valleycruises.co.uk

## Grand Union Canal (Mids)

**ANGLO WELSH WATERWAY HOLIDAYS**
Narrowboat holiday & day hire.
North Kilworth. T:0117 3041122
www.anglowelsh.co.uk

**CALCUTT BOATS**
Narrowboat holiday hire.
Stockton. T:01926 813757
www.calcuttboats.com

**FOXTON BOAT SERVICES**
Trip boat and day boat hire.
Foxton. T:01162 792285
www.foxtonboats.co.uk

**KATE BOATS**
Narrowboat holiday hire.
Warwick & Stockton. T:01926 492968
www.kateboats.co.uk

**SAISONS**
Narrowboat holiday hire.
Whilton Marina. T:01327 844442
www.saisons.co.uk

**SILEBY MILL**
Narrowboat holiday & day hire.
Sileby. T:01509 813583
www.surftech.co.uk/canal/sileby

**UK BOAT HIRE**
Narrowboat holiday hire.
Gayton, Market Harborough & Rugby.
T:0845 1264098
www.ukboathire.com

**UNION CANAL CARRIERS**
Narrowboat holiday & day hire.
Braunston. T:01788 890784
www.unioncanalcarriers.co.uk

## Shropshire Union Canal

**ANGLO WELSH WATERWAY HOLIDAYS**
Narrowboat holiday & day hire.
Bunbury. T:0117 3041122
www.anglowelsh.co.uk

**CHAS. HARDERN BOATS**
Narrowboat holiday hire.
Tarporley. T:01829 732595
www.chashardern.co.uk

**CHESHIRE CAT NARROWBOAT HOL**
Narrowboat holiday hire.
Nantwich. T:07867 790195
www.cheshirecatnarrowboats.co.uk

**COUNTRYWIDE CRUISERS**
Narrowboat holiday hire.
Brewood. T:01902 850166
www.countrywide-cruisers.com

**NAPTON NARROWBOATS**
Narrowboat holiday hire.
Autherley Jct. T:01926 813644
www.napton-marina.co.uk

**NORBURY WHARF**
Narrowboat holiday & day hire.
Norbury. T:01785 284292
www.norburywharfltd.co.uk

**WELSH GATEWAY CANAL HOLS**
Narrowboat holiday & day hire.
Nantwich. T:01270 624075
www.welshgatewaycanalholidays.co.uk

## Staffs & Worcs Canal

**ANGLO WELSH WATERWAY HOLIDAYS**
Narrowboat holiday & day hire.
Great Haywood. T:0117 3041122
www.anglowelsh.co.uk

**UK BOAT HIRE**
Narrowboat holiday hire.
Gailey. T:0845 1264098
www.ukboathire.com

## Stratford-on-Avon Canal

**ANGLO WELSH WATERWAY HOLIDAYS**
Narrowboat holiday & day hire.
Wootton Wawen. T:0117 3041122
www.anglowelsh.co.uk

**LYONS BOATS**
Narrowboat holiday hire.
Warstock. T:0121 474 4977
www.lyonsboats.co.uk

## Trent & Mersey Canal

**ANDERSEN BOATS**
Narrowboat holiday hire.
Middlewich. T:01606 833668
www.andersenboats.com

**AQUA NARROWBOATS**
Narrowboat holiday hire.
Willington. T:01283 701041
www.aquanarrowboathire.com

**BLACK PRINCE NARROWBOAT HOLIDAYS**
Narrowboat holiday hire.
Acton Bridge & Stoke-on-Trent.
T:01527 575115
www.black-prince.com

**CANAL CRUISING CO.**
Narrowboat holiday hire.
Stone. T:01785 813982
www.canalcruising.co.uk

**CREST NARROWBOATS**
Narrowboat holiday hire.
Stoke-on-Trent. T:01691 774558
www.crestnarrowboats.co.uk

**MIDDLEWICH NARROWBOATS**
Narrowboat holiday hire.
Middlewich. T:01606 832460
www.middlewichboats.co.uk

**UK BOAT HIRE**
Narrowboat holiday hire.
Anderton. T:0845 1264098
www.ukboathire.com

## Worcester & Birmingham

**ANGLO WELSH WATERWAY HOLIDAYS**
Narrowboat holiday & day hire.
Tardebigge. T:0117 3041122
www.anglowelsh.co.uk

**BLACK PRINCE NARROWBOAT HOLIDAYS**
Narrowboat holiday hire.
Stoke Prior. T:01527 575115
www.black-prince.com

**BROOK LINE**
Narrowboat holiday hire.
Dunhampstead. T:01905 773889
www.brookline.co.uk

**UK BOAT HIRE**
Narrowboat holiday hire. Alvechurch &
Worcester. T:0845 1264098
www.ukboathire.com

# Waterways people

Haley Shurmer
Marketing Manager, UK Boat Hire

"My career at ABC Leisure Group commenced almost three years ago now but my involvement with the waterways started long before. In 2001 my partner Russ suggested that we try living afloat on a narrowboat. Having never lived together or even taken a holiday on a narrowboat this was perhaps a recipe for a break up! It turns out this was something he had been dreaming of since he was a young boy. So not wanting to disappoint him I agreed! We started searching

for our new home in the waterways press and six months later we found 'Emily Gray'. Once purchased we quickly began updating her to our own taste and managed to find residential moorings in various locations including central Birmingham and Worcester. We took every opportunity to get away at weekends and holidays, and cruised most of the Midland waterways. The amazing thing about the canals is that you really feel as if you are away from everything almost immediately and your worries float away while you enjoy the ever changing scenery.

After two years living afloat, the time had come to find a land-based location and we were lucky enough to find an old farm worker's cottage literally a few minutes' walk from Austcliffe on the Staffordshire & Worcestershire Canal and found a mooring for her close by. This was to be her mooring for more than five years.

My canal knowledge and experience has really helped me in my role at ABC Leisure Group as I can speak to customers with genuine passion about canals, cruising and my experience living afloat.

You will be pleased to know that Russ and I are still together although Emily Gray is no longer with us as we now enjoy holidays from one of UK Boat Hire's start locations whenever we can."

# Waterways people
Mollie Lloyd
and her two dogs, Lenny and Meg

# My local canal
Staffordshire & Worcestershire Canal

"I often walk my two dogs along the canal near Kidderminster. It's a pocket of countryside in the middle of the town. The dogs can run free off the lead and get really excited by all the smells and open space to run around together. Meg can't resist a swim though! And Lenny likes to get his feet wet in shallow bits on the banks if he can too. I love watching the wildlife and, even this close to town, I often see herons, geese, ducks, swans and lots of birds in the hedgerows.

My canal is only metres away from the town's busy ring-road, yet somehow it's like a rural walk. The dogs and I sometimes carry on walking until we reach the surrounding villages... and the Lock Inn at Wolverley always welcomes me, even when the dogs are soggy with mud in winter.

I think the best thing about going to the canal for my dog walks is that I can carry on walking as far as I like and never get lost. I'm hopeless at directions and the canal is great because I can just follow the towpath instead of having to concentrate on maps. I take in the surroundings and watch my dogs enjoying themselves! The canal is our favourite walk... And the towpath is a particularly friendly place when we meet other dog walkers."

# WILDLIFE & NATURE

Canals were built for boats, but have become a vital habitat for wildlife too. As our towns and cities sprawl greedily and our once green gardens become concrete parking lots, the canals are increasingly important for British wildlife. These green corridors rambling through every corner of the land create an everyday haven for wild plants, insects, fish and wild creatures. Badgers to barn owls, bats to butterflies, water voles to bumble bees, crayfish to dragonflies, rabbits to ladybirds, robins to squirrels, hedgehogs to grass snakes. A Bellamy of a place with an awesome diversity of life.

## British Waterways' Wildlife Survey

Every year the Wildlife Survey is a chance for water-loving nature enthusiasts to head for the canals and record sightings of wildlife. Kingfishers, newts, toads and otters were spotted in record numbers in the 2010 survey. The results also showed curlews, merlins, water voles, otters and song thrushes.

With the fashion for low maintenance gardens, Britain's towns are slabbing over lost beds of flowers and insects - and so house sparrows have been a declining species. Luckily the canals still skip joyfully with miles of hedgerows and grassy towpaths giving the much-adored house sparrow respite from the arid urban jungle. This little bird was the 5th most sighted species in the 2010 survey.

## Factfile

### British Waterways' Wildlife Survey

British Waterways want everyone to get involved with their annual wildlife survey. It records all wildlife from insects to birds spotted along the waterways. Nobody is too young or old to get involved.
Takes place annually from March/April to September. Wildlife spotting goes on throughout the summer.

www.waterscape.com/wildlifesurvey

# DAYS OUT
### in the Heart of England

## Birmingham
## The canal capital

New York has Central Park... Birmingham has Brindley Place.

When it comes to canals, Birmingham is the capital, usurping London. With its fanfare of waterways charm, Birmingham owns more canals than Venice - and what it lacks in Gondola panache, it makes up for with romantic English narrowboats.

Right in the heart of the city, this waterways oasis is secretly hidden from the crowds. A retreat from the furore of shopping and noise, a place to sit and stare, somewhere to escape for lunch with the ducks.

The city is too busy to notice the waterways basin quietly under the bridge... and a collision of the two worlds is miraculously unlikely.

### BRINDLEY PLACE AND GAS STREET BASIN
The canal hub that was once vital for the Industrial Revolution. Gas Street Basin got its name from being the first zone in the city to have gas lighting. This was a measure of the importance of the place in the canal era. Narrowboats would have loaded and unloaded along the water's edge with cargoes of coal, chocolate crumb, raw materials heading to factories, and products on their way from the industries of the Midlands to world markets.

### LUNAR SOCIETY
The name for a group of learned and creative thinkers meeting in Birmingham between 1765 and 1813. Amongst them were eminent names including Erasmus Darwin, Matthew Boulton, Josiah Wedgwood, James Watt. Many conversations about the creation of canals and development of industrialisation were cannoned from here in Birmingham. www.lunarsociety.org.uk

## Factfile

**Birmingham Canal Navigations**
Birmingham OS SP061866

Birmingham Tourist Info
T:0121 202 5115 www.visitbirmingham.com

Canalside pubs, bars and restaurants around Brindley Place and Gas Street Basin.

The National Indoor Arena, the National SEA LIFE Centre and Symphony Hall are all canalside in Brindley Place.

Boat trips and water bus
Catch the water bus or take a boat trip through the heart of Birmingham (daily Easter-Oct & winter weekends)
T:0121 4556163 www.sherbornewharf.co.uk

# Days out

in the Heart of England

## The Potteries

Stoke doesn't pretend to be as attractive as Cornwall or the Cotswolds, nor does it bother garlanding its grimiest urban truths with fake sequins for tourists. What you get from a day out in the Potteries is a priceless peek into the innovative genius of Britain's pottery businesses spanning over two centuries.

The English cliché, 'a nice pot of tea', couldn't be more at home than around this part of the country. It was here in this area called the Potteries where pots for almost everything, including the original good old-fashioned teapot, were first mass-produced during the Industrial Revolution. And it's still ceramics heaven with living heritage shaping the skyline with charismatic bottle ovens and museums to visit, but also offering modern-day factory tours and factory shops galore.

The area of the Potteries was one of the main reasons the Trent & Mersey canal was built. Josiah Wedgwood (the world-renowned pottery manufacturer) was in the business of producing delicate products and, in his era of the 1700s, bumpy packhorse transportation was painfully slow and precarious over the existing rugged tracks. Wedgwood needed a better way to transport his finished products to buyers and also a more commercially efficient mode of getting the raw materials of coal, china clay and flint he needed for his factories.

With Wedgwood as one of the main benefactors, the great engineer James Brindley was employed and, after an 11-year build, the Trent & Mersey Canal was opened in 1777. The Potteries could now explode into mass production and export to the world, starting their journey by canal boat.

## Factfile

**Trent & Mersey Canal**

**THE WEDGWOOD MUSEUM & VISITOR CENTRE**
Barlaston OS SJ886394
A short walk from the canal, the Museum is in the grounds of the Wedgwood Factory and is home to a vast collection of ceramics, Fine art, manuscripts and documents dating back up to 250 years. The Visitor Centre offers an opportunity to see craftsmen at work and even try your own hand at some of the skills on show.

Open daily all year apart from Christmas and New Year. Mon-Fri 0900-1700, Sat-Sun 1000-1700

Restaurants, tea room and gift shops. Admission charge. Wheelchair access.

T:01782 371919 www.wedgwoodmuseum.org.uk
T:01782 282986 www.wedgwoodvisitorcentre.com

**GLADSTONE POTTERY MUSEUM**
Stoke-on-Trent OS SJ912432
The only intact pottery factory from the Victorian era (the height of the production of fine bone china), it still has its huge bottle kilns and cobbled yards. Daily workshops.

Open daily all year 1000-1700 apart from 24 Dec-4 Jan.

Tea room and gift shop. Admission charge. Wheelchair access to most areas.

T:01782 237777 www.stokemuseums.org.uk/gpm

**EMMA BRIDGEWATER**
Stoke-on-Trent OS SJ912432
The only modern working pottery housed in one of original 19th-century potteries. FREE factory tours, gift shop & factory outlet or you can decorate your own pots.

Open Mon-Sat 0930-1730 (2000 Thu), Sun 1100-1600.

Café, gift shop & factory outlet. Decorating Studio charge.

T:01782 201328 www.emmabridgewater.co.uk

# Days out
in the Heart of England

## Foxton Locks & Inclined Plane Museum

Canal history is wrapped up in an outdoor experience that is alive and kicking at Foxton. This staircase flight of 10 locks tumbles 75ft downhill, with soaring views over real scarecrow countryside.

The scene at Foxton remains vitually unchanged since the heyday of the canals over 200 years ago - except that the canal boats laden with cargoes of sugar, tea, soap, tinned food, chemicals and paper that once passed through the locks, have now been replaced by leisure boats that give a good show for gongoozlers. And the visitor can explore the canal attractions that lie behind the doors of old canalside buildings.

## Factfile

**Grand Union Canal - Leicester Section**
Foxton OS SP691897

**FOXTON INCLINED PLANE MUSEUM**
Open daily in summer 1000-1700
Nov-Mar weekends 1000-1600 (except Christmas).
Contact them for winter weekday hours.

Gift shop. Small admission charge. Wheelchair access.

T:01162 792657 www.fipt.org.uk / www.foxtonlocks.com

**DAY BOATS, BOAT TRIPS & BRIDGE 61 PUB**
T:1162 792285 www.foxtonboats.co.uk

**FOXTON LOCKS INN & THE OLD BOATHOUSE**
T:01162 791515 www.restaurantfoxtonlocks.co.uk

### Foxton Inclined Plane & Museum

Follow the way-marked trail that takes you from the bottom of the locks to the remains on the hill of Foxton Inclined Plane. Old tracks creak from the grassy hill through the rubble of history. The plane once lifted boats from the canal at the bottom of the hill, and hauled them over dry land to the water at the higher level. The inclined plane lifted the boats in a fraction of the time that it took to work through the 10-lock staircase. But after just 10 years in service, in 1911, the plane was deemed too expensive to maintain and was abandoned. Plans are afoot to reopen the lift, and Foxton Inclined Plane Trust who are behind the restoration, have their headquarters in the old lift's boiler house, where there is a small museum too.

### Boat trips

A 25-minute boat trips is available aboard 'Vagabond', a vintage boat, reputed to be over 100 years old. Sundays, Bank Holidays, some Saturdays & school holiday weekday afternoons (weather permitting)

### Day boats

Foxton Boats offer day boats for full day or half day hire. Boats are for up to 12 people (and you can take your dog too)

### The old stables

The old stables now house a discovery room with displays about the 50-60 horses and boats that once travelled through the locks every day.

### Coffee Stop

You can have tea and cake or a farmhouse ice cream - and meet John Cryer standing with his cap on his head and rock solid cup of tea in his hand, gazing nostalgically out of the window overlooking his lock. John is a life-sized model of the former lock keeper from the original era of canalmania. If you're willing to listen, he'll tell you about the old days (in a recorded monologue of his job as a lock keeper).

### Pubs

There is a pub on either side of the water at the junction at the bottom of the flight. Foxton Locks Inn is a foodie pub serving good real ales. Bridge 61 is an unusual mini-pub where you can get a pint of milk and a loaf of bread to go with your pint if you choose (dogs & muddy boots are welcome).

# Days out
## in the Heart of England

## Braunston
## Historic Boat Rally

Braunston, just like any English village, knows instinctively how to throw a jolly good fete. But when folk flock here for the annual Braunston historic boat rally, it's a day that turns out to be much more than just a fete: it's a party, a convention, a festival, a nifty excuse for a get-together, and a felt-tipped diary date to celebrate Britain's unsung heroes of the waterways... the nation's fabulous historic canal boats. Go, and you'll be treated to a tumultuous floating display of living heritage in an outdoor parade of around 100 historic canal boats, all arriving by water-road from across the corners of Britain to congregate in Braunston. A day out of unquantifiable pleasure.

It's a day to see wooden narrowboats that were once tugged by horses, unpowered butty boats, steel steam boats, diesel-powered narrowboats, canal craft from every era from the birth of canals to those used for the war effort, as well as plenty of today's leisure boats stuffed with mod cons luxuriating in Braunston Marina.

It's easy to get nostalgic. These are not just hoards of old boats, these are restored, preserved and cherished British treasures. Touchable, living history uncorked in this parade with immense pride. Braunston is the day of days for historic canal boats.

Gongoozlers hover, expelling star-struck sighs of relief as prestigious 70ft boats slither, unscathed, into mooring spaces scarcely big enough for a Smart Car-sized boat. Then, like after watching a golfer's birdie, the crowds chirp in awe.

Enthusiasts will like to show you the difference between the putt-putt of a Gardner engine and a Lister engine, and chap-ish celebrations inevitably unravel the oily rags with unbridled glee. But whether you give two hoots about boat engines or not, the smiles are infectious and feed the good spirit of the day.

Braunston's historic boat festival isn't just a fun day out, it's a living documentary of a nation's history and a bold parade of pride, endurance, British bulldog spirit and stalwart humour. Every year the crowds turn up with typical boaty camaraderie, serenaded with a background soundtrack of deep throated putt-putts.

## Beer tent

The side-hub of any waterside event is usually the beer tent. Form an orderly British queue for your beer, and you're guaranteed to get chatting while you wait for your pint of tepid ale from an obscure brewery's barrel. The accompaniment of spontaneous merriment with live folkie music, and a handful of out-of-key audience participants (with or without a tambourine) is all part of the English constitution we call tremendous fun.

## Factfile

Grand Union Canal
Braunston OS SP540658

**BRAUNSTON RALLY & MARINA**
The Rally is organised by the marina, and usually takes place on the last weekend of June. Open 1000-1700 with boat parades twice daily. Trade stands, canal societies, beer tent, food and Morris dancers. Shops, workshops and chandlery in the marina.

FREE admission if on foot. Charge for cars.
T:01788 891373 www.braunstonmarina.co.uk

The Historic Narrow Boat Owners' Club
www.hnboc.org.uk

The Friends of Raymond
www.friendsofraymond.org.uk

# Days out

in the Heart of England

## Crick Boat Show

Every May, a sleepy picturesque corner of Northamptonshire bursts at the seams with festival goers. Crick Marina on the Grand Union Canal becomes the outdoor venue for a much-coveted waterways event that's infamous amongst boaters.

Hundreds of boats line the water, from canoes to wide beam boats, but narrowboats are always the stars of this show. This is your chance to wander through dizzy numbers of spanking new narrowboats and dream (or scheme) to buy. There's plenty of stuff to do from free boat trips to boot-stomping music with hundreds of stalls heaving with anything from the latest boat paraphernalia to the obligatory festival fudge, as well as finger food and the happy beer tent. Kids get storytelling, craft workshops and plenty of grassy space to do what kids do.

Britain being Britain, rain has been known to blight the event, some years with mud swamps to rival Glastonbury's worst. Other years have seen picnickers melting with strawberries and cream on sun-toasted grass. But whatever the weather, the tradition is stalwart good humour.

## Factfile

**Grand Union Canal**
Crick. OS SP595726

**CRICK BOAT SHOW**

Held on the Bank Holiday at the end of May.

Admission charge.

T:01283 742971 www.crickboatshow.com

## IWA Festival

This is the festival of fun and fundraising that anyone who cares about the waterways goes to. The crowds can rely on the dedication of IWA members and the WRG team to make the annual festival a regular success. The venue changes every year, but the camaraderie and boaty spirit is carved in stone. Boats are part of the spectacle and the water bobs with everything from historic vessels to the newest designer narrowboats, and the happy hoards of boat owners all peacocking together. It's a day of flags and gazebos, music and dancing, stalls, talks, fudge, burgers in buns, fun for the kids and, of course, the compulsory beer tent for grown ups.

### Factfile

**IWA FESTIVAL**
Organised by the Inland Waterways' Association (IWA)
'Campaigning for the use, maintenance and restoration of Britain's inland waterways'.

Used to be held on the Bank Holiday at the end of August, but changed to last weekend in July for 2011. Location varies each year.

Admission charge goes to the IWA.

T:01494 783453
www.waterways.org.uk

# Days out
## in the Heart of England

## Ashby Canal

### BOSWORTH FIELD
A place that affected England's history. The famous Bosworth Field where the battle that is considered to have ended the Wars of the Roses was fought in 1485, lies by the canal. War was waged between Yorkist King Richard III and Lancastrian Henry Tudor - Richard was the last king of England to die in battle, leaving Henry to found the Tudor Dynasty.

Battlefield Trail & Country Park OS SP400999

Info boards, Visitor Centre, restaurant & gift shop. Wheelchair access to Centre - difficult around Trail & Park. Admission charge (Country Park Free).

T:01455 290429 www.bosworthbattlefield.com

### MOIRA FURNACE MUSEUM
19th-century blast furnace, boat trips, craft village & park. Tea rooms.

Moira. OS SK315155

Open May-Sep Tue-Fri 1200-1500, Sat-Sun 1200-1600. Oct-Apr Wed-Fri 1200-1400, Sat-Sun 1200-1500. School Hols daily. Admission charge. Wheelchair access.

T:01283 224667 www.nwleics.gov.uk

## Caldon Canal

### CHEDDLETON FLINT MILL
Grade II-listed complex with water mills, flint kilns and other outbuildings.

Cheddleton. OS SJ970525

Phone for opening times. FREE admission.

T:0161 4085083
www.people.exeter.ac.uk/akoutram/cheddleton-mill

## Cromford Canal

### CROMFORD MILL
A Grade I-listed site which is part of the Derwent Valley Mills World Heritage Site. The mill was the world's first successful water-powered cotton spinning mill, built in 1771 by Richard Arkwright. Tours can be arranged (charge).

Cromford. OS SK298569

Open all year daily 1000-1700. FREE admission (small parking charge). Restaurant. café and gift shops.

T:01629 823256 www.arkwrightsociety.org.uk

## Dudley Canal

### BLACK COUNTRY LIVING MUSEUM
Canals themselves are only half the story; the industries that they were built for is the other. An area in the Midlands, aptly nicknamed The Black Country, grew up in the boom years of the Industrial Revolution manufacturing chains, ships' anchors, nails, locks and keys. Significantly for the workforce, the Black Country is also renowned for its breweries and boasts more pubs per mile than almost anywhere in Britain. The canal networks are dense in the Midlands with reminders of urban heritage along many water miles.

For an authentic experience of yesteryear, visit the 26-acre Black Country Museum. The region's historic buildings were saved from demolition and rebuilt brick by brick at the museum site creating an urban canalside village. Staff dress in costume and craftsmen demonstrate Black Country skills. Shop in the traditional sweet shop, take a lesson in an old-fashioned school, see the underground coal mine, visit exhibition halls, see limestone caverns, take a boat trip into the Dudley Tunnels and explore much more. The whole package sounds a bit bizarre, yet manages never to stoop into crass tourism. Black Country humour and a traditional bag of fish and chips with mushy peas, swilled down by a pint of the Black Country's best mild ale will make the day.

Dudley. OS SO950915

Open every day March to October, rest of year closed Mon-Tues. Wheelchair access. Food, drink and shopping.

T:0121 5579643 www.bclm.org.uk
T:01384 236275 www.dudleycanaltrust.org.uk

## Grand Union Canal (Midlands)

### BRAUNSTON
Fascinating village where the Grand Union meets the Oxford Canal. Marina, book & gift shops, boat hire, pubs and cafés.

Braunston. OS SP540658

### HATTON LOCKS
21 locks with the nickname 'Stairway to Heaven'. Views over Warwick, interactive displays and a canalside café with gifts.

Hatton. OS SP242668

## Stourbridge Canal

### RED HOUSE GLASS CONE
Stourbridge was once world renowned for its glassmaking and the Red House Glass Cone still beckons from the skyline like a cathedral of the glass industry. One of only 4 still standing in Britain and the best preserved across Europe, it ceased production in 1936 and now offers glass-making demonstrations, displays of historic tools, audio and visual exhibitions, a shop and canalside café evocatively on the spot where narrowboats once loaded cargo from the Cone. In contrast to the industrial darkness and heat inside the Cone, the adjacent shop sparkles delicately with light and shelves of fine glass artefacts. Purchases are hard to resist.

Stourbridge. OS SO894864

Open daily all year 1000-1600. FREE admission (charge for guided tours). Tea room and gift shop. Wheelchair access.

T:01384 812750 www.dudley.gov.uk

## Stratford-on-Avon Canal & River Avon

### SHAKESPEARE COUNTRY

There are plenty of pretty places along the Avon Ring, but one place attracts more visitors every year than any other. A 16th-century playwright's unwitting epitaph said his birthplace, Stratford-upon-Avon, would become a world renowned tourist attraction. It is now the second most visited tourist destination in Britain after London. Stratford is a destination that's as proud and passionate as Juliette's kiss. Wisteria-clad historic buildings with dwarfed front doors waft images of Shakespearian cloaks brushing through.

But don't let Shakespeare, or the shocking number of tourists who turn up here, fool you. Stratford is more than a shrine to Shakespeare. Victorian lamp posts, the canal, war memorials, oaks that stood before the bard was born and still outlive some buildings. all tell another story of Stratford. The bard's hometown has aged into a magnificently overblown symbol of English zest. It's a beacon for England, an every-day festival of Englishness, a place folk flock to - to laze all day at the water's edge or mess about in boats, go sightseeing or shopping, or even to go to the theatre.

### ROYAL SHAKESPEARE COMPANY (RSC)
The RSC are probably the most famous theatre company in the world and aim to keep modern audiences in touch with Shakespeare. T:01789 403444 www.rsc.org.uk

### SHAKESPEARE BIRTHPLACE TRUST
Working to preserve and maintain properties, manuscripts, books and other records connected with, or relating to, Shakespeare. They also promote the appreciation and study of his plays and works across the world.

T:01789 204016 www.shakespeare.org.uk

### HOLY TRINITY CHURCH
Shakespeare is buried here. www.stratford-upon-avon.org

### TOURIST INFORMATION CENTRE
T:0870 1607930 www.shakespeare-country.co.uk

## Trent & Mersey Canal

### ETRURIA INDUSTRIAL MUSEUM
Two ghastly words to horrify the ordinary day-tripper or tourist. 'Industrial' and 'museum' are two killer words that should never be allowed to sit together in a 'come here to have fun' type of guide book. But don't be put off, force the kids to go too. Nobody leaves with a glum face - this industrial museum is a gem.

There's a lively annual programme of events. Some days, visitors are greeted with an unholy stench of boiling bones (part of the traditional process), other days are quieter. But for the best experience, go when the Etruscan Bone and Flint Mill is in action on one of their 'Steaming Weekends'. You'll have the thrill of seeing the simplicity of Victorian genius at work. Cogs, that turn cogs, that turn cogs, that crush bones, and grind flint stone as if it was butter. The steam engine behind the drama puffs along with the watching crowds. The museum's workers are friendly and on steaming weekends, enthusiasm bounces from their faces. Volunteers and visitors, side by side, stand wide-eyed with respect for the working physics and nostalgic heritage.

Stoke-on-Trent. OS SJ872468

Opened to the public by Fred Dibnah in 1991. Open Wed-Sun 1200-1630. Closed Dec-spring. Admission charge. Contact for details of Steaming Weekends. Craft classes.

T:01782 233144 www.stokemuseums.org.uk

### SHARDLOW HERITAGE CENTRE
The Salt Warehouse is the oldest canal warehouse in the village and, fittingly, now houses Shardlow Heritage Centre. For a very small entrance fee, you can learn about the fascinating history of this area. Among its exhibits is a replica of a working boat family's cabin. It's the sort of heritage centre that is a labour of love and manned with passion, so anything you can think of to ask is enthusiastically answered!

Shardlow. OS SK435303

Open Easter-Oct Sat, Sun & Bank Hols. Ring for exact opening times. Small admission charge (accompanied children FREE). Wheelchair access.

T:01332 793368

## Worcester & Birmingham Canal

### TARDEBIGGE LOCKS
The longest flight of locks in the UK, with 30 locks raising the canal 220 feet in just over 2 miles. Tardebigge Top Lock is one of the deepest in Britain, with a rise of over 11 feet. Originally a boat lift was built on the site but it was replaced by an extra deep lock for technical reasons and to save money for the company building the canal.

Tardebigge. OS SO951670 (Walk page 118-119)

# FOOD & DRINK

## Pubs
in the Heart of England

## Caldon Canal

### BLACK LION

Short walk from the canal over the Churnet Valley Railway. Large gardens with steam trains passing almost by your table.
Consall Forge. T:01782 550294
www.blacklionpub.co.uk

## Grand Union Canal (Mids)

### FOXTON LOCKS INN

Canalside at foot of Foxton Locks.
Foxton. T:01162 791515
www.restaurantfoxtonlocks.co.uk

## Shropshire Union Canal

### ANCHOR INN
Canalside by bridge 42. Traditional unspoilt pub with campsite.
High Offley. T:01785 284569

### DYSART ARMS
Traditional English pub worth the ½-mile walk from Bunbury Locks. Wooden floors, bookshelves, huge fireplace and a village church overlooking the pub's garden.
Bunbury. T:01829 260183
www.dysartarms-bunbury.co.uk

### SHROPPIE FLY

Canalside at the wharf. Traditional local with book-lined walls, and a boat forming part of the bar.
Audlem. T:01270 811772
www.shroppiefly.co.uk

## Staffs & Worcs Canal

### THE LOCK INN
Canalside with a patio alongside Wolverley Lock. Flagstone floor and huge fireplace in the bar.
Wolverley. T:01562 850581
www.thelockwolverley.co.uk

### THE VINE
Canalside by Kinver Lock. Traditional bar and conservatory restaurant. Huge sprawling garden
Kinver. T:01384 877291

## Stratford-on-Avon Canal

### FLEUR DE LYS
Canalside near Lock 31. Rambling pub with flagstone and wood floors and a huge garden by the canal.
Lowsonford. T:01564 782431
www.fleurdelys-lowsonford.com

## Trent & Mersey Canal

### THE BUBBLE INN
Canalside by lock 19. Modern bar/ restaurant in historic stone building with huge fireplace. 4-star rooms in former farm building.
Stenson. T:01283 703113
www.thebubbleinn.com

### HOLLY BUSH INN
Thatched and oak-beamed award-winning pub a short walk from the canal. Ancient pub, reputedly the second to be licensed in the UK.
Salt. T:01889 508234
www.hollybushinn.co.uk

### STAR INN

Alongside Star Lock (no.27). Historic pub with wood floors, and bars on three levels. Outside area great for watching boats in action.
Stone. T:01785 813096

### SWAN INN
Canalside on the junction of the Trent & Mersey and Coventry Canals. Traditional pub with cosy corners and great gongoozling.
Fradley Junction. T:01283 790330
www.theswanatfradley.co.uk

## Worcester & Birmingham Canal

### CROWN INN

Canalside by bridge 61, up a quiet cul de sac. Traditional local with real ales and typical bar meals. People spill out towards the canal at busy times and in the summer.
Alvechurch. T:0121 4452300

### THE WEIGHBRIDGE
In Alvechurch Marina. Award-winning historic pub. Interesting home-cooked meals. Large garden and terrace.
Alvechurch. T:0121 4455111
www.the-weighbridge.co.uk

# Teashops
in the Heart of England

### Ashby Canal

**SUTTON WHARF**
Canalside café/bistro a short walk from the famous site of the Battle of Bosworth, and home to the Ashby Trip boat. Homemade cakes and meals. Available for private evening functions. Dogs and muddy boots welcome!
Sutton Cheney. T:01455 213838
www.suttonwharf.com

### Birmingham Canal Navigations (BCN)

**CANALSIDE CAFÉ**

Vegetarian cafe with a reputation for its quirky ambience and real ales. Tiny interior but plenty of tables along the canal.
Birmingham. T:0121 2487979

**'GEORGE'**
Floating Coffee Company, a surprisingly roomy barge moored in Brindley Place.
Birmingham. T:0121 6330050
www.sherbornewharf.co.uk

### Shropshire Union Canal

**WATERSIDE CAFÉ**
Canalside in Nantwich Marina. Award-winning café well-known for breakfasts and cream teas.
Nantwich. T:01270 626171
www.nantwichmarina.co.uk

### Staffs & Worcs Canal

**OLD SMITHY TEAROOM**
Canalside by Wolverley Lock. Run by the Lock Inn nearby. Large sunny garden and patio.
Wolverley. T:01562 850581
www.thelockwolverley.co.uk

**SHUGBOROUGH HALL**
Lady Walk Tearoom & Restaurant in the grounds of Shugborough Hall, a short walk from the canal.
Great Haywood. T:01889 881388
www.shugborough.org.uk

**THE WINDLASS**
Victorian-themed café/restaurant in Grade II-listed former workshop and stables in Stourport Basin.
Stourport. T:01299 871742

### Trent & Mersey Canal

**LOCK HOUSE RESTAURANT**
Canalside by Haywood Lock. Large canalside garden and plenty of room inside. Full meals as well as cakes and snacks.
Great Haywood. T:01889 881294

**CANALSIDE CAFÉ**

Canalside between locks
In a courtyard of traditional buildings including the info and gift shop. Homemade cakes & snacks.
Fradley Junction. T:01827 252000

**WILLOW TREE TEA ROOMS**
Canalside in the marina. Tea rooms by day, bistro restaurant in the evenings with interesting local and organic food menu.
Willington. T:01283 703700
www.merciamarina.co.uk

For listings of waterside pubs & teashops in the UK, visit our website:
www.greatwaterwaysoutdoors.com

# WATERWAYS LIFE
## The chocolate canal

Britain's chocolate canal launched our nation's iconic indulgence. Birmingham's canal network gave us the chocolate bar with the world famous label on it - Cadbury's.

Our 'sinful' pleasure comes from the work of a clean living Quaker family. In the 1800s, exotic cocoa beans arriving on our shores from afar could be carried inland by canal boat and turned into chocolate at Cadbury's canalside chocolate factory. The Cadbury's factory took the bean, added milk and stirred up a recipe that was destined to melt in the mouths of generations to come.

### The inland trade route

In the 20th century, cocoa beans were carried inland by boat along the Gloucester & Sharpness Canal to Frampton on Severn. Milk was brought along the canal from local farms and the process of turning the cocoa beans into chocolate crumb began in the Cadbury's factory at Frampton. The crumb then continued its journey to Bournville to be made into chocolate.

### Did you know?

The first mass-produced chocolate bar in Britain was made by Fry's.

### Who discovered cocoa?

Ancient Mayan and Aztec civilizations were sucking drinks from cocoa beans before the rest of the world had discovered the Americas. When Columbus first stumbled on the bitter bean in his travels, he didn't realise its rich potential as a future Nigella-sweet recipe ingredient. In the early 1500s, when the conquistador Hernan Cortes brought the beans back to Europe, kings and queens indulged themselves on the new frightfully posh beverage. Chocolate houses started opening across Europe and by 1800 the craze had arrived in London.

l Tardebigge - Gloucester Docks
- Gloucester & Sharpness Canal
mooring dolly & milepost l

## What made Cabury's special?

Apart from the family recipe that gives
Cadbury's chocolate its distinctive flavour,
the Cadbury's brand was built on its Quaker
principals. The Industrial Revolution was driven
by many Quaker businesses. Amongst them
were Wedgwood pottery, Clarks Shoes, Bryant
and May matches, Rowntree's confectionary,
Fry's chocolate, Huntley and Palmer biscuits.
Quaker dynasties included Quaker bankers and
financiers too. Quaker entrepreneurs were hugely
successful. But Quaker businesses insisted profit
shouldn't be in conflict with ethics and social
responsibility. In an era of commercial growth,
dark times often fell on the poorest workers.
While many ruthless businesses left their
workforce in poverty with few rights and unsafe
factory machinery, Quaker reformers campaigned
to stop child labour, improve working and living
conditions and support the early trade union
movement. On the outskirts of the city, Cadbury
built Bournville Village for his workers, with
his canalside factory in the village. Cadbury's
mission was to give his workers quality housing,
open spaces with green air, somewhere grassy for
family frolics and to bat a cricket ball. Arguably
everything working families could want...
except a pub of course! In a bid to 'escape' from
reality, drunkenness was a social plague in the
overcrowded cities of the Industrial Revolution
- and Cadbury planned to offer his workers a
healthier alternative. Brave Bournville is still a
pub-free zone today.

## Cadbury's big dates

1824 - John Cadbury opened a grocery shop
in Birmingham selling drinking chocolate and
cocoa.
1831 - Cadbury brothers John and Benjamin
started manufacturing chocolate as a brand.
1847 - The Birmingham factory opened for
business.
1861 - John Cadbury retired and his sons
Richard and George took over.
1893 - Bournville Village was created.
2009 - Kraft takeover.

## Founded on ethics

On ethical grounds,
the Cadbury business
controversially boycotted
cocoa beans from
African plantations
where slavery was rife.
John Cadbury also
campaigned to form the
Animal Friends Society,
which was a forerunner
to the RSPCA.

## Factfile

### Worcester & Birmingham Canal
Cadbury World brings the chocolate experience to life.

Bournville OS SP048813 Canalside near bridge 77.

Opening times vary throughout the year. Booking
recommended to guarantee entry.

Restaurant and gift shops.

Admission charge. Wheelchair access.

T.0844 880 7667 www.cadburyworld.co.uk

# NORTH

Ordinary people curve into a warm smile to utter the words, "the North". It's a place that stirs the soul with untamed moors, Pennine tufts and dreamy Dales.

At a latitude of human resilience and non-mediocrity, the North is fertile home ground for locals including Wordsworth, Lowry, Beatrix Potter, Harold Wilson. William Wilberforce led the struggle for the abolition of slavery, and another lad born and bred 'up north', Captain Cook, born 1728 in Marton, sailed the seas in his ship 'Endeavour', earning a place in history books.

But the North really belongs to the canal boat. Inland waterways made the textile industry possible with trade routes opening to the world. Canals in the north were the backbone of the Industrial Revolution, scrambling from the River Mersey, twisting through Manchester, Rochdale, Huddersfield, Skipton, Calderdale and tunnelling bull-faced through the Pennines.

The industrial towns of the north were built along canals. Back to back on a skyline where Godly countryside rubbed next to Dark Satanic Mills. Now the lost era of textile mills has left crowds of lonely chimneys reaching for the sky, brick monuments of the reality of the Victorian worker's lot. Stark beginnings add to the appeal of Lancashire's cotton mills and Yorkshire's woollen mills as visitors turn up for a free day out sightseeing, discovering new respect for nostalgia.

Wherever you roam, the story of the water is never far away. Liverpool, perched on the left wing of England's coast, still bounces on its past heyday as a thriving port of world significance. From left to right, the north is cut by wild waterways that defy the landscape. Heavily-locked canals crawl up and down hill from every edge, spinning the traveller between the downright revolting and the unspeakably beautiful.

Explore these parts and you'll meet some of England's most dynamic waterscapes. A Yorkshire wind might be your solitary companion on the moorlands, but there's always a place beyond where unbuffed friendliness and a Yorkshire cup of tea awaits, brewed without asking and poured hot from the pot.

# WATERWAYS
## of the North
boat, bike, boot

LANCASTER

SKIPTON    YORK

LEEDS

MANCHESTER

HUDDERSFIELD

MACCLESFIELD

## Highlights

**STANDEDGE TUNNEL** on the Huddersfield
Narrow Canal - **LUNE AQUEDUCT** on the
Lancaster Canal - **SKIPTON** on the Leeds
& Liverpool Canal - **HEBDEN BRIDGE** on
the Rochdale Canal - **MARPLE LOCKS  &
AQUEDUCT** on the Peak Forest Canal

### Huddersfield Narrow Canal

Standedge Tunnel    **HUDDERSFIELD**

**ASHTON-UNDER-LYNE**

Ashton-under-Lyne to Huddersfield
20 miles, 74 locks

It might not win top prize for scenery, but every
canal enthusiast's pride shines through in every
mile of this 20-mile canal. The Huddersfield
Narrow Canal is a restoration success and has
been hailed as one of 'The' achievements of the
canal restoration era. With 74 locks and a 3-mile
tunnel, it is never mediocre. Standedge Tunnel is
one of the 7 Wonders of the Waterways and the
crowning glory of the Huddersfield, being the
longest, deepest, highest canal tunnel in Britain
(and a grand day out all on its own).

### Lancaster Canal

**CARNFORTH**

**LANCASTER**

**GARSTANG**

**PRESTON**

Preston to Tewitfield
41¼ miles, 0 locks

Slithering along the northwest coast of England,
this is the canal that wants to reach the Lake
District again. It currently halts at Tewitfield,
tantalisingly close to the Lakeland dream, but the
Lancaster Canal is strumming restoration hopes
to reopen its route all the way to Kendal. In the
meantime the canal remains a quiet waterway
with other highlights doing their best to allay
the mutterings of the Lake District. Only a hop
from the canal, the wide sands of Morecambe
Bay serpent the traveller and, as well as the rural
views along the route, Rennie's Lune Aqueduct is
an eye-catcher too.

## Leeds & Liverpool Canal

Liverpool to Leeds
127 miles, 91 locks

Simply the very best canal in Britain and the very worst canal in Britain. The Leeds & Liverpool Canal is a sitting duck for Lancashire's worst hooligan towns one minute and, in another, it escapes in euphoria to virgin tufts of wild Pennine grass.

## Macclesfield Canal

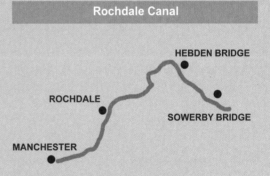

Hardings Wood Junction to Marple Junction
27¾ miles, 13 locks

The canal with the unique 'USP' of swirling bridges. These so-called Snake Bridges once allowed the horses towing canal boats to cross on the towpath to the other side of the water, without needing to be uncoupled from the boat. But there is much more to this canal than its quirky bridges - it's a master of mixed identity. The Macclesfield Canal blows north from the mild-mannered Midlands into the chunkier stoned canals of the north. Neither here nor there, it owns its space gloriously. Attractive, unspectacular, blissfully uninterrupted, the greenery is in charge and doesn't let anything disturb the status quo. Here, thrill seekers will find it takes little more than a moorhen to stir the pulse.

## Peak Forest Canal

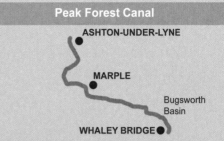

Whaley Bridge to Dukinfield Junction
14½ miles, 16 locks

Trespassing into England's woolly hat walking territory, the Peak Forest Canal lets anyone taste the sheer pleasure of this remote landscape. A delicious canal with big views over the Goyt Valley and uplifting whiffs of the countryside. Marple Locks do their bit to spice the way with stonework screaming with history. A peaceful narrow canal, with memorable moments.

## Rochdale Canal

Manchester to Sowerby Bridge
32 miles, 92 locks

A canal that stands out from the crowd, not because it has any of the facilities and fancies of the busier canals in the south, but because it is a canal of extraordinary uncluttered charisma. The Rochdale Canal is the rugged beauty of the Pennines. This waterway parties through Manchester's glitzy gay village and after enduring a few urban blemishes, the route beyond is a feisty delight. The water climbs through the friendliest villages on earth and seizes the heights of the Pennines with the full glory of no less than 92 locks in 32 miles. A thriller.

# Waterways
## of the North
boat, bike, boot

## The Four Counties Ring

MIDDLEWICH

KIDSGROVE

STOKE-ON-TRENT

MARKET DRAYTON

NORBURY

AUTHERLEY JUNCTION

110 miles, 94 locks

by boat - an energetic cruise takes one week
by bike - a leisurely slow ride takes around 3 days
by boot - a walk with time to sightsee takes around one week

Trent & Mersey Canal, Shropshire Union Canal and Staffs & Worcs Canal

A glorious route for explorers with plenty to enjoy along the way - including rural Shropshire, the Potteries of Stoke-on-Trent, the challenge of 'Heartbreak Hill' and the red water of the canal through the famous Harecastle Tunnel.

## The Cheshire Ring

MANCHESTER    ASHTON-UNDER-LYNE

MARPLE

PRESTON BROOK

MACCLESFIELD

ANDERTON

MIDDLEWICH

Hardings Wood Junction

97 miles, 92 locks

by boat - an energetic cruise takes one week
by bike - a leisurely slow ride takes around 2-3 days
by boot - a walk with time to sightsee takes around one week

Macclesfield Canal, Peak Forest Canal, Ashton Canal, Rochdale Canal, Bridgewater Canal, Trent & Mersey Canal

A journey from the party in the heart of Manchester, into a more rural waterscape with the Pennine Range overlooking the canal. The Cheshire Ring treads the Peaks and the Cheshire Plain in an uplifting trail. The route is packed with thrills that include the Anderton Boat Lift and the fascinating Marple locks.

## The South Pennine Ring

SKIPTON

BURNLEY

LEEDS

SOWERBY BRIDGE

ROCHDALE

HUDDERSFIELD

MANCHESTER

70 miles, 198 locks

by boat - an energetic cruise takes two weeks
by bike - a leisurely slow ride takes around 2 days
by boot - a walk with time to sightsee takes around one week

Rochdale Canal, Calder & Hebble Navigation, Huddersfield
Narrow Canal and Ashton Canal

A feisty route with the richest rewards for the
hardy traveller. The drama of this ring unfolds
as it journeys defiantly through the Pennines.
Be prepared to encounter the Standedge Tunnel
- the longest, deepest and highest tunnel in the
country. The entire ring is heaving with scenery.

# ROUTES
## along the towpath

## SOME DESIGNATED TOWPATH ROUTES

### Lancaster Canal

**NATIONAL CYCLE NETWORK (NCN) ROUTE 6**
Will run from London to Keswick (once fully open)
Follows the canal towpath from Lancaster to Carnforth.

**NATIONAL CYCLE NETWORK (NCN) ROUTE 62**
Will run from Glasson to Selby (once fully open)
Follows the canal towpath for a short while out of Preston.

### Leeds & Liverpool Canal

**NATIONAL CYCLE NETWORK (NCN) ROUTE 6**
Will run from London to Keswick (once fully open)
Follows the canal towpath from Blackburn to Rishton.

**AIRE VALLEY TOWPATH**
National Cycle Network (NCN) Route 66 & 69
Leeds to Bingley
Follows the canal towpath all of the way from Leeds through to Bingley.

**PENNINE CYCLEWAY**
National Cycle Network (NCN) Route 68
Derby to Berwick-upon-Tweed
Follows the canal towpath all of the way from Colne to Barnoldswick (or join the canal at Burnley for longer stretch).

**PENNINE WAY**
Total trail 268 miles
Crosses the canal at Gargrave.

**NATIONAL CYCLE NETWORK (NCN) ROUTE 69**
Morecambe to Grimsby
Follows the canal towpath all of the way from Silsden to Shipley (becoming Route 66 from there to Leeds).

### Macclesfield Canal

**CHESHIRE RING CANAL WALK**
27¾ miles (total trail 97 miles)
Follows the canal towpath all the way from Kidsgrove to Marple Junction.

### Peak Forest Canal

**CHESHIRE RING CANAL WALK**
8 miles (total trail 97 miles)
Follows the canal towpath all the way from Marple Junction to Dukinfield Junction (the Ashton Canal).

### Rochdale Canal

**CALDER VALLEY CYCLEWAY**
National Cycle Network (NCN) Route 66
Sowerby Bridge to Warland
Follows the canal towpath much of the way from Sowerby Bridge through to Warland.

### More info

For more detailed information and maps of all National Cycle Network Routes, go to www.sustrans.org.uk

For more walks and trails, go to www.ramblers.org.uk

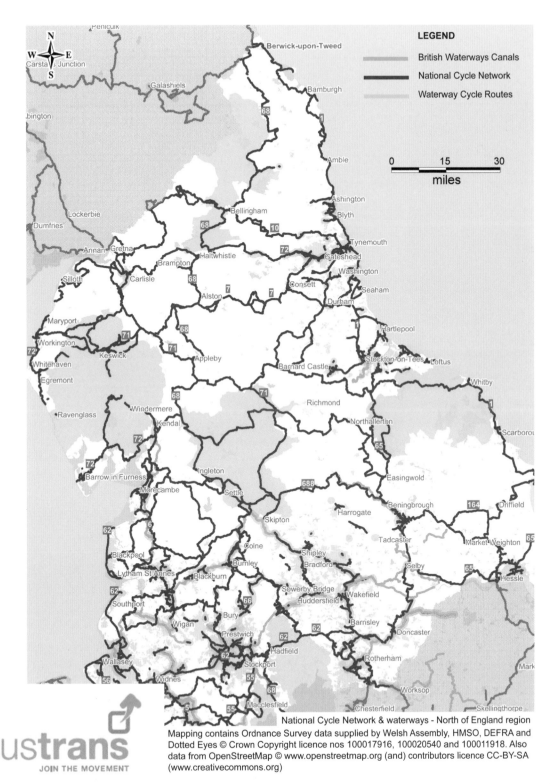

LEGEND

British Waterways Canals

National Cycle Network

Waterway Cycle Routes

0    15    30
miles

National Cycle Network & waterways - North of England region
Mapping contains Ordnance Survey data supplied by Welsh Assembly, HMSO, DEFRA and
Dotted Eyes © Crown Copyright licence nos 100017916, 100020540 and 100011918. Also
data from OpenStreetMap © www.openstreetmap.org (and) contributors licence CC-BY-SA
(www.creativecommons.org)

sustrans
JOIN THE MOVEMENT

# Routes
## along the towpath

JOIN THE MOVEMENT

**Martyn Brunt**
**Sustrans NCN Development Manager**

## My favourite bike ride
### Leeds & Liverpool Canal

"Looking for a day that takes in beautiful countryside, rich industrial history, stunning scenery, galleries, shops, museums, the longest canal in the country and even a World Heritage site? Then it's the Aire Valley Towpath for you!

When I was first told by a friend that we were going for a day out riding our bikes along a canal in Leeds, I was sceptical to say the least. By the end of the day I was a total convert to the extent that I've been back twice to take other friends along the same ride.

The 17-mile Aire Valley Towpath in Yorkshire provides a wonderful opportunity to explore part of the Leeds & Liverpool Canal, the longest canal in Britain. It passes through urban areas and tranquil countryside, connecting the shopping

Mecca of central Leeds with nearby Bingley.

With gentle gradients and smooth surfaces along the length of the route, you'll find the route ideal if you want an easy day's pedalling, or if you have small children or are a wheelchair user. You'll also find the route is growing in popularity - one section of the path near Kirkstall Brewery has recently been improved to the extent that students from the nearby Leeds Metropolitan University are using it as their main means of getting from halls of residence to the campus.

Along the way you travel past such attractions as Kirkstall Abbey, Bramley Fall, Rodley, Calverley Woods, Apperley Bridge, Buck Wood at Thackley, Shipley, Hirst Wood, Dowley Gap and the Three and Five Rise Locks at Bingley. Any one (or preferably all) of these is worth lingering at to take in the views and soak up the atmosphere, and it seems almost unfair to single some out for special mention, but if you're pushed for time then I'd suggest the following as "must do" attractions on your day out.

So go and try it for yourself – 1000 students and a man full of Cascadian Black Beer can't all be wrong!

### Leeds Industrial Museum at Armley Mills

This was once one of the world's biggest woollen mills, today it gives an insight into the city's rich industrial heritage. Genuinely fascinating.

### Kirkstall Abbey

One of the best preserved Cistercian monasteries in the country, with a brand new Visitor Centre to boot.

### West Wood at Calverley

Owned by the Woodland Trust, this beautiful wood defies description. All I can say is go and see it for yourself, and be rendered similarly speechless.

### Five Rise Locks at Bingley

An 18th-century engineering masterpiece, these five locks operate as a 'staircase' flight in which the lower gate of one lock forms the upper gate of the next. When completed in 1774, thousands gathered to watch the first boats make the 60 foot descent. Now, over 200 years later, the flight is still in daily use.

### Saltaire

Perhaps the highlight of the route. Saltaire has been declared a UNESCO World Heritage Site due to its preservation as a Victorian Industrial Village. Named after Sir Titus Salt, the area has amazing architecture, galleries, boutiques and antique shops aplenty. It's also well worth stopping in at the Saltaire Brewery Visitor Centre, where a pint of Cascadian Black is recommended. Or two if it's a cold day."

**Bingley Five Rise Locks**
**Bingley Three Rise Locks**
**SALTAIRE**
**LEEDS**

### Factfile

Start: Leeds OS SE297332
Finish: Bingley OS SE107400
National Cycle Network (NCN) Routes 66 & 69
17 miles, 28 locks

#### Highlights

Saltaire World Heritage Site (Days Out page 184-185)
Bingley Five Rise & Three Rise Locks (Days Out page 188-189)

#### More info

For more detailed information and maps of all National Cycle Network Routes, go to www.sustrans.org.uk

| Signpost at Bingley Five Rise Locks
- Saltaire |

# Routes
## along the towpath

We've rambled fervently for more, hunting round the next bend in the water, following the water, and stopping to sightsee as often as we want. On foot it's oh so slow, and beautifully fulfilling.

### A walk along the Peak Forest Canal

Canal walking can be a great cheat's way to some of England's hardiest walking territory - the Peak Forest Canal merrily takes you on an easy walk through territory meant for beefy-calved hikers.

From the start at Marple Locks, views of the Peak Forest spread before you. The landscape is remote, yet the canal never feels lonely. Watch out for the herons around these parts, they're so laid-back, they trip you up on the towpath.

Marple Lock flight is fascinating, with local stonework and history climbing every step of the flight with you.

As you head off along the canal from Marple Locks, bridges and leafiness mark the way. The green miles ahead belong only to you, and then, as you approach Whaley Bridge, you bump into liveaboard boats on their moorings (it's hard not to enjoy being secretly nosey as you pass - even if you know you shouldn't).

Whaley Bridge awaits at the end of the walk on the edge of the Peak District National Park. This is your chance to spend some time pottering around, going window shopping, resting your feet in a teashop or just going straight to the pub.

Phillippa & Martine
Some of the highlights of our epic canal walk from Cornwall to Scotland

## Our favourite walks

Walking the canals of the North has brought us face to face with both the beauty and the beast. The Leeds & Liverpool Canal, the Manchester Ship Canal, the Huddersfield Narrow, the Lancaster Canal, the Rochdale Canal... the cities and their canals are inseparable. But the canal names don't spoil the sweet secret of rural rambles that lie between busy cities, flinging the willing walker in and out of Heathcliffian landscapes.

In the North, where there are some of the most heavily locked canals in Britain, the boater's journey might be exhausting, but locks add easier interest and welcome companions to the walker.

With engineering marvels, rustic mileposts and landmarks, canal walks in the North are trails in the great outdoors to discover history... or just a fabulous place to take a stroll, looking ahead, facing the wind.

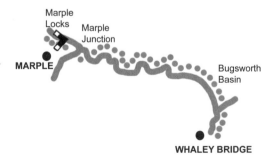

## Secret passages

Near the top of Marple Locks, you'll find two tight tunnels carved into the hill at lock 13. Here, so typical of Britain's canals, it thrusts its most humble sightseeing at you when you least expect it - and it is thrilling. England's real history is there to touch at lock 13. Walk through the tiny cobblestone tunnel, and you're inside a passage built for the horses that pulled working boats over two hundred years ago. Don't just carry on walking though — look harder and you'll discover the second, even tinier, passage hiding by the lock side. It was for the boatmen working the lock and leads down to the bottom gates of the lock. If you get the chance to scramble into that dark spiralling passage and stand alone, silently for a while - for that moment, you can live the everyday experience of a boat man in the great days of the 'canal mania'.

## Bugsworth Basin

At the end of a short arm near Whaley Bridge is the restored complex of basins - the remains of a once busy terminus (the original end of the Peak Forest Canal), where tramways brought stone down from the hills to be loaded onto boats for transportation along the canal.

## Factfile

### Peak Forest Canal
Start: Marple Bottom Lock OS SJ961891
Finish: Whaley Bridge OS SK011816
7 miles, 16 locks

### Highlights
Marple Locks
Marple Aqueduct
Bugsworth Basin

### Did you know?
It's worth a quick detour to see Marple Aqueduct, just beyond Marple Bottom Lock. It's Grade I-listed (as are Marple Locks). The aqueduct is 300ft long, over 100ft above the River Goyt below, and took nearly 7 years to complete.

# Routes
## along the towpath

### A walk along the Leeds & Liverpool Canal

You'd swear the cows chew slower and the swans smile wider here. Despite the occasional hateful noise pollution of cars that somehow even manages to follow the canal into the Pennines, this section of the Leeds & Liverpool Canal blows you off your feet with some of the best open countryside anywhere on the canal networks in England. Heart-filling, mind clearing, and a soul full of sheer pleasure.

You can arrive by car, go for a walk for the day, and then go home to a comfy sofa. Or if the whim takes you, bring a tent and sleep under the stars at the campsite in Gargrave... then wake at dawn for an early start.

There's an earnest euphoria in the air around these parts, with people on bikes and in well-waxed walking boots doing any of the challenging long-distance trails - the Pennine Way, Trans Pennine Trail. We like to listen to their stories, and share tales of our end-to-end canal walk with them too - but we rarely keep up with the fittest because there are too many distractions on the canals for us to rush.

The reward after a slow walk from Gargrave to Skipton is a pint of ale in the Narrowboat pub, tucked down a cobbled alley near the hubbub of Skipton Basin.

**GARGRAVE**

**SKIPTON**

## Factfile

### Leeds & Liverpool Canal
Start: Gargrave OS SD934545
Finish: Skipton OS SD987516
5 miles, 3 locks

### Highlights
Far-reaching views
Skipton Basin and the canal arm to the castle

### Did you know?
The Dalesman Café Tearooms has become famous for stamping the route cards of pilgrim cyclists on the 355-mile Pennine Cycleway (Sustrans National Cycle Network Route 68).

### Gargrave village
This is idyllic England. Gargrave pulls out all the stops with cute cottages, tearooms, 3 pubs and a church. Come on Sunday when the church bells ring and it's a scene that stops the clocks. You won't think of anywhere else you'd rather be.

### Campsite at Gargrave
Neat and tidy, and stuffed to the brim with caravans, motorhomes and tents. An intimate site right on the waterside. Caravans probably get the best pitches with backpacking tents content to fit in without a fuss. But what the site lacks in 'real' camping je ne sais quoi, it amply makes up for in its warm welcome and unrivalled position smack on the Leeds & Liverpool Canal in Gargrave. An overnight meeting place for passing strangers with backpacks walking the Pennine Way or bike panniers cycling the end-to-end Sustrans Route 68.

### The canal basin in Skipton
Skipton is Saxon for sheep, but today the canal basin in Skipton is a hub for boats, bikes and boots. Dayboat hire, boat trips, ice cream boat, fish and chips, pubs and inviting places to eat galore.

Sam's Now Running
Departures every
15 minutes

NARROW BOAT
LEO
NEXT TRIP
30 min Trip
Behind & Under Castle
Adults £3.00 Children £2.00
PLEASE
Q
THIS SIDE OF BOARD

WEAK
BRIDGE
267
WE
BRI
2
m/t

CRAY

THORP

# Routes
## along the towpath

### A walk along the Macclesfield Canal

If you start in the town of Macclesfield, the canal is just a short trot from the train station via cobbled roads signposted with names like 'Coronation Street'. As you reach the canal, you pass the original Hovis Mill where your mind tricks you into hearing Dvorak and watching sepia images of a knobbly-kneed boy on his bike delivering bread. After only a few strides, the bricks and mortar of Macclesfield are left behind and the further north you go, the more peaceful this walk becomes. The towpath is refreshingly tufty underfoot in parts, less trampled by the touristy-shoes of more busy towpaths.

You can be sure that the Macclesfield Canal always calls a spade a spade, so when you stumble on its treasures, the rewards are genuine. Heritage is rife, and beautifully understated. Keep your eyes peeled for the magnificent milestones along the way. They are unusually large for canal milestones, and made from Kerridge stone. The stones typically seclude canal secrets - once they would have informed working boat crews on how any miles they had travelled, but during the Second World War, they were buried to stop potential enemy invaders from finding their way around. After the war, many were lost until canal enthusiasts in the 1980s found and restored the majority of them to their modest glory.

This is a leafy walk, far away from the crowds and as close to the secrets of the canals as you can get.

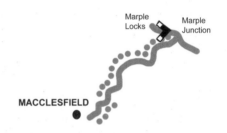

## Factfile

### MacclesfieldCanal
Start: Macclesfield OS SJ925731
Finish: Marple Junction OS SJ961884
11 miles, 0 locks

### Highlights
Clarence Mill in Bollington
Bridges 29 & 2 - snake bridges
Marple Junction

### Did you know?
The National Trust's Lyme Park, a short walk from bridge 17, featured s Darcy's house 'Pemberley' in the BBC's 1995 adaptation of 'Pride & Prejudice'.

### Snake bridges
The Macclesfield is most renowned for its unique snake bridges, so watch out for them along the way. They swirl with perfectly spiralled brickwork once enabling boat horses to swap sides on the towpath without needing to be uncoupled from their narrowboats.

### Marple Junction
Marple Junction is where the Macclesfield and Peak Forest Canals meet, surrounded by views towards the Goyt Valley and wistful mountain peaks.

### Bollington
Known by locals as the Happy Valley, Bollington feels more like a village than a town. Bollington Discovery Centre is in the canalside Clarence Mill. A gallery, displays and an image database tell the story of the town, the mill (and other cotton mills in the area), the Macclesfield Canal and their historic importance to the town. Regular exhibitions of art and local history.

### Cheshire Ring
The Macclesfield Canal is part of the Cheshire Ring, both a popular boating route and towpath walk. The Ring, 97 miles, covers all of the Macclesfield Canal and parts of the Rochdale, Bridgewater, Peak Forest, Ashton and Trent & Mersey Canals.

I Bridge 36 outside Macclesfield - Bollington Aqueduct I

# ROUTES
boating

SHIRE CRUISERS
SOWERBY BRIDGE

**Shire Cruisers, Sowerby Bridge**

## Our customers' favourite routes
A cruise along the Rochdale Canal

### DAY 1 - 4 MILES, 5 LOCKS, 3 HOURS

Leaving our historic canal basin, you ascend the deepest lock in the country, and sail along the side of the valley, through two more locks, to Mytholmroyd, where you moor for the night. Here you have two pubs with food, an upmarket café and convenience stores.

## Factfile

**RochdaleCanal**
Start & Finish: Sowerby Bridge OS SE065237
20 miles, 34 locks, 3-night break (16 hours cruising)

**SHIRE CRUISERS**
T:01422 832712 www.shirecruisers.co.uk

**Highlights**
Hebden Bridge
Todmorden and its views

**Did you know?**
Tuel Lane Lock, in Sowerby Bridge, is the deepest lock in the UK. It is over 19½ft deep, and has to be operated by a lock keeper.

### DAY 2 - 6 MILES, 12 LOCKS, 5 HOURS

Next morning, travel on to Hebden Bridge. This old mill town nestles in a fork in the hills, houses piled tier upon tier. Hebden is the original plastic-bag-free town, and has not succumbed to a big supermarket, so has an amazing variety of shops, cafés, restaurants and pubs. It's full of surprises – everything from horsey clothing to hand-made pottery, and not one but two bookshops.

Keep on through the town and gradually wind up the valley, with woods, crags and the Calder running alongside, and views of the moors high above. Pause perhaps at the Stubbing Wharf pub, but keep going in order to reach Todmorden, a town schizophrenic as to whether it's Yorkshire or Lancashire, wool or cotton. Moor at the Fielden Wharf visitor moorings below Lock 19, just beside one pub - though don't neglect the other pubs, restaurants and the busy market. Don't miss the Town Hall and many other fine Victorian, and much older, buildings, all dominated by a curving railway viaduct.

### DAY 3 - 8 MILES, 14 LOCKS, 6 HOURS

Turn below Lock 19 and head back to Luddenden Foot (pub and Indian restaurant). The valley looks quite different on the way down, and you'll see things you missed on the way up.

### DAY 4 - 2 MILES, 3 LOCKS, 2 HOURS

You need to get up early to be at the top lock for 8am, then head back to base.

| Hebden Bridge - Sowerby Bridge -
Sowerby Bridge (overleaf) |

## Pets

Many live-aboard boaters have dogs and cats who share their floating lifestyle, and the canals have a distinct dog-friendly culture. So there's no need to leave the furriest member of the family behind when you go on a narrowboat holiday. They'll love the outdoor fun!

Most hireboat companies welcome well-mannered pets. Some make a small charge.

A cruise along the Calder & Hebble Navigation, Aire & Calder Navigation and Selby Canal

Sail down the leafy Calder & Hebble Navigation past Brighouse, and through wide river sections and narrow cuttings to Wakefield, where there are good moorings close to the new Hepworth gallery. Then on to Stanley Ferry to see the famous aqueducts and two very convenient and contrasting pubs.

You are now on the Aire & Calder Navigation, which is still a thriving commercial waterway, although there are now many more pleasure boats than barges. Electric locks and a wide channel help you speed to Castleford - keep on the main line towards Knottingley. This section briefly passes through an industrial hinterland,

but is full of interest because much water-borne freight comes through. At Bank Dole you leave the main line and its electric locks, to drop into the Aire as it winds through farmland, stopping occasionally at pretty brick-built villages. And so to Selby, where you can explore the ancient Abbey and market, before taking the train to York – you could have time for a full day there.

## Factfile

**Calder & Hebble Navigation, Aire & Calder Navigation and Selby Canal**
Start & Finish: Sowerby Bridge OS SE065237
96 miles, 68 locks, 7-night break (40 hours cruising)

### Highlights
The Hepworth Wakefield
Brand new gallery celebrating Yorkshire's unique artistic talents, including 40 sculptures by Barbara Hepworth.
www.hepworthwakefield.org
Selby Abbey (almost 1,000 years old)

### Did you know?
Stanley Ferry has two aqueducts - a new one was built in 1981 alongside the old one, which was believed to be too endangered by the large boats which travel this area.

# Boats

in the North

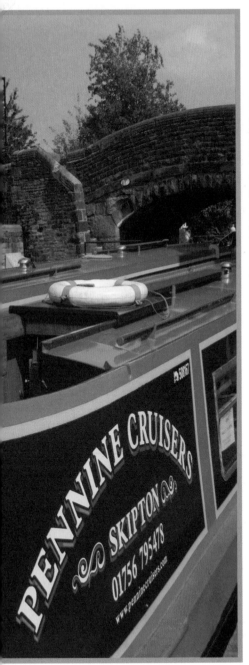

## Bridgewater Canal

**CLAYMOORE NARROWBOATS**
Narrowboat holiday hire.
Preston Brook. T:01928 717273
www.claymoore.co.uk

## Calder & Hebble Navigation

**SHIRE CRUISERS**
Narrowboat holiday hire.
Sowerby Bridge. T:01422 832712
www.shirecruisers.co.uk

## Huddersfield Narrow Canal

**MARSDEN SHUTTLE**
Water Taxi Marsden to Standedge.
Marsden. T:01457 871800
www.huddersfieldcanal.com

**STANDEDGE TUNNEL**
Boat trips into the tunnel.
Standedge. T:01782 785 703
www.standedge.co.uk

## Lancaster Canal

**ARLEN HIRE BOATS**
Narrowboat holiday hire.
Preston. T:01772 769183
www.arlen-hireboats.co.uk

**LANCASTER CANAL CRUISES**
Boat trips and water bus.
Lancaster. T:01524 389410
www.budgietransport.co.uk

## Leeds & Liverpool Canal

**CANAL BOAT CRUISES**
Narrowboat holiday hire and restaurant
trip boat.
Riley Green. T:01254 667412
www.canalboatcruises.co.uk

**CANAL BOAT ESCAPES**
Narrowboat holiday & day hire.
Barnoldswick. T:01282 813097
www.canalboatescapes.co.uk

**HAPTON VALLEY BOATS**
Narrowboat holiday hire.
Reedley. T:01282 771371
www.canal-cruises.co.uk

## PENNINE BOAT TRIPS
Daily March to October. Private charter
& day boat hire available.
Skipton. T:01756 790829
www.canaltrips.co.uk

**PENNINE CRUISERS**
Narrowboat holiday & day hire.
Skipton. T:01756 795478
www.penninecruisers.com

**SHIRE CRUISERS**
Narrowboat holiday hire.
Foulridge. T:01422 832712
www.shirecruisers.co.uk

**SILSDEN BOATS**
Narrowboat holiday hire.
Silsden. T:01535 653675
www.silsdenboats.co.uk

**SNAYGILL BOATS**
Narrowboat holiday & day hire.
Skipton. T:01756 795150
www.snaygillboats.co.uk

## Macclesfield Canal

**BRAIDBAR BOATS**
Narrowboat holiday hire.
Higher Poynton. T:01625 873471
www.braidbarboats.co.uk

**FREEDOM BOATS**
Day boat hire and trip boat.
Macclesfield. T:01625 420042
www.freedomboats.co.uk

**HERITAGE NARROW BOATS**
Narrowboat holiday & day hire.
Scholar Green. T:01782 785700
www.heritagenarrowboats.co.uk

## Peak Forest Canal

**PHOENIX**
Day boat hire.
Whaley Bridge. T:01663 747808
www.trafalgarmarineservices.co.uk

## Rochdale Canal

**BRONTE BOATS**
Narrowboat holiday & day hire.
Hebden Bridge. T:01706 815103
www.bronteboathire.co.uk

**SHIRE CRUISERS**
Narrowboat holiday hire.
Sowerby Bridge. T:01422 832712
www.shirecruisers.co.uk

**STUBBING WHARF**
Boat trips. Private charter too.
Hebden Bridge. T:07966 808717
www.stubbingwharf.com

## Waterways people
Nigel Stevens
co-owner of Shire Cruisers

Nigel's first encounter with the waterways was being stung by a wasp on a family picnic by a French canal. The canal bug itself struck later, before Operation Ashton in 1968, the first giant restoration weekend which geared up the campaign to restore the Ashton and lower Peak Forest – with such success that today's boaters don't know these canals were ever closed.

Much work with the Waterway Recovery Group and the IWA, and on the upper Avon, followed.

In 1980, Nigel and his wife Susan (they met on a dig!) bought a hire fleet in Yorkshire. They thought they could easily do it better than the professionals, and 30 years later are still trying… Their company put a hire boat on the first land-locked section of the Rochdale Canal, allowing boaters to explore a magic six-mile section.

Nigel has always thought the most important thing about the waterways was how to secure their future, and while chairman of the British Waterways Advisory Forum worked with many others on the plans for the National Waterways Charity. Exciting stuff, and an opportunity for each of us to make a difference if we all pull together.

# WILDLIFE & NATURE

## Wildfowl & Wetlands Trust - Martin Mere

**WWT**

Martin Mere is home to over 100 species of rare and endangered ducks, geese, swans and flamingos. There are beavers, otters, wildflowers and insects too. With impromptu feathered displays and a symphony of nature's noises, the centre has all the elements that add up to a cracking day out with smiles ear-to-ear and heart-to-heart.

The Wetland Centre is a family friendly day out all year round, with a calendar of activities and jaw-dropping attractions - from wintering birds, to an outdoor spring nursery for the fluffiest babies on earth.

### Avocet

In 2004 WWT Martin Mere created new land to encourage summer migrants. Avocets were a rare bird at Martin Mere up until that point and numbers have steadily increased year on year to us having 40 pairs in 2009 that successfully fledged a number of chicks. We have since created small islands and duck marshes so that we can provide avocets with a safe environment from predation. Avocets spend much of the winter in Mediterranean countries and migrate to the UK for the summer breeding season. They can often be viewed as early as March at Martin Mere through to September.

## Kingfisher

Kingfishers are resident at WWT Martin Mere all year round although they are yet to nest on site. They do nest locally and use the reserve as a feeding site as our ponds have large populations of fish which has resulted in popular sightings throughout the year from a designated kingfisher hide. The bright blue markings on the kingfisher make the bird popular for all visitors.

# Wildlife & Nature

### Pink-footed Goose

Pink-feet breed in Iceland over the summer and can be commonly seen at WWT Martin Mere in September and October. The numbers of pink-footed geese have been steadily rising in the country for many years. The last couple of years, in particular, has seen record numbers of geese in the agricultural areas around Lancashire because of the abundance of food available, particularly on the Lancashire mosses which might have up to a quarter of the Icelandic population of pink-feet pass through during the migration. Populations have increased mainly due to successful breeding seasons over in Iceland with an increase of protected areas to provide safe shelter for the geese

Martin Mere has welcomed almost 40,000 geese in the winter of 2010 which was a record for the reserve. The reserve is perfect for the geese to use as a refuge because it is free of disturbance with large open areas of water that allow the geese to roost overnight without the fear of predators such as foxes. We manage the reserve using Long-horn cattle to graze, ensuring that the grass in the right condition for them (2 – 3 inches long) as well as having correct water levels. Basically we provide everything for them to get a decent night's sleep!

### Whooper swan

Whooper swans breed in Iceland over the summer and will spend the entire winter at WWT Martin Mere from November to March. Martin Mere is an attractive site for the swans due to the presence of a large food source in

the form of the surrounding agricultural land which provides grass for grazing, stubble fields containing grain and waste potatoes left over from harvesting. The Mere provides a safe roosting spot, and most of the birds can be found here in the evening and overnight, heading out in the day to feed in surrounding areas.

The number of whoopers at Martin Mere was 1,700 in 2007, and can reach 2,000 birds in the depths of winter. Overall population in Iceland is c27,000 so approximately 8% of the Icelandic population can be using the site at one time. We feed grain and waste potatoes to the swans which can be seen from the hides. This is a sample of what they forage in the wild and is purely supplemental feeding. It encourages the birds to stay on site so people can see them and enable us to educate people about them. It also keeps them off farmer's fields which prevents conflict with our neighbours and lessens energy loss through constant disturbance if they are scared off when people see them as pests.

## Factfile

**Leeds & Liverpool Canal**

Burscough OS SD427142
A short walk from the canal at bridge 31.

Open daily all year (only closes on Christmas Day)
End Oct-Feb 0930-1700 (Christmas Eve to 1500)
Mar-end Oct to 1730.

Last admission an hour before closing.

Café and gift shop.

Admission charge. Wheelchair access.

T:01704 895181
www.wwt.org.uk

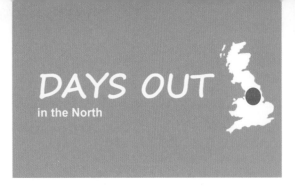

# DAYS OUT
## in the North

# NATIONAL WATERWAYS MUSEUM

Some museums encase their treasures behind glass and glare at visitors who dare to touch, yet this museum is unmistakably visitor-friendly. But this isn't any old museum, it's a waterways museum. No starch or "sssh", just the promise of something spectacular for any generation of the family and an authentic waterways welcome. An amazing day out that lets rip with nostalgia, intrigue, education, play, pride and a good dose of patriotism. Definitely not to be missed!

In 1836, most traffic through Ellesmere Port was iron ore, brought on coastal ships from Cumberland mines, to be loaded onto canal boats heading for the Midlands. Now the site is home to the National Waterways Museum. The museum is housed in the old wharf, built in 1844, offering a maze of waterside buildings to explore. It's a museum with as much to see outside as inside. The texture and patterns of the brickwork make the old buildings exhibits themselves. And the lock alongside marks the dramatic end of Shropshire Union Canal, where the Manchester Ship Canal and the famous River Mersey sprawl into a Liverpudlian backdrop.

The whole site is fascinating, yet the water is the keeper of the real heroes - the museum's collection of historic boats. Everything from restored narrowboats to rotten sinking barges that have to be regularly pumped to stay afloat.

### For kids

There's stuff to turn and touch, rub and read, look up to and roll around on. There are audio sets, video games, models of leggers and navvies. The whole museum is a life-sized story of the canals to play with.

### Friendship

Working narrowboats were owned by companies such as Fellows Morton & Clayton or Grand Union Canal Carrying Company (GUCC). But there were also the indelible No1s - a proud few owned by the families that crewed them. Joe and Rose Skinner owned the last of the No1s and the museum invites visitors inside their narrowboat Friendship to listen to recordings of them. "Bonnets gave me a headache" Mrs S tells us, "I wore a man's cap!" The intimacy of politely listening to the Skinners' real life whilst sitting inside Friendship is a moving privilege. The only thing missing is the cup of tea Mrs S would have surely brewed specially for you.

### The stables

The smells have gone but the imagination is let loose as you tread the cobbled floor into empty stables, the power house of the Industrial Revolution. Tack hangs from the walls and the sweet ghosts of giant souls fill the space.

### Pump House

An unassuming brick building that houses bold and unfathomable engineering. Fabulously exciting. Steam engines do something to the voyeur and reliably make little boys out of men.

### Climb aboard Ferret

A Fellows Morton & Clayton narrowboat that is powered by a 15-horsepower Bolinder engine. Crouch inside the boatman's cabin and imagine an entire family eating and sleeping there. Don't be shy about being nosy - do open the cupboard and peek at the pots, pans, jugs and old tins of Ovaltine all lurking inside. Spin round and see decorative roses and castles spilling into every crevice of woodwork. Then give a moment for the old kettle standing on the iron stove silently telling its story of comfort once lent to a hardworking boat family.

### Porters Row

The museum authentically presents a terraced row of houses kitted with domestic paraphernalia. As you tour from house to house, you travel from the 1950s, 1930s, 1900s to 1830s. Set in the context of the canals, Porters Row not only uncovers intriguing social history, it also unleashes the inexplicable pleasure of domestic nosiness blended with nostalgia.

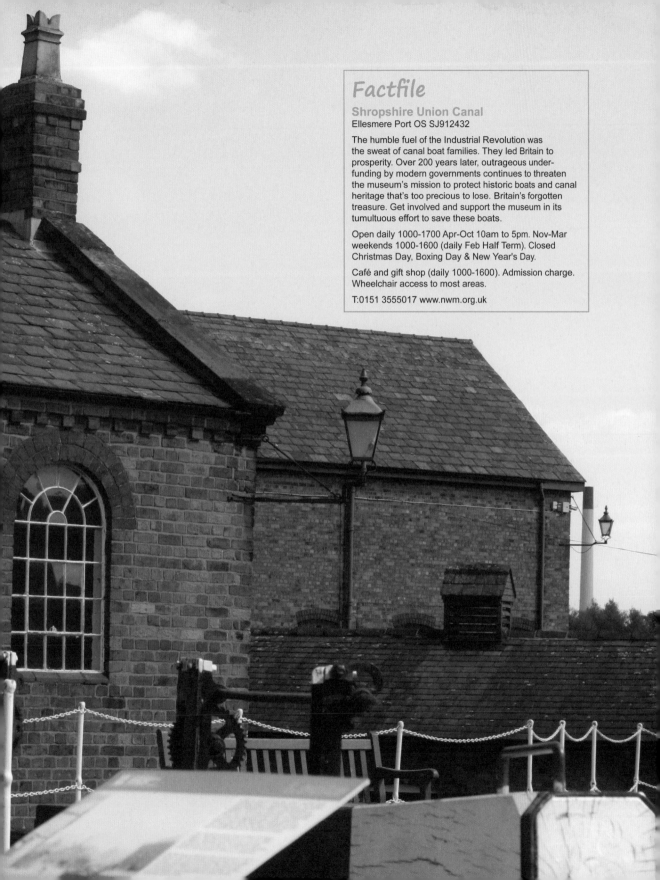

## Factfile

### Shropshire Union Canal
Ellesmere Port OS SJ912432

The humble fuel of the Industrial Revolution was
the sweat of canal boat families. They led Britain to
prosperity. Over 200 years later, outrageous under-
funding by modern governments continues to threaten
the museum's mission to protect historic boats and canal
heritage that's too precious to lose. Britain's forgotten
treasure. Get involved and support the museum in its
tumultuous effort to save these boats.

Open daily 1000-1700 Apr-Oct 10am to 5pm. Nov-Mar
weekends 1000-1600 (daily Feb Half Term). Closed
Christmas Day, Boxing Day & New Year's Day.

Café and gift shop (daily 1000-1600). Admission charge.
Wheelchair access to most areas.

T:0151 3555017 www.nwm.org.uk

# Days out

in the North

## STANDEDGE TUNNEL

Even the Pennines, the cloud-brushing backbone of Britain, couldn't stop the defiant route of Britain's canal... navvies simply blasted through. Standedge Tunnel is the longest, highest and deepest tunnel on Britain's inland waterways, furrowing 3¼ miles from one side of the Pennines to the other.

**British
Waterways**

"I've been working on the Huddersfield Narrow Canal and Standedge Tunnel & Visitor Centre for over 41 years now and am a Senior Waterway Operative and Pilot Guide.

When I left school I began working in textiles. This wasn't for me, so by chance one day I was walking around Hill Top reservoir and began chatting to some British Waterways staff. The morning after I went down to Standedge and asked if there was any jobs. I was asked if I had a motorbike licence – I did, and the rest is history. I got a job working on water control as much of the water was being used to supply local factories.

I guided the first ever trip into the tunnel 2001, but my favourite moment was meeting Prince Charles during the reopening of the canal. I was guiding the boat that day and very nervous, but he was extremely interested in the heritage of the canal and asked me lots of interesting questions. I was also recently given an honorary lifetime membership to the Huddersfield Canal Society which was a very touching moment for me.

I love the canals; there's nothing better. The wildlife and the heritage are fantastic, but the best thing about canal life is the people. Meeting the public at Standedge and getting them fascinated about the history of the canal and tunnel makes the job so very special."

## Factfile

**Huddersfield Narrow Canal**
Standedge OS SE040120

30-minute passenger boat trips into the tunnel, in glass-roofed boats with a specialist guide. 3-hr through boat trip only available 1st Sat of month.

Open Mar-Nov Tues-Fri 1030-1600, Sat-Sun 1000-1700 Closed Mon except School and Bank holidays.

Café and gift shop.

Entry FREE to Visitor Centre, grounds, café & gift shop. Boat Trips (charge). Wheelchair access.

No dogs. Disabled access to glass-roofed boat trips and Visitor Centre but no access on the through-tunnel trip.

T:01484 844298 / 01782 785703 (Nov-Mar)
www.standedge.co.uk

# Days out

## SALTAIRE

**A World Heritage Site**

Saltaire is a UNESCO-designated World Heritage Site. Sir Titus Salt's mill stands boldly as a statement of the best of British entrepreneurship, workmanship and determination. It's a place where weavers worked for a modest wage in the textile industry that led the world. The mill's redundant chimney rises skywards (almost to its former 250ft) as a modern-day monument to the Industrial Revolution.

As with any revolution, the Industrial Revolution brought upheaval and chaos to this island. The mid-19th century was a time of radical social change as rural communities were brought (often by barge) to new urban towns built for industry. Capitalism was the wild fire of the nation. Some mill owners were greedily blind to the wrongs of child labour and the social and economic slavery of workers miserably crammed into urban slums of disease and smog. Thankfully, Quaker families such as Cadbury, and other non-conformist church reformers such as Titus Salt valued their workers' human rights more.

### Tour the village

For his mill workers, Salt built an entire village with neat rows of houses, schools, a workers' institute, a park and more. The houses must have seemed grand and solid to Salt's workers. Reliable patterns of windows and doors offer security and comfort and a quality of life that was better than many other mill workers might expect. The new industrial capitalism was the cauldron for Britain's class structure. Dizzily looking up and down at each other, Britain created an order and stamped it clearly with invisible labels. The heyday of the Dark Satanic Mills depended on the so-called lower class. Britain paved itself with class structure, but Saltaire managed to cement its pavements with respect for one common cause - the mill. His cobbled street community is still alive today, except now it's occupied by private residents who go about their own daily business whilst tourists tiptoe around. It is a site of immaculate heritage (except for the back allies that are now littered with armies of wheelie bins, for a throw-away culture that Saltaire's original inhabitants wouldn't grasp).

### Visit the mill

Inside the mill, the cathedral acoustics that once bellowed with looms have been replaced by background recordings of soft classical music. Naked bricks arch overhead and stone floors echo the atmosphere. The void between is filled with the largest permanent collection of David Hockney paintings. And 'Hockney-cool' shopping covers several floors with books, jewellery and a certain type of experience.

> The mill once housed 1,200 looms producing 30,000 yards of alpaca and other cloths daily. Steam-driven machinery needed 50 tons of coal per day and water drawn from the River Aire through pipes running under the building and canal.

### Food and drink

Titus Salt thought alcohol was 'a source of social evil' and he deliberately omitted to build a local boozer for his workers. What would he have said when over a hundred years after his death, the Boathouse Inn was opened right next to his mill. The pub overlooks the park where white dots of cricket speckle the green and families push prams and kick balls. Titus probably would aprove of the views at least. A second pub had the audacity to open in the tree-lined main street of Saltaire. It is cheekily called 'Don't Tell Titus'. Saltaire now even has its own ale to show off - a good pint of Saltaire Blonde is unashamedly delicious with a citrusy aftertaste.

## Factfile

### Huddersfield Narrow Canal
Saltaire OS SE139381

**SALTS MILL**
Open daily 1000-1730 (1800 Sat-Sun) all
year, except Christmas Day, Boxing Day
& New Year's Day. (Top Floor Wed-Sun)
Shops, cafés and exhibitions.
FREE admission.

T:01274 531163 www.saltsmill.org.uk

**SALTAIRE**
www.saltairevillage.info

# Days out
## in the North

## FESTIVALS

### Rushbearing Festival

Tradition teams up with English madness as the countryside drums to life with a procession of clog-clonking feet and men wearing Panama hats. The merry herd of folk set off early for a full day tugging a cart of rushes around Yorkshire's landscape. One poor lucky lass gets the honour of perching precariously on top of the 16ft-high cart of rushes. She is willing to cling on throughout the episode with hilarity, humour and as much dignity as she can muster.

The festival has practical roots since it originally served as a yearly method of replacing old rush floors in the local village churches surrounding Sowerby Bridge. The procession follows the trail of the churches but, of course, where there's an English church, there's usually an English pub

- and the hopeful carry their own tankards with intent. Each pub fuels the procession until the final post at the canal basin in Sowerby Bridge.

A day of accordian merriment and plenty of stick clonking for authentic effect, with tales of the past and the best of British community spirit.

### Middlewich Folk and Boat Festival

A weekend of music, water, boats and even canalside camping for the complete festival deal. Traditional narrowboat crafts, street performers, dance, workshops and lots of fringe events are on offer. Wholesome folkie fun for all the family.

### Rake the moon from the canal

Wrap up warm, follow the crowd and go moon-raking along the Huddersfield Narrow Canal. A festival pumped with quirky canal history, big on atmosphere and a dose of British eccentricity. The villagers of Slaithwaite come together (with outsiders gate-crashing) to bring back to life the dastardly story of two Slaithwaite rogues. The tale goes that, one frosty day in 1802, said duo were smuggling barrels of liquor from a boat when patrolling soldiers disturbed them. The rogues hid the barrels in reeds and returned later under cover of darkness. Soldiers again disturbed them, but the quick-witted rogues yelled, "Cans tha noon seah? T'mooin fell int watter an we'ar rekkin er aht!". The soldiers went off sniggering at the duo's stupidity. The smugglers' triumph is a nifty excuse for a weekend of carnival over two centuries on. Lanterns float down the canal, toe-tapping music rings in the air and of course the giant Mr Moon makes his appearance.

### Imbolc Fire Festival

Something in the Pennine air keeps old legends alive and, for the locals of Marsden, one story has become an annual tradition with all sorts of canalside shenanigans. A procession from Standedge Visitor Centre to Tunnel End Inn ends in a battle between Jack Frost (winter) & Mr Green (spring) as they come to loggerheads over the passing seasons. Luckily the inn serves real ale and home-cooked food so the hearty celebrations can last as long as it takes.

## Factfile

**SOWERBY RUSHBEARING FESTIVAL**
September. Sowerby Bridge.
Rochdale Canal.
www.rushbearing.co.uk

**MIDDLEWICH FOLK & BOAT FESTIVAL**
June. Middlewich.
Trent & Mersey Canal.
www.midfest.org.uk

**MOONRAKING FESTIVAL**
February. Slaithwaite.
Huddersfield Narrow Canal.
www.slaithwaitemoonraking.org

**IMBOLC FIRE FESTIVAL**
February. Marsden.
Huddersfield Narrow Canal.
www.kirklees.gov.uk

## Other festivals in the North

**LIVERPOOL BOAT SHOW**
End of April/early May. First one held in 2011. Mersey.
www.liverpoolboatshow.com

**SKIPTON WATERWAY FESTIVAL**
May. Skipton.
Leeds & Liverpool Canal.
www.penninecruisers.com

**ETRURIA CANALS FESTIVAL**
May. Stoke-on-Trent.
Trent & Mersey Canal.
T:01782 233144

**SALTAIRE FESTIVAL**
September. Saltaire.
Leeds & Liverpool Canal.
www.saltairefestival.co.uk

**MARSDEN JAZZ FESTIVAL**
October. Marsden.
Huddersfield Narrow Canal.
www.marsdenjazzfestival.com

# Days out
## in the North

## Calder & Hebble Navigation

### SOWERBY BRIDGE CANAL BASIN

The canal basin at Sowerby Bridge is where the Calder & Hebble seamlessly turns into the Rochdale Canal.

In the days of 'canal mania', the basin would have been the scene of narrowboats unloading from long 72ft boats on the Rochdale Canal and reloading onto shorter boats on the Calder & Hebble Navigation, which could only carry narrowboats of a maximum length of 60 feet.

Today it's home to holiday hireboat company Shire Cruisers and, in a cobbled setting, canalside bars with outside seating.

Look out for the sculpture of the man and boy working at the lock arm by the entrance to the basin.

Sowerby Bridge. OS SE065237

## Huddersfield Narrow Canal

### STANDEDGE TUNNEL AND VISITOR CENTRE
The longest, deepest, highest tunnel on the canal networks (Days Out page 182-183).

## Leeds & Liverpool Canal

### BINGLEY FIVE RISE & THREE RISE

A staircase climb, 60ft above the woollen mills of Bingley. An intriguing view down into the locks from the towpath and a chilling journey for the boater (although the reward for the boater is almost 17 miles of lock-free cruising on the canal's summit). This is canal drama at its best.

Unspoilt lockside cobbles and brickwork dredge thoughts of hurrying cargo in bygone days. But now this hardy, and frankly not the prettiest, stretch of the Leeds & Liverpool Canal is for dedicated thrill-seekers after the water's richest rewards.

At the top of the lock flight, the old stables have been turned into a small shop and inviting café, with ice cream, cakes, coffees and teas.

Bingley Five Rise was awarded the Transport Trust's Red Wheel plaque (the first one in Yorkshire) in 2010 - it is the steepest lock staircase in Britain, one of the 7 Wonders of the Waterways, and the only Grade I-listed structure on the Leeds & Liverpool Canal.

Bingley. OS SE107399

### SALTAIRE
A World Heritage Site. Mill and workers' village (Days Out page 184-185).

### WEAVERS' TRIANGLE

The Weavers' Triangle Trust are working to preserve Burnley's textile heritage & one of the finest surviving Victorian industrial landscapes in the country. See an original mill engine working in Oak Mount Mill, have a go at weaving in the Visitor Centre. There are also guided towpath walks, and visits to the Burnley Embankment, one of the 7 Wonders of the Waterways.

Burnley. OS SD838322

FREE admission. Visitor Centre, café, pub next door. Limited wheelchair access.

T:01282 452403 www.weaverstriangle.co.uk

## Macclesfield Canal

### SILK MUSEUMS

At the height of the Silk Industry, there were 120 mills and dye houses in Macclesfield and silk is still being produced there, albeit on a much smaller scale. The history of the silk industry and Macclesfield's role in it is now best understood by visiting one of the four Silk Museums, with exhibits ranging from restored Jacquard handlooms and a huge collection of silk ties to a photo archive containing over 20,000 photographs relating to Macclesfield and the silk industry.

Macclesfield. OS SJ916734

Opening times vary. Admission charge. Heritage Centre, Coffee Shop and Silk Shop. Events and exhibitions. Some wheelchair access.

T:01625 612045 www.macclesfield.silk.museum/

## Trent & Mersey Canal

### ANDERTON BOAT LIFT

The Anderton Boat Lift is impressive enough from the ground but you can enjoy a 30-minute boat trip and get a boat's eye view from inside the lift. The 'Edwin Clarke' is a glass-topped trip boat taking you 50 feet up from the River Weaver to the Trent & Mersey Canal above. The boat masters are waterways oracles, willingly answering any questions about the Lift. One of the 7 Wonders of the waterways.

Anderton, Northwich. OS SJ647753

Opening times vary. Admission FREE to Visitor centre, exhibition area, café and gift shop (car park charge). Charge for Boat trips. Wheelchair access.

T:01606 786777 www.andertonboatlift.co.uk

# FOOD & DRINK

## Pubs
in the North

### Huddersfield Narrow Canal

**TUNNEL END INN**

A short walk from the canal, overlooking the entrance to Standedge Tunnel. Popular traditional pub, real ales, real fire, pub food and a real welcome.
Marsden. T:01484 844636
www.tunnelendinn.com

### Lancaster Canal

**ANCHOR INN**
Friendly historic inn whose original bar was below the waterline. You can see stalactites & stalagmites in what is now the cellar.
Salterforth. T:01282 813186

**WATER WITCH**
Converted canalside stables between bridges 98 & 99. Award-winning pub serving a great range of real ales and pub meals.
Lancaster. T:01524 63828
www.thewaterwitch.co.uk

### Leeds & Liverpool Canal

**NARROW BOAT**
Short walk from the canal up a tiny cobbled street. Wooden floors, real ales and a large range of continental beers.
Skipton. T:01756 797922
www.markettowntaverns.co.uk

**THE BOATHOUSE INN**

Overlooking Roberts Park, with its back to the canal. Just over the canal bridge from Saltaire village, a World Heritage Site.
Saltaire. T:01274 585690
www.theboathouseinn.co.uk

### Macclesfield Canal

**RING O' BELLS**
Canalside by bridge 2. Traditional local with lots of cosy corners.
Marple. T:0161 4272300
www.ringobellsmarple.co.uk

### Peak Forest Canal

**NAVIGATION INN**
Overlooking Bugsworth Basin at the end of the original main line.
Buxworth. T:01663 732072
www.navigationinn.co.uk

### Rochdale Canal

**STUBBING WHARF**

Canalside near Stubbing Upper Lock, with the river at the other side. Boat trips from just outside. Real fire, real ales, dogs welcome
Hebden Bridge T:0870 0348443
www.stubbingwharf.com

# Teashops

in the North

## Huddersfield Narrow Canal

### MOONRAKER FLOATING TEAROOM

Café on a narrowboat moored by
Dartmouth Lock (23E).
Slaithwaite. T:01484 846370

### THE LITTLE BRIDGE

Café wine bar, canalside by bridge 44.
Open Wed-Sun.
Slaithwaite. T:01484 846738

### WATER'S EDGE CAFÉ

Canalside by the entrance to
Standedge Tunnel.
Marsden. T:01484 844298
www.standedge.co.uk

## Leeds & Liverpool Canal

### DALESMAN CAFÉ & TEAROOMS

A short walk from the canal.
Grade II-listed café renowned among
walkers and cyclists for its warm
welcome, good food & jars of sweets.
Pilgrim cyclists on the 355-mile
Pennine Cycleway (Sustrans National
Cycle Network Route 68) can get their
route cards stamped here.
Gargrave. T:01756 749250

### FIVE RISE LOCKS CAFÉ

Canalside at the top of Bingley Five
Rise Locks. Plenty of indoor space and
some tables outside to watch boats
tackling the locks.
Bingley. T:01274 562221

## Macclesfield Canal

### WATERSIDE CAFÉ

Canalside (cross the footbridge 27A)
on the ground floor of the imposing
Clarence Mill.
Bollington. T:01625 575563

## Rochdale Canal

### GABRIELS COFFEE LOUNGE

A friendly, tiny teashop with a handful
of seats inside and a few more outside
tables. Fairtrade coffees, teas, cakes
and snacks. Just opposite Sowerby's
'Jack O' The Locks' sculpture.
Sowerby Bridge. T:01422832233
www.gabrielscoffeelounge.co.uk

For listings of waterside pubs & teashops
in the UK, visit our website:
www.greatwaterwaysoutdoors.com

## WATERWAYS LIFE
## Mikron

**Probably the coolest theatre company in the world.**

Mikron is the Greek word for small, and this theatre company is so small its cast turns up in a narrowboat, puts on a show, and then leaves by boat as quietly as it arrived.

No fuss, no over-fancy props and definitely no luvvie-tiaras. An audience gets the impression Mikron wouldn't like red carpets rolled out, and if they were, the cast would prefer jute rugs at least. Home is up north in Marsden, where the Huddersfield Canal nudges the Pennines, but when the company is on tour, the cast live aboard Tyseley, the 1936 narowboat that once belonged to the Grand Union Carrying Company.

Since 1972, Mikron has toured the waterways performing all across Britain. Sometimes outdoors on the waterside, or in canal pubs, at festivals, boat rallies, in village halls and even inside a canal tunnel if they are asked to.

## Factfile

**Huddersfield Narrow Canal**
Based in Marsden OS SE045115

Mikron tour all summer in their narrowboat, Tyseley, and by road in the autumn.

You can support them by going to see one of their shows, becoming a 'Friend of Mikron', sponsoring a show, buying merchandise from their online shop, or just spreading the word...

T: 01484 843701
www.mikron.org.uk

You don't have to dress up or need pots of money to see Mikron perform live. Often their plays are free, with just a bucket passed round for your best donation at the end.

Over the years they've played to hundreds of thousands of people. Each audience is usually a laid-back mix of boaters, locals, curious theatregoers and waggy-tailed dogs.

Mikron describes itself as "A little theatre company with a reputation for tackling large-scale subjects and turning history into vivid and dramatic entertainment." Their plays are original and accessible to diverse audiences. Lines flow with the ease of an un-ironed performance that bears no creases. Intelligent, educational, moving and crisply funny, Mikron treats us to plays that are rousting and issue-based, digging the best and worst of Britishness from under the rug. Expect unconventionally classy performances that speak simply, yet yield deeper than the surface.

Travelling in a narrowboat and performing along the waterways is a way of life for the cast. This, combined with the company's dedication to live theatre in non-theatre venues, gives Mikron its unique and unmissable zest.

# WALES

Plain signposts mark the borders: 'Croeso i Gymru', they say, 'Welcome to Wales'. Understated, almost modest. But Wales doesn't need to shout, the excitement is there in the landscape for all to see.

Beyond the borders, high open spaces tease you to explore off the beaten track and discover country lanes down in the valleys speckled with place names that the English can't grasp.

Inevitably, the Welsh coastline doesn't escape the occasional pustule of kitsch clutter, but Wales isn't ruined by plastic entertainment - instead, it's grounded with the call of its wild Celtic heritage wilfully beckoning you to pull on a woolly hat and find an adventure.

Wales has the ancient landscapes of Snowdonia, the natural beauty of the Brecon Beacons National Park, the wilderness of the Black mountains. And notably, Britain has 28 World Heritage Sites, 3 of which are in Wales. The breathtaking Pontcysyllte Aqueduct is a World Heritage Site, and the included 11-mile stretch of Llangollen Canal can claim to cross from one country into another. Blaenavon is a humble town with World Heritage status too. Here, in the 18th and 19th centuries, migrant workers helped make Blaenavon one of the most important producers of iron, coal and steel in the world.

While the Irish Sea throws its mood swings along the coastline, some of Britain's greatest rivers crawl inland. The River Severn, the Wye, the Dee, all carve their distinctive trails and, alongside them, the Welsh canals bring the gentlest routes of all.

North, south, east and west, Wales is passionate about its identity. Never just a westerly corner of Britain, Wales is the Big Country deliciously trapped in a small body. Welsh castles, choirs of male voices singing as sweetly as the hills, generations of farmers and their sheep dogs, and unspoilt beaches building family trees on childhood memories.

# WATERWAYS
## of Wales
### boat, bike, boot

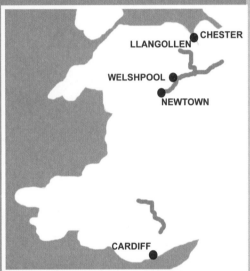

## Highlights

**PONTCYSYLLTE AQUEDUCT** on the Llangollen Canal - **PEN Y FAN** views on the Mon & Brec Canal - **BRYNICH LOCK & AQUEDUCT** on the Mon & Brec Canal - **CHIRK AQUEDUCT & VIADUCT** on the Llangollen Canal - **MAESBURY MARSH** on the Montgomery Canal

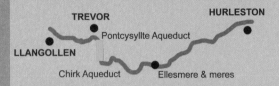

Hurleston Junction to Llantysilio (near Llangollen)
46 miles, 21 locks

A narrow fantastically exciting canal that deservedly attracts boaters and towpath tourists in droves. The Llangollen Canal sets off innocuously enough from Cheshire's soft surroundings, working its way towards the mountains of North Wales. Just before it reaches its famous destination at the Eisteddfod town of Llangollen, the canal does its best to half scare you to death - it takes you over Pontcysyllte Aqueduct. Mice and men cross white-faced, and tourists with cameras from across the globe turn up to click away with one hand whilst holding on to the railings tightly with the other. A World Heritage Site - not to be missed.

## Montgomery Canal

Frankton Junction to Aberbechan (near Newtown)
32½ miles, 21 locks

Nicknamed the Monty, this canal is itching to do the full Monty again. It closed in the early 1900s after a breach and is one of the many canals across Britain that battle for full restoration. The canal is navigable in parts with plenty to enjoy, and where boats can't go yet, the towpath is the trump card into deepest Wales. And because the Monty has been unnavigable and undisturbed in sections, it is a special haven for wildlife too.

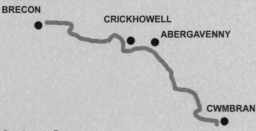

## Monmouthshire & Brecon Canal

BRECON

CRICKHOWELL

ABERGAVENNY

CWMBRAN

Cwmbran to Brecon
35¾ miles, 6 locks

The DIVA of Britain's canals, set in the Brecon Beacons National Park with the Black Mountains as a spectacular backdrop. The Mon & Brec Canal is isolated from the cruising rings of the mainstream canal networks, and that leaves an intimate cohort of boats free to roam to and fro at will. With only a handful of locks, this is utterly lazy water. But don't be fooled by the tranquillity, its tumultuous scenery is a heart stopper. The route twists under canopies of leaves and then, with an innocent bend in the water, it will thrust you into the sort of sublime panorama that only Wales can do.

# ROUTES
## along the towpath

## SOME DESIGNATED TOWPATH ROUTES

### Llangollen Canal

**OFFA'S DYKE PATH**
Chepstow to Prestatyn (total trail 177 miles)
Follows the towpath all the way from just outside Chirk to just beyond Trevor Basin.

### Mon & Brec Canal

**LÔN LAS CYMRU**
National Cycle Network (NCN) Route 8
Cardiff to Holyhead (Anglesey)
Follows the Taff Trail from Cardiff to Brecon and the canal towpath from Brynich to Brecon.

**TAFF TRAIL**
Brecon to Cardiff (total trail 55 miles)
Follows the canal towpath all the way from Brecon to Brynich Lock (trail walkers can continue along the towpath as far as Talybont-on-Usk to rejoin the Route there).

### Montgomery Canal

**OFFA'S DYKE PATH**
Chepstow to Prestatyn (total trail 177 miles)
Follows the towpath much of the way from just outside Welshpool to Llanymynech.

**SEVERN WAY**
From its source to the sea (total trail 210 miles)
Follows the towpath all the way from Newtown to Welshpool.

### More info

For more detailed information and maps of all National Cycle Network Routes, go to www.sustrans.org.uk

For more walks and trails, go to www.ramblers.org.uk

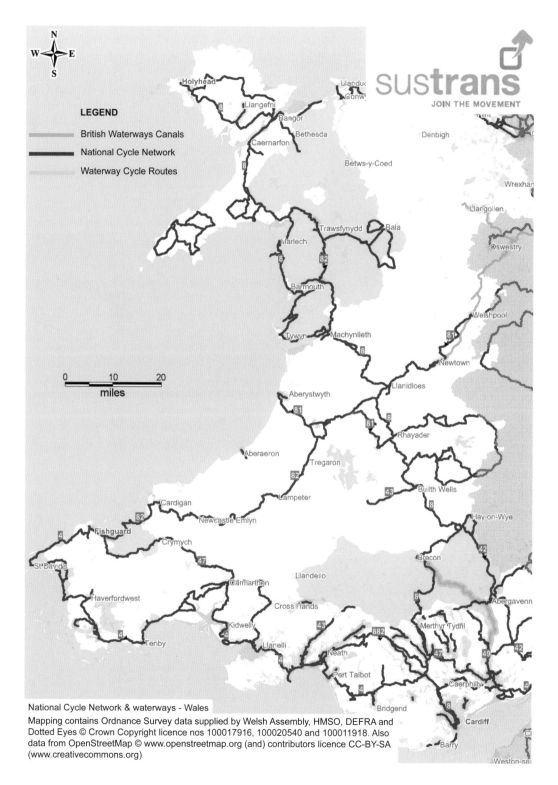

National Cycle Network & waterways - Wales
Mapping contains Ordnance Survey data supplied by Welsh Assembly, HMSO, DEFRA and
Dotted Eyes © Crown Copyright licence nos 100017916, 100020540 and 100011918. Also
data from OpenStreetMap © www.openstreetmap.org (and) contributors licence CC-BY-SA
(www.creativecommons.org)

# Routes
along the towpath

JOIN THE MOVEMENT

**Gwyn Smith**
**Sustrans Area Manager for South Wales**

## My favourite bike ride
Monmouthshire & Brecon Canal

"Have you ever seen the black crest of a heron close up? Well, I get the opportunity almost every evening. Being on a bike you can sneak up quickly and quietly and get a short opportunity to see them in all their glory. The Mon & Brec Canal forms part of my commute between Usk and Pontypool and I have been up close, and personal, with fishing herons almost every evening.

The canal for me, since I joined Sustrans over 6 years ago, has on reflection had quite an effect on my travel habits between my home and our office in Cardiff.

I love riding along the Crumlin Arm (National Cycle Network Route 47) from Newport to Fourteen Locks - feeling very smug as I pedal along looking at the queues of standing traffic on the motorway. I never feel as smug as I struggle up the incline that is the 14 locks, cursing the barriers that are supposed to stop motorbikes. However, being an engineer, I still marvel at the flight of locks and look forward to the day they are fully restored. (www.fourteenlocksetr.co.uk)

At least at the top I can stop at the Visitor Centre for a cuppa and a well-earned rest. (www.fourteenlocks.co.uk)

My favourite stretch is from Govilon to Pontypool. I join the canal where it passes under the excellent NCN Route 46, usually after coasting down the spectacular Clydach gorge from Brynmawr. Once on the canal, I let my mind wander until I reach the boat house at Llanfoist. The contrast always surprises me as I pass from the tree-lined waterway to what appears to be an immaculate lawn. On the one side is the canal and the magnificent boat house (where I would love to live), and on the other, magnificent views of Abergavenny and the surrounding hills of the Black Mountains.

With time pressing I leave this idyllic place travelling along the canal, sometimes passing the time of day with visitors on hired canal boats and other walkers and cyclists.

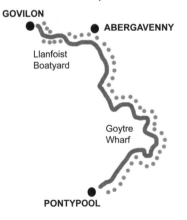

GOVILON

ABERGAVENNY

Llanfoist
Boatyard

Goytre
Wharf

PONTYPOOL

I Llanfoist Boat House I

What I am always on the lookout for is the magical flash of bright blue of the exotic jewel-like bird, the kingfisher. I remember my first sighting of this magnificent bird some 20 years ago on this very canal and we still laugh at the tale. We... my wife, my mum and dad hired a boat to explore the canal. We were sitting in the front window of the boat when suddenly it veered toward the bank and there, on a tree stump, was the kingfisher. My mum, who was driving at the time, got so excited she steered the boat towards the bird. We had a great view but sore necks after the impact. Luckily the bird escaped unharmed and we have a great memory."

# Factfile

Start: Govilon OS SO265137
Finish: Pontypool OS SO293002
12 miles, 0 locks

### Highlights
Llanfoist boat yard - base for Beacon Park Boats
Goytre Wharf - Visitor Centre, gift shop and café in large site with marina, boat hire base and former lime kilns

### Bike hire
**PEDALAWAY**
Mountain bikes, tourers and tandems. Also trailer bikes and child seats. Hopyard Farm, Govilon. T:01873 830219
www.pedalaway.co.uk
www.hopyardcourtyardcottage.co.uk

### More info
For more detailed information and maps of all National Cycle Network Routes, go to www.sustrans.org.uk

# Routes
along the towpath

**Phillippa & Martine**
Some of the highlights of our epic canal
walk from Cornwall to Scotland

## Our favourite walks

Some canals that we have walked have asked to
be visited only once, but the canals of Wales beg
us to keep coming back... and we do. These aren't
'once in a lifetime' experiences, they are to be
savoured at every opportunity. Come any time
of year and the views will be different. Never
boring, always demonstratively reaffirming of
life. As an instant remedy for the stresses of daily
life, we always recommend a comfy pair of shoes
and a walk along a Welsh canal.

### A walk along the Monmouthshire &
Brecon Canal

Brecon is thought of as the outdoor capital of
Wales and the Monmouthshire & Brecon Canal
is a secret hideaway running through the heart of
the Brecon Beacons National Park.

This Welsh canal is remote - distanced from the
noise of roads, and the void that scratches from
daily 9-to-5 grind.
Despite being a high trail, the towpath is

easily accessible, which makes it popular with
strollers and extreme outdoor enthusiasts alike.
If you prefer solitude, avoid Bank Holidays and
weekends.

A walk with big Welsh views, and the taste of real
air to fuel your boots. Mountains, cormorants,
red kites, sheep, blankets of Welsh grass – and
canopies of leaves that change colour with the
seasons (irresistible for us secret tree-huggers!)

This isn't a canal walk for lock enthusiasts,
since most of the way is lock free. Features of
interest include several lift bridges and Brynich
Aqueduct. Built by the engineer Thomas
Dadford, the four-arched aqueduct elegantly
carries the canal over the River Usk below.

Towpath walks usually have enough canal
highlights to make up for any stretches of
monotony, but the Mon & Brec spoils you
with delicious scenery every step of the way.
And, no matter how grateful you are for each
satisfying waterways mile, just when you think
the views couldn't get any better, they do. A
lunch break stop, picnicking on the towpath with
cheese sandwiches, looking over the water at the
mountainous peak of Pen y Fan is amongst the
most memorable moments of our end-to-end
canal walk across Britain.

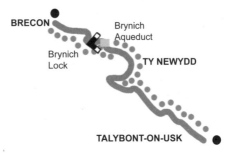

i Brynich Lock - Pen y Fan -
Talybont-on-Usk i

### Ty Newydd

Ty Newydd boatyard is set in a 360° panorama, with the Brecon Beacons and Pen y Fan standing majestically in the distance.

### Signposts

Spot the rusting diamond-shaped signposts peeping over many stone bridges on the Mon & Brec. A world without cars seems inconceivable today, yet of course canals preceded our carbon-burning noise polluters. With the arrival of the motor car, new pressure was put on canal bridges originally constructed for foot passengers or horse & cart. These signs warned drivers of the newfangled motors to beware of weight limits over the bridges.

## Factfile

**Monmouthshire & Brecon Canal**
Start: Brecon Basin OS SO046281
Finish: Talybont-on-Usk OS SO111229
6 miles, 1 lock, 5 lift bridges

### Highlights
Brynich Lock
Brynich Aqueduct
Ty Newydd
Views of Pen y Fan

### Did you know?

The Taff Trail Cycle Route follows the Mon & Brec Canal from just outside Brecon to Brynich Lock where cyclists head off on the road, though walkers on the Trail can continue on the canal as far as Talybont-on-Usk.
www.tafftrail.org.uk

# Routes
along the towpath

## A walk along the Llangollen Canal

The big walk along Britain's canals - a mere handful of miles, yet a riot of excitement.

Start in historic Llangollen, at the busy wharf. You might want to explore Horseshoe Falls (created by Thomas Telford to provide water for the canal) or take a short horse-boat trip from the wharf before you head off away from town to experience the marvel of this canal. Expect crowds of people and boats if you arrive on a Bank holiday. But don't be too put off by the company, since a traffic jam on a canal is a different affair from one on a road. It's usually a good excuse to natter with strangers and for boaters to show off their rope work.

Only a short way into the walk, you'll leave the crowds behind and the solitude of Wales bleats aloud with herons, sheep, kites and green space. Dinas Bran castle, built in the 1260s, is high on the hill, and there are dynamic views over the River Dee with picnic spots to die for. Then there are bridges and boats, and if you come in July you'll find yourself serenaded by heavenly voices too, as the air fills with the annual Eisteddfod chorus.

## Factfile

**Llangollen Canal**
Start: Llangollen Wharf OS SJ214422
Finish: Pontcysyllte OS SJ270420
4 miles, 0 lock

### Highlights
Pontcysyllte Aqueduct (Days out page 220-221)
Views over the Dee valley

### Did you know?
The long-distance National Trail, Offa's Dyke Path, joins the Llangollen for a short stretch from Chirk, with walkers able to choose between walking across the Pontcysyllte Aqueduct, or (for the less brave) walking down the road to the floor of the valley and back up the other side.

LLANGOLLEN   Trevor Basin   Pontcysyllte Aqueduct

The walk is idyllic enough already, but the highlight is yet to come. Brace yourself as you approach Pontcysyllte Aqueduct... an extreme experience awaits. It was awarded World Heritage Site status in 2009 and is one of the Seven Wonders of the Waterways.

Nothing prepares you for the colossal drama of Pontcysyllte Aqueduct. It's pure adrenalin... An inspirational feat of engineering carrying the canal over the river Dee. Eighteen arches held together with ox blood and Welsh flannel have kept the Llangollen Canal suspended in flight for over 200 years. The non-vertiginous can brave the slim towpath hugging the water with 127-foot sheer drops either side.

"Don't look down", walkers whisper to each other as they paw their way across the aqueduct, clinging with all their body to the railings that stop the fall. And boaters steer into the flying bathtub, white-faced, with sheer drops without even railings on their side. Everyone is talking about the adventure - chivvying each other, and gingerly clicking one-handedly with cameras.

An extraordinary walk with high moments almost every step of the way.

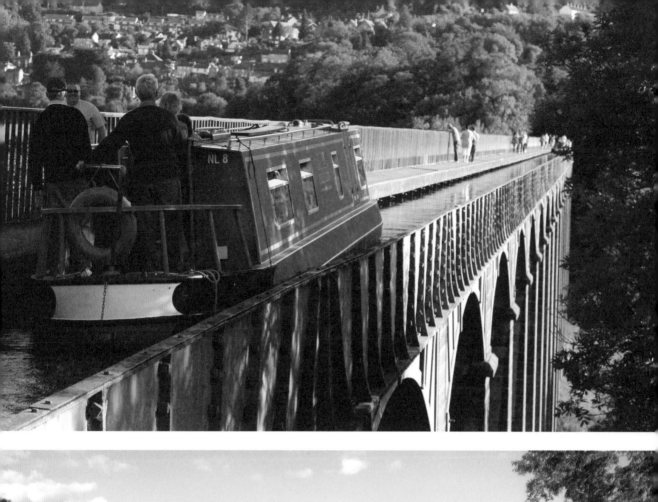

# ROUTES
## boating

## Favourite boating routes

When canals reach the far edges of England, boaters can carry on cruising across the borders to explore Wales... and even navigate the amazing Pontcysyllte Aqueduct on the Llangollen Canal. But one Welsh canal remains isolated from the rest and quietly potters about the countryside in the heart of the Brecon Beacons National Park.

The navigable whole of the Monmouthshire & Brecon Canal is only just over 35 miles long, of which 22 miles are lock free - making this the route to choose for utterly lazy cruising.

There are plenty of friendly canalside pubs along the route to tempt you to linger, and views over the Black Mountains call for unhurried lunch stops. The simplicity of this landlocked canal means there's no panic over a crammed itinerary - just moor where and when you want, and turn around to return the boat when you have to.

Whatever time of year you choose to visit, the 'Mon & Brec' begs you to come back again to see another season. The entire canal is a blaze of colours that change with the seasons under its intimate tree-lined route.

Holiday hire narrowboats are comfortable and warm, even when the weather isn't kind, so boating out of the hot season is still fun. And some of the boats on the Mon & Brec are wide beam with extra space for luxury.

### The lazy route for a one or two-week break

Start from Beacon Park Boats at Llanfoist Wharf. Cruise to Govilon to moor overnight, and then head for Llangynidr. Travel through the locks, the swing bridges and the tunnel on the following day, then moor in Brecon. Spend the fourth day cruising to Talybont, crossing the aqueduct along the way. Return through the tunnel and five locks to Llangattock. On the sixth day, head for Gilwern and on the seventh day make a leisurely return journey to Llanfoist.

### Brecon

The outdoor capital of Wales. The town is lively with a busy turnover of walkers, cyclists and boaters. Has a museum, cathedral and canal basin.

### Crickhowell

A small town of welsh vintage that is now notorious for its walking festival that takes place at the beginning of March each year.

### Too shy to ask?

It's the question we polite Brits don't dare to ask. But what are the loos like? Don't worry, the old-fashioned boater's bucket-and-chuck-it has been usurped by full flush facilities. Most modern narrowboats are like luxurious floating cottages.

### Factfile

**Monmouthshire & Brecon Canal**
Start: Cwmbran OS ST291953
Finish: Brecon OS SO046281
35¾ miles, 6 locks

**Highlights**
Llangynidr Locks
Brynich Lock
Goytre Wharf
Llangattock Wharf

**Did you know?**
At the height of the Industrial Revolution, iron and coal were transported from the ironworks at Blaenavon along horse-operated tram roads down to the Mon & Brec Canal, where they were stored in canalside warehouses before being loaded onto canal boats. The wharves and canal at both Llanfoist and Govilon form part of the Blaenavon Industrial Landscape World Heritage Site.

www.world-heritage-blaenavon.org.uk

## Waterways people

John Pugh has been an IWA member for over 30 years and cruised the networks extensively.

Canals are a linear park and we all have to share and help protect the waterways environment for everybody. John knows that this can at times cause a conflict of interests.

"The towpath is great for families enjoying gentle bike rides" John explains, "but if parts of the canal towpaths have been hard-surfaced and speeding cyclists use them, it can be a nightmare!"

Many of us who love the canals are concerned that the slow culture should be protected and hard-surfacing of the towpaths be limited to appropriate sections.

Luckily the canal community is a friendly beast and, when they can, differences are ironed out over a pint in a waterside pub.

# Boats
## in Wales

## Llangollen Canal

### ANGLO WELSH WATERWAY HOLIDAYS
Narrowboat holiday & day hire.
Trevor Basin. T:0117 3041122
www.anglowelsh.co.uk

### BETTISFIELD BOATS
Narrowboat holiday hire.
Bettisfield. T:01948 710398
www.bettisfieldboats.com

### BLACK PRINCE NARROWBOAT HOLIDAYS
Narrowboat holiday hire.
Chirk. T:01527 575115
www.black-prince.com

### CREST NARROWBOATS
Narrowboat holiday hire.
Chirk Marina. T:01691 774558
www.crestnarrowboats.co.uk

### 'EIRLYS', JONES THE BOATS
Trips across Pontcysyllte Aqueduct.
Daily Easter to October. Charter trips
also available.
Trevor Basin. T:01691 690322
www.canaltrip.co.uk

### LLANGOLLEN HORSE-DRAWN BOATS
Horse-drawn boat trips. Daily Easter to
October.
Llangollen Wharf. T:01978 860702
www.horsedrawnboats.co.uk

### MAESTERMYN & WELSH LADY CRUISERS & MID WALES NARROWBOATS
Narrowboat holiday hire and day boat
hire.
Whittington. T:01691 662424
www.maestermyn.co.uk

### 'THOMAS TELFORD'
Trips along canal and across
Pontcysyllte Aqueduct. Daily Easter to
October.
Llangollen Wharf. T:01978 860702
www.horsedrawnboats.co.uk

### UK BOAT HIRE
Narrowboat holiday hire.
Blackwater Meadow (Ellesmere),
Whitchurch & Wrenbury.
T:0845 1264098
www.ukboathire.com

## Mon & Brec Canal

### BEACON PARK BOATS
Narrow & widebeam holiday hire.
Llanfoist Wharf. T:01873 858277
www.beaconparkboats.com

### BEACON PARK DAY BOATS
Day boat hire and Canadian canoes.
Includes expert tuition.
Brecon Basin. T:0800 6122890
www.beaconparkdayboats.co.uk

### BRECON BOATS
Day boat hire.
Talybont. T:01874 676401

### CAMBRIAN CRUISERS
Narrowboat holiday hire.
Ty Newydd. T:01874 665315
www.cambriancruisers.co.uk

### CASTLE NARROWBOATS
Narrowboat holiday hire and day boat
hire.
Gilwern. T:01873 830001
www.castlenarrowboats.co.uk

### COUNTRY CRAFT NARROWBOATS
Narrowboat holiday hire.
Llangynidr. T:01874 730850
www.countrycraftnarrowboats.co.uk

### DRAGONFLY CRUISES
2½-hour boat cruises from Brecon
to Brynich. Timings and days vary.
Wheelchair access.
Brecon Basin. T:07831 685222
www.dragonfly-cruises.co.uk

### PONTYMOILE MARINA
Day boat hire.
Pontymoile. T:01495 752420
www.pontymoilemarina.co.uk

### ROAD HOUSE NARROWBOATS
Narrowboat holiday hire.
Gilwern. T:01873 830240
www.narrowboats-wales.co.uk

### UK BOAT HIRE (RED LINE BOATS)
Narrowboat holiday & day hire.
Goytre Wharf. T:0845 1264098
www.ukboathire.com

| Llangollen Canal - Chirk Aqueduct
(overleaf) |

**British Waterways**

Howard has worked for British Waterways for over 30 years looking after the Llangollen and Montgomery Canals. His day can hardly be described as routine, involving anything from meeting celebrities through assisting customers to rather less glamorous routine maintenance.

Howard has seen many changes during his three decades as a waterway operative and supervisor, although working in the shadow of mighty Pontcysyllte Aqueduct has been a constant inspiration.

"Probably one of the most memorable times was assisting in draining the aqueduct," Howard recalls. "This involved draining the cast iron trough by pulling out a giant plug. The water took nearly two hours to drain away, sending a huge cascade into the River Dee nearly 130 feet below. Very impressive indeed".

Howard has played an increasingly important role in promoting the aqueduct since it became a World Heritage Site last year.

"I recall it being a very long and tense summer's day waiting for the result to come in from Seville. But when the news finally broke, the looks on everyone's faces told you 10 years of preparation had all been worthwhile," Howard fondly recalls.

So what's next?
"Helping everyone who passes over this stunning structure whether by boat or on foot, is a truly memorable experience."

## Waterways people
Piers Warburton, Community Development
Officer. Llangollen Canal

**British Waterways**

Piers Warburton is the man tasked with driving an ambitious waterway partnership, forging closer links between local communities along the Llangollen Canal and their waterway heritage.

'Pontcysyllte Aqueduct & Canal Project' is a community-focused project with its roots in the successful World Heritage bid of 2009, which placed the iconic structure alongside legendary sites like the Taj Mahal and the Statue of Liberty.

Now the two-year project is coming to fruition, providing individuals and groups along the 11-mile World Heritage Site corridor with a range of hands-on environmental conservation skills.

Piers has spent his time working closely with individuals, businesses, schools and interest groups engaging them in a range of activities and improvements to the canal. These range from heritage and environment sessions to towpath

improvements. He says the most memorable part of his job has been the creation of 'Aqueducks' – Friends of the World Heritage Site – who will continue with the project's work into the future.

"The launch day was particularly exciting when we launched hundreds yellow rubber ducks into the canal to mark the occasion. The friends group went on to organise their own community fun day and I felt honoured to be a part of it. I've derived a huge sense of satisfaction from the project, particularly forming 'Aqueducks' and seeing how the various individuals and groups have benefitted from the project".

In his spare time Piers enjoys mountain biking and walking pretty much anywhere, from on the canal to taking part in the mountain bike marathon.

# WILDLIFE & NATURE

**Dr Sean Christian –
RSPB Cymru Head of Conservation**

"Wales has an embarrassment of riches when it comes to magnificent waterways", says Dr Sean Christian. "From the River Severn that runs through the heart of the country, to the beautiful Llangollen and Montgomeryshire Canals, Wales can boast rich habitats and internationally important ecosystems in and around these waterways."

RSPB Cymru recognises the importance of canals and rivers to the birdlife of the country. Not only do canals provide an important food source for many species, but the banks and verges also provide shelter and breeding areas which, after years of decline, are reviving and thriving.

Dr Christian is a biologist by qualification and he likes nothing more than walking the riverbanks and towpaths of Wales' waterways, observing the wildlife that lives and breeds on them.

He explains: "My favourite stretch of canal is the old "Monty" – the Montgomeryshire Canal – a wonderfully scenic canal up in Powys that meanders through the most beautiful parts of the Welsh Marshes. I say "canal" but it's really only partly restored. The route actually runs for about 30 miles from the stunning Llangollen Canal junction down to Newtown but only bits of it are still navigable.

The route was derelict for many years after it burst its banks in the 30's and was officially abandoned during the War. The section I like best - 12½ miles or so of easy walking from Newtown to Welshpool are currently being renovated. A large part of the route follows the Severn Way along the old towpath. You can join the Severn Way at the Severn footpath near the middle of Newtown and follow it all the way up to Welshpool.

What is unique about this canal route is that it is almost entirely rural and was always a rural canal designed and funded by the landowning community to provide the Upper Severn Valley with agricultural lime.

The Monty is a haven for wildlife such as wildfowl, kingfishers and grey wagtails, herons and reed warblers, and is a wonderful place to find a bit of peace and tranquillity. It's a place for slow boats, fishermen, walkers and birdwatchers. In a way the closure of the canal was a chance for wildlife to recover and flourish and the Montgomeryshire Canal and the nearby River Severn are among Wales' most important waterways for wildlife.

Fortunately, nature conservation seems to have been given a high priority during its restoration. The whole of the Welsh section of the canal is now designated with Sites of Scientific Interest, particularly freshwater plants (like the floating water plantain).

During restoration British Waterways and the canal restorers worked very closely with the Countryside Council for Wales, Natural England and a variety of other conservation organisations, in particular the Montgomeryshire Wildlife Trust which runs several excellent nature reserves along the route (Pwll Penarth, Dolydd Hafren and the wet meadows and wet woodlands at Red House).

Access is great along almost all of the canal. As well as being on the route of the Severn Way, some parts of the towpath are also part of the Offa's Dyke long-distance footpath.

You know when you are getting close to Welshpool because soon after Belan you come into the parkland that surrounds the National Trust's impressive and imposing Powis Castle which watches over this lovely old market town."

From source to estuary mouth, the River Severn is one of Britain's great natural treasures. As an RSPB advocate against the proposed Severn Barrage, Dr Sean Christian has studied the possible effects on habitat and species on the River.

He says "The proposed Cardiff to Weston barrage would have destroyed huge areas of estuary marsh and mudflats used by up to 69,000 birds each winter, and blocked the migration routes of countless fish, such as Atlantic salmon, trout and eels."

He goes on, "Our rivers and canals represent valuable wildlife corridors. They are nature's way of allowing the spread of species into new feeding and breeding grounds. The great thing for humans is that we can observe these natural events right in front of us, while enjoying all the benefits that our countryside offers."

Clearly passionate about what he does, Dr Sean Christian is in that enviable position of earning his living doing something he loves and believes in.

Dr Sean Christian is RSPB Cymru's Head of Conservation. He is responsible for the management and development of RSPB Cymru's conservation policy and campaigns throughout Wales.

RSPB Cymru is part of the RSPB, and speaks out for birds and wildlife, tackling the problems that threaten our environment. The conservation charity relies upon memberships and donations to fund its work.

# Wildlife & Nature

## Little Grebe (Tachybaptus ruficollis)

A small, dumpy grebe which often appears to have a 'fluffy' rear end. It readily dives when disturbed, surfacing unseen some distance away. In summer it has a bright chestnut throat and cheeks and a pale gape patch at the base of the bill. It can be noisy, with a distinctive whinnying trill.

It is found across the UK although is largely absent from upland areas. Look for it wherever there are suitable lakes, gravel pits, canals and slow rivers with plenty of vegetation. In winter it can be found on more exposed lakes, as well as sheltered coasts and estuaries. Winter concentrations can be found in places like the Thames Estuary, Chew Valley Lake and Rutland Water.

When to see them: All year round.
What they eat: Insects and larva.

**Dipper (Cinclus Cinclus)**

A short-tailed, plump bird with a low, whirring flight. When
perched on a rock it habitually bobs up and down and
frequently cocks its tail. Its white throat and breast contrasts
with its dark body plumage. It is remarkable in its method of
walking into and under water in search of food.

Found along fast-flowing rivers, mainly in upland areas
but also on lowland rivers in SW England. Look for tell-tale
droppings on stones in the river.

When to see them: All year round.
What they eat: Insect larvae and freshwater shrimps.

# DAYS OUT
## in Wales

## LLANGOLLEN HORSE-DRAWN BOAT

Imagine a world without cars - a lost time, a quieter place when the slow sounds of traffic clip-clopped only with the unhurried rhythms of horses' hooves. Canals were built before the engine was invented and canal boats were traditionally pulled along from the towpath by sturdy horses. Boat families valued their steed as part of the family crew, and took pride in keeping their horse's paraphernalia decorated in traditional colours.

Horse-drawn boats have become a rare sight on today's waterways, with only a handful still operating for tourism. Hitching a ride on a special horse-drawn trip boat is a ridiculously romantic way to slow down and drift into days gone by. In the absence of noise, every other sense gets its chance... and the sweet smell of horse downwind wraps up the experience perfectly! Heavy horses are the gentle giants that once owned the towpaths and, even though they are few today, wherever they grace our canals they command our respect.

### Secret waterways heritage

Look closely under many bridges and tight corners of the canals and you will see where towing ropes once gouged into the masonry as horses tugged their heavy cargo along.

### Our visit to Llangollen

We arrive early. Three heads peep from the stable doors with routine morning expressions as everyone prepares for the day's work ahead. From the water, the ducks flap as the excitement builds and passengers turn up for the first trip of the day. The horses' handlers introduce the gang:

"This is Geordie, the mellow, most loveable one." (Geordie dozes through the attention.) "Taff, the naughty one." the gathering crowd send a baton of smiles.

"And this is Stanley, the alpha male." Stanley chomps a handful of scones and accepts fuss with disregard.

Today, cyclists and walkers are encouraged to use the towpaths of course, but when the canals were first built they would have been mere trespassers because the path was built for horses. As Stanley sets off down the towpath effortlessly towing his cargo of passengers, he leaves an indent of hoof prints in the dust. His mark is a reminder of proud heritage.

## Factfile

**Llangollen Canal**
Llangollen OS SJ215422

Horse-drawn boat trips are available from the Wharf towards the end of the canal (a World Heritage Site).

45-min return trips, and a 2-hr trip which includes a visit to Chain Bridge (across the river Dee) and Horseshoe Falls at the head of the canal (built by Thomas Telford)

Daily from 1100 Mar-Oct. Timings vary. Wheelchair access.

Motorised 2-hr return cruises to Pontcysyllte Aqueduct are also available.

Teashop and gift shop.

T:01978 860702 www.horsedrawnboats.co.uk

There are only three other horseboat companies still operating in the UK, and the Horseboating Society works to promote horseboating and preserve its heritage and skills.

www.horseboating.org.uk

# Days out

## PONTCYSYLLTE AQUEDUCT
### One of the 7 Wonders of the Waterways

Pioneering, brave and outrageously satisfying to cross. The Pontcysyllte Aqueduct is the ultimate dazzler of British canal engineering. 18 pillars stretch to the heavens, suspending a great bathtub of water in the sky that ludicrously allows narrowboats to fly. 127 feet of fresh air holds white-faced boaters and walkers above the valley of the River Dee. Whatever the weather is doing, there's always a high cloud of adrenalin from wide-eyed people who seem compelled to share jokes of fear with each other. Sheer drops are the peril of the clumsy helmsman one side... and walkers on the snake-thin towpath hip-bump as they pass anyone daring to come the other way.

If you close your eyes, you can feel your feet sway, but be reassured that the pillars holding the aqueduct up will stand as boldly as they have done for over 200 years - reliably still held together by just ox blood and Welsh flannel. Utterly amazing. Not to miss.

## Factfile

### Llangollen Canal
Trevor Basin OS SJ270420
Built by Thomas Telford and William Jessop, the aqueduct was completed in 1805. The Aqueduct and 18km of the Llangollen Canal were awarded World Heritage Site status in 2009.

### Pontcysyllte boat trips
'Thomas Telford'
Cruises the canal from Llangollen with the highlight of crossing the Pontcysyllte Aqueduct.
T:01978 860702 www.horsedrawnboats.co.uk

'Eirlys', Jones the Boats
In Trevor Basin. 45-minute cruises across the aqueduct and back with full commentary.
T:01691 690322 www.canaltrip.co.uk

Seating is inside the narrowboats with clear window views (if you dare look). Luckily for the vertiginous, both boats have a well-stocked bar onboard.

# Days out
in Wales

**PONTCYSYLLTE AQUEDUCT**
A World Heritage Site (Days Out pages 220-221).

**LLANGOLLEN WHARF HORSE-DRAWN BOAT TRIPS**
Horse-drawn boats, motorised cruises to Pontcysyllte, a tea room and gift shop (Days Out pages 218-219).

**INTERNATIONAL MUSIC EISTEDDFOD**
Llangollen's International Music Eisteddfod is one of the world's greatest music festivals. It's been held every July for the past 60 years and, with musicians and dancers from over 50 countries, there are daily music and dance competitions, and spectacular evening concerts.

Llangollen. OS SJ215421

Held over a week in early July. Day and evening sessions. Admission charge.

www.llangollen2010.co.uk

## Monmouthshire & Brecon Canal

**GOYTRE WHARF**
Large site with woodland walks (the name means 'place in the woods'), a small heritage exhibition and huge stone limekilns from its industrial heritage. There's a hireboat base with day and holiday boats, a small gift shop and a restaurant bar with large conservatory overlooking the canal.

Goytre. OS SO312064

T:01873 880516 www.goytrewharf.com

**TRIP BOAT**
Regular boat trips from Brecon Basin to Brynich Aqueduct and back. Sit back and enjoy the stunning backdrop of the Brecon Beacons. The boat goes through a lock and over the aqueduct before turning round for the return journey. Refreshments on board.

Brecon. OS SO047281

Mar-Oct. Timings vary. Wheelchair lift. Charter also available.

07831 685222 www.dragonfly-cruises.co.uk

## Montgomery Canal

**POWYSLAND MUSEUM & CANAL CENTRE**
Housed in a former warehouse, the museum explores the history of canals, railways and crafts with displays and exhibits including maps, photos and other items relating to Montgomeryshire's heritage.

Open May-Sep Mon-Tues, Thu-Fri 1100-1300 & 1400-1700, Sat 1000-1300 (not Oct-Apr) & 1400-1700.

www.powyslandclub.co.uk

# FOOD & DRINK

## Pubs

in Wales

### Llangollen Canal

**BRIDGE INN**
Overlooking Chirk Aqueduct. Traditional pub with real fires & a patio outside to soak up the view.
Chirk Bank. T:01691 773213

**DUSTY MILLER**
Characterful converted corn mill by Wrenbury Lift Bridge. Huge windows and a canalside garden give gongoozling opportunities whatever the weather.
Wrenbury. T:01270 780537
www.thedusty.co.uk

**SUN TREVOR**

Overlooking the canal at bridge 41. Large garden with valley views
Sun Bank. T:01978 860651
www.suntrevor.co.uk

### Mon & Brec Canal

**COACH & HORSES**

Canalside by bridge 133. Traditional pub with large garden overlooking the canal. Guest rooms available.
Llangynidr. T:01874 730245
www.coachandhorses.org

**ROYAL OAK**
Canalside by bridge 153. Attractive pub with flagstones, beams and real fires, and there's a pretty canalside garden too.
Pencelli. T:01874 665396

**STAR INN**

Canalside by the aqueduct. Cosy traditional pub with a huge fireplace, ever-changing choice of real ales and a large garden by the river below the canal.
Talybont-on-Usk. T:01874 676635
www.starinntalybont.co.uk

**WHITE SWAN**
17th-century coaching inn, a short walk from bridge 157. Flagstone floors, beams and real fires. AA-Rosette food. They run luxury holiday cottages nearby.
Llanfrynach. T:01874 665276
www.the-white-swan.com

### Montgomery Canal

**THE NAVIGATION INN**
Friendly pub in 18th-century warehouse, canalside by bridge 79. Dogs and boots welcome!
Maesbury Marsh. T:01691 672958
www.thenavigation.co.uk

**POWIS ARMS**
Canalside near Pool Quay Lock. Traditional local handy for walkers on the Offa's Dyke Path.
Pool Quay. T:01938 590255
www.powis-arms.co.uk

# Teashops
in Wales

### Llangollen Canal

**@29 COFFEE SHOP**
Canalside by Grindley Brook staircase locks. Useful stores for boaters or anyone on the towpath, as well as a perfect gongoozling spot. Internet café and gift shop.
Grindley Brook. T:01948 663385

**WHARF TEA ROOM**
By the wharf with the trip boats and horse-drawn boats. Patio with views over Llangollen and tables by the canal. Homemade cakes and snacks. Small gift shop.
Llangollen Wharf. T:01978 860702
www.horsedrawnboats.co.uk

### Mon & Brec Canal

**THE MARINA TEAROOM**
Canalside in Pontymoile Marina. Converted narrowboat on land. Day boat hire at the marina.
Pontymoile. T:01495 752420
www.pontymoilemarina.co.uk

**TIPPLE 'N' TIFFIN**
Canalside in Brecon Basin. Part of the Theatr Brycheiniog. Coffees, teas, snacks and full restaurant meals daytime and evening.
Brecon. T:01874 611866
www.brycheiniog.co.uk

**WATERSIDE REST**
Large conservatory-style café/restaurant next to a small heritage exhibition and shop. Patio overlooking the canal and the former lime kilns. Boat hire.
Goytre Wharf. T:01873 881069
www.goytrewharf.com

### Montgomery Canal

**CANAL CENTRAL**
Canalside near bridges 80 & 81. Tea room & shop with an emphasis on locally sourced produce. Holiday accommodation above. Cakes, teas and snacks.
Maesbury Marsh. T:01691 652168
www.canalcentral.co.uk

For listings of waterside pubs & teashops in the UK, visit our website:
www.greatwaterwaysoutdoors.com

# WATERWAYS LIFE
## Engineering marvels

Over 200 years ago, Britain built a network of water roads that were the motorway routes of the Industrial Revolution.

### Made in Britain

The great British manufacturing businesses of the Industrial Revolution built factories and mills wherever the necessary raw materials happened to be. Salt in Cheshire, coal in the Midlands, limestone, grain and cotton - a canal system was built to create a transport system that could carry materials and cargo across the country, and send goods to every corner of the globe. Britain's beautiful landscape threw every contrary contour it could to make the canal engineers' job impossible.

### Mission Impossible

The engine hadn't been invented and there were no cranes or electricity. And to make the task even more ludicrous, the only tools the canal builders had were hand shovels and barrows.

So how did they cut a line out of the earth that outrageously scrambled impossible corners of this island, and made unpowered narrowboats climb up and down hill on still water?

The Great Engineers - Brindley, Telford, Jessop, Dadford... were responsible for the success of innovative canal structures. Their determination, bravery and staggering Victorian arrogance has left an engineering legacy that is amongst the very best treasures of British heritage.

Britain's manmade waterways defied the rules of nature, taking water up over mountains and down into sea coves - carrying canal boats in suspended flight in aqueducts over vast valleys, and blasting through mountains in tunnels. Lock flights, swing bridges and all manner of ingeniously simple engineering feats allowed a water road to carve Britain.

### Navvies

Navvies set out with shovels and sweat to dig a line out of the earth linking city to city, distant quarries to lonely mines and mill to mill. Over Welsh hills, Cornish beaches, the Pennines and even daring the wild Highlands of Scotland. For barely a wage to survive on, he dug a line out of the earth, filled it with water and called it our nation's canal network. To save water, the cut was often only 3 feet deep and 7 feet wide and narrowboats were designed to haul cargo along the narrow water-road.

I Marple Aqueduct - Marple Locks - Napton Top Lock I

## 7 Wonders of the Waterways

Over fifty years ago Robert Aickman, founder of the Inland Waterways Association (along with Tom Rolt) declared 7 monumental engineering works the 7 Wonders of the Waterways:

### Anderton Boat Lift

The 'cathedral' of the canals lifts boats from the Trent & Mersey Canal to the Weaver.
Anderton, Northwich. Trent & Mersey Canal/Weaver Nav OS SJ647753
Visitor Centre open from February, boat lift and river trips Mar-Oct.
T:01606 786777
www.andertonboatlift.co.uk

### Burnley Embankment

The 'straight mile' carries the canal over the rooftops of Burnley, near the Weavers' Triangle. Almost a mile long and up to 60ft high in places.
Burnley
Leeds & Liverpool Canal OS SD844325

### Barton Swing Aqueduct

A canal full of water amazingly swings out of the way for ships on the canal below. Carries the Bridgewater Canal over the Manchester Ship Canal. Operates all year.
Barton upon Irwell
Bridgewater Canal OS SJ767976

### Caen Hill Flight

16 wide locks pounded closely together take boats miraculously up and down hill. The highlight of 29 locks in the 2¼ miles leading to Devizes.
Devizes.
Kennet & Avon Canal OS ST983614

### Standedge Tunnel

3¼ mile-long tunnel through the Pennines.
Marsden
Huddersfield Narrow Canal OS SE040120
Open April-Oct. Visitor Centre with café, guided & through boat trips.
Standedge Tunnel & Visitor Centre
T:01484 844298 www.standedge.co.uk

### Bingley 5 Rise

Unique 5-lock staircase to heaven carries the canal up 60ft above Bingley's mills. Boat passage through the flight Mon-Fri needs to be booked.
Bingley
Leeds & Liverpool Canal OS SE107399
T:0113 2816860

## How a lock works

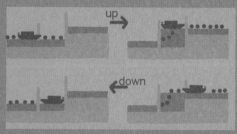

up

down

# SCOTLAND

An unforgiving North Sea scratches at Scotland's ferocious coastline whist the romantic Highlands and Lowlands storm inland. Snow peaks, peat bogs, an unspoilt wilderness... this land knows the rare freedom of space unembarrassed by silence, and in its remoteness, some parts of Scotland still let you be alone.

Water flings itself any way you can turn with the rampaging sea at every edge, while serene lochs, rivers and canals steal inland from coast to coast.

Holidaymakers make pilgrimages across the world to experience Scotland. They come on the tartan tourist trail in search of irrestistible legends - Scotland The Brave, The Soulful, The Endurer.

Clans, bagpipes, gritty heritage and wild whisky mix well in the souvenir shops. And who escapes from a visit to Scotland without carrying the mark of tartan? Souvenir hats, scarves, table mats, postcards, kilted dolls... all chequered in graffiti for your pleasure.

Scotland is the location of films such as Braveheart, Rob Roy, 39 Steps and Harry Potter, and it's easy to see why the mists of the Highlands blend legends and truths. Nessie, Britain's most famous monster, would surely never get the same press coverage if she appeared in a pond in the Midlands.

It's the great waterways of Scotland that give tourists what they really want. The Great Glen began as a geological fault line in the earth, stretching from Fort William to Inverness, the land mass to the north and the south slid in opposite directions and, around 8,000BC, glaciers in retreat helped shape the famous lochs that muster starry-eyed visitors every year. The Caledonian Canal was built to join the lochs together, creating a navigable coast to coast inland waterway. Probably the greatest waterways outdoors of all with unforgettable scenery, Neptune's Staircase, Ben Nevis, and midges from June to September.

Scotland's canals don't come bland. Moody skies, mountains and lochs reign mournfully, yet never miserably. This is a landscape of extreme pleasure.

# WATERWAYS
## of Scotland
### boat, bike, boot

## Highlights

**FALKIRK WHEEL** on the Forth & Clyde /
Union Canals - **NEPTUNE'S STAIRCASE**
on the Caledonian Canal - **LOCH NESS**
on the Caledonian Canal - **CRINAN
SEA LOCK** on the Crinan Canal - **AVON
AQUEDUCT** on the Union Canal

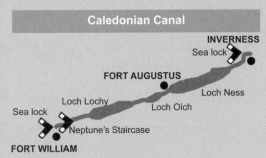

## Caledonian Canal

Fort William to Inverness
60 miles, 29 locks & 10 swing bridges (all manned)

An ecstatic Highland journey, coast to coast,
following the Great Glen Way. Along the trail,
the Caledonian Canal laps up the drama of
Ben Nevis, the romance of Scotland's lochs
and a potential encounter with Nessie! This
canal is the calm path set in a storm of remote
Scotland's wild Highlands that once whistled
with mournful pipes of the Clans. A sublime and
deeply beautiful experience.

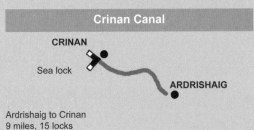

## Crinan Canal

Ardrishaig to Crinan
9 miles, 15 locks

A jagged coastline on the extreme west side of
Scotland needed its own short cut to help sailors
avoid the murderous seas. The Crinan Canal is
only for seagoing vessels and towpath visitors
wrapped up in woollies. The most stunning short
cut in Britain, and anyone would travel miles out
of their way to get to it.

## Forth & Clyde Canal

Firth of Forth to Firth of Clyde
35 miles, 39 locks

Glasgow's proud canal and another of Scotland's coast-to-coast routes, the Forth & Clyde links the Irish Sea to the North Sea. The canal connects to the Union Canal via the Falkirk Wheel.

## Union Canal

**FALKIRK**
●Falkirk Wheel
**LINLITHGOW**
Falkirk
Tunnel
**EDINBURGH**
**RATHO**

Falkirk to Edinburgh
34 miles, 2 locks, 3 aqueducts

A canal that touches Edinburgh, yet is most celebrated for its connection to the Falkirk Wheel. The world's first rotating boat lift was opened by the Queen in 2002 and has become one of Scotland's top tourist attractions. This modern-day marvel of engineering was built to join the Union Canal and the Forth & Clyde Canal. The 8th Wonder of the Waterways. Long before the Falkirk Wheel, even when the canal was first being built, it managed to cause a stir - the owners of Callendar House couldn't bear the new water-road to be seen on their estate, so insisted on a tunnel being clawed out of the hill behind the house (Falkirk Tunnel). The Union is the only surviving contour canal in Scotland, so has no locks beyond Falkirk. But it has 3 aqueducts, and Avon Aqueduct is the 2nd longest in Britain (after Pontcysyllte in Wales).

# ROUTES
## along the towpath

## SOME DESIGNATED TOWPATH ROUTES

### Caledonian Canal

**GREAT GLEN WAY**
Fort William to Inverness
79 miles
Follows the canal towpath and lochside paths all the way from Corpach to Inverness, with a short route from the start at Fort William to Corpach.
www.greatglenway.com

**GREAT GLEN MOUNTAIN BIKE TRAILS**
Corpach to Inverness
Several trails of various lengths along the route of the Caledonian Canal, which follow the canal and loch towpaths much of the way from Corpach to Inverness.

**CAMPBELTOWN TO INVERNESS**
National Cycle Network (NCN) Route 78
Will run from Campbeltown to Inverness (once fully open)
Follows the canal towpath all the way from Corpach to Fort Augustus.

### Crinan Canal

**BELLANOCH TO DUNARDRY LOCKS**
Approx ¾ mile
Great views of the Moine Mhor National Nature Reserve alongside the canal.

**CAMPBELTOWN TO INVERNESS**
National Cycle Network (NCN) Route 78
Will run from Campbeltown to Inverness (once fully open)
Follows the towpath all the way from Ardrishaig to Crinan.

### Forth & Clyde Canal

**FORTH TO FIRTH CANAL PATHWAY**
Firth of Clyde to Firth of Forth
31 miles (total trail 66 miles)
Follows the canal towpath all the way from Bowling Basin to the Falkirk Wheel.

**GLASGOW TO EDINBURGH**
National Cycle Network (NCN) Route 754
Clydebank to Edinburgh
Follows the canal towpath all the way from Clydebank through to Falkirk.

### Union Canal

**CLYDE TO FORTH CYCLE ROUTE**
National Cycle Network (NCN) Route 75
Gourock (near Glasgow) to Leith (near Edinburgh)
Follows the canal towpath from Slateford Aqueduct to Edinburgh Quay.

**FORTH TO FIRTH CANAL PATHWAY**
Firth of Clyde to Firth of Forth
34 miles (total trail 66 miles)
Follows the canal towpath all the way from the Falkirk Wheel to Edinburgh Quay.

**GLASGOW TO EDINBURGH**
National Cycle Network (NCN) Route 754
Clydebank to Slateford
Follows the canal towpath all the way from Falkirk through to Slateford Aqueduct before joining Route 75.

**LINLITHGOW TO AVON AQUEDUCT**
**4 miles return**
Follow the towpath west from Linlithgow to see the 2nd longest aqueduct in Britain (after Pontcysyllte in Wales).

### More info

For more detailed information and maps of all National Cycle Network Routes, go to www.sustrans.org.uk

For more walks and trails, go to www.ramblers.org.uk

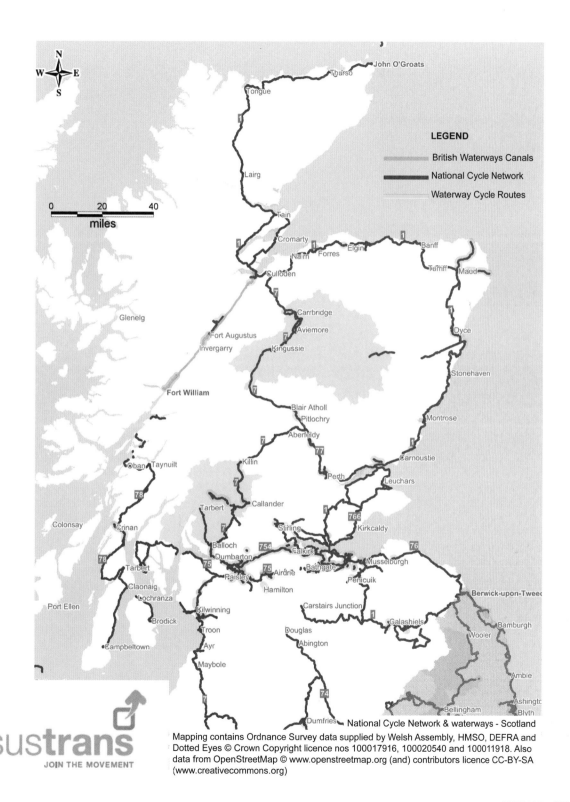

LEGEND

British Waterways Canals

National Cycle Network

Waterway Cycle Routes

National Cycle Network & waterways - Scotland

Mapping contains Ordnance Survey data supplied by Welsh Assembly, HMSO, DEFRA and Dotted Eyes © Crown Copyright licence nos 100017916, 100020540 and 100011918. Also data from OpenStreetMap © www.openstreetmap.org (and) contributors licence CC-BY-SA (www.creativecommons.org)

sus**trans**

JOIN THE MOVEMENT

# Routes
along the towpath

JOIN THE MOVEMENT

Katharine Taylor
Sustrans NCN Development Manger
Scotland

## My favourite bike ride
Crinan Canal

"The Crinan Canal is a delight for cyclists of all ages and abilities. It was originally built for commercial shipping and was completed by Thomas Telford in the early 19th century, but its wide, peaty waters are now used mainly by pleasure craft. Before the railways were built, the fastest way to travel between Glasgow and Inverness was by steamer using the Crinan and Caledonian Canals. Bypassed by modern transport modes, the Crinan now provides a wonderful slow and peaceful journey through beautiful countryside. Info boards along the way tell the canal's history.

You can join the canal at the sea lock at Ardrishaig where the canal spills out into Loch Gilp. After passing several locks (the first of 15

on this canal), follow it northwards for two miles past residential gardens and open countryside to Lochgilphead. It's also possible to join at Lochgiphead at one of the access points off the A816 which runs along the west side of the town. If joining here, turn right and follow the canal as it meanders inland across open country to Cairnbaan, where there are several more locks and an attractive hotel for refreshments.

Onward to Dunardry where a series of locks and winding holes mark the highest point of the canal – 65 feet above sea level. A mile further on at Bellanoch is a very interesting detour if you have time. Turn right onto the B8026 which heads straight over the flat plain of the Moine Mhor (The Great Bog) towards the village of Kilmartin (5 miles). Kilmartin Glen has hundreds of ancient monuments – stone circles, standing stones and cairns – giving an indication of its antiquity. In the village there's a fascinating museum, with a café attached, which explains the area's history. A traffic-free path to the west of Kilmartin takes you past several of the ancient burial cairns and up to 16th-century Carnasserie Castle.

Back on the canal, at Bellanoch you can see the sea again, but the canal doesn't join it here. Instead it runs alongside the shore of Loch Crinan, past another large winding hole, towards Crinan. Where the B841 comes to an end by the canal you can see Crinan Ferry on the opposite shore, although no ferry has run here for 40 years. The canal enters Crinan along the shore, past Crinan Harbour, which was originally the sea lock until the current one was excavated in the 1930s. Crinan is a beautiful place to relax after your ride, with boats at their moorings, shops, a hotel and superb views out over Loch Crinan."

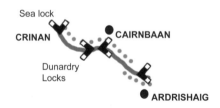

## Factfile

Start: Ardrishaig OS NR855855
Finish: Crinan OS NR788944
National Cycle Network (NCN) Route 78
9 miles, 15 locks

### Highlights
Crinan Harbour and the sea lock
Moine Mhor nature reserve

### Bike hire
**CRINAN CYCLES**
Large range of bikes, also trailer bikes
and child seats.
Lochgilphead. T:01546 603511
www.crinancycles.co.uk

### More info
For more detailed information and maps
of all National Cycle Network Routes,
go to www.sustrans.org.uk

# Routes
## along the towpath

JOIN THE MOVEMENT

Richard Toleman
Sustrans Volunteer Ranger

## My favourite bike ride
### Union Canal

"I live close to the Union Canal near Linlithgow and the towpath is a favourite ride of mine. Linlithgow is a historic town and its Palace has royal connections being the birth place of Mary, Queen of Scots. The town sits astride both the Union Canal and the Edinburgh to Glasgow & Stirling railway. This railway connection allows easy access to the canal for cycling from other parts of Scotland. Start from Manse Road Canal Basin just up the hill from the station. It's the location for the Linlithgow Union Canal Centre, operated by the Linlithgow Union Canal Society. The Society runs canal boat trips, a museum, tearoom and shop from a converted canal stable. All are worth a visit before you set off for Falkirk.

The canal follows the 240ft (73m) contour and, as you head west out of the town, there are good views to the NW over the Forth valley towards the Ochil Hills. After passing the golf course and Woodcockdale canal stables, you ride along a high embankment, the approach to the Avon aqueduct. This 12-arch structure, 810ft long and 85ft high, is magnificent with splendid views. It is the second highest in Britain after the Pontcysyllte Aqueduct in Wales and is a cast-iron trough set in masonry. A short side walk at the west end allows you to see it from below. Just beyond can be seen the remains of an original barge in an abandoned dry dock. A few yards beyond the next bridge you can detour to the south to cycle through Muiravonside Country Park. Riding on, you pass the entrance to Causewayend or Slamannan Basin, constructed as an exchange between the now abandoned railway and the canal. Coal was delivered along this line to be transhipped by barge to Edinburgh, while lime from a nearby kiln was delivered to adjacent farms.

You now ride into wide open country, once more with extensive rural views, although the industry of Grangemouth can be seen far away. Cycling through Polmont the station is close by - another access point. As you continue westward, the scene alternates between modern suburbia and remote countryside, but is no less enjoyable. You will know when you are approaching the outskirts of Falkirk, as you go through a deep cutting and into a tunnel (which has a laughing face at one end and a frowning face at the other!). When the canal was being dug the then owner of Callendar House, William Forbes, refused to allow it to pass within view of his house so the canal engineers were obliged to tunnel for 690yds under the hill. A fence protects the towpath and the tunnel is illuminated which gives it a magical and mysterious air. However, it can be a bit gloomy, so best to bring a torch. It's too difficult to cycle – I tried and hit the wall! Just push your bike, but look out for the drips from the roof, or cascades after heavy rain.

Emerging from the tunnel, Falkirk High station is signed to the right, the last rail access point. On the south side of the canal is Bantaskine Park and the Seagull Trust, which run boats for disabled people, both accessible over a bridge, and a pleasant detour. Over the last two miles there are frequent extensive views over Falkirk with the Highlands in the far distance. Look carefully as you cycle and you will see the remains of some of the 11 locks which took the original canal down to join the Forth & Clyde Canal. From here a new length of canal was cut when the 'Millennium Link' reopened in 2000.

And now for the last and most spectacular part of the ride. You first come to a small staircase of two locks which lowers the canal below the railway. Beyond is a short tunnel under both the railway and the Antonine Wall. As you cycle out you emerge on the approach aqueduct of the Falkirk Wheel to a vast view over the Forth valley. It is unforgettable. The Wheel is 115ft in diameter with two gondolas which can transfer up to four boats between the two canals. It is a

suitable destination for my favourite ride. There is always plenty of hustle and bustle with the movement of people and boats and there are often special events. There is one more lock at the canal junction which takes you into the Forth & Clyde canal and that's it. You can take a rest at the visitor centre with a shop, toilets and a café.

Although that's the end of my ride, there is more. It can also be the start of towpath rides on the Forth & Clyde Canal eastwards through Falkirk to join the Forth at Carron sea lock, or westwards to Glasgow and the Clyde at Bowling. What are you waiting for, keep cycling!"

## Factfile

Start: Linlithgow OS NT005770
Finish: Falkirk OS NS851802
National Cycle Network (NCN) Route 754
12 miles, 2 locks, 1 tunnel, 1 aqueduct

### Highlights
Falkirk Wheel (Days Out page 252-253), Linlithgow Canal Centre and Avon Aqueduct

### More info
For more detailed information and maps of all National Cycle Network Routes, go to www.sustrans.org.uk

# Routes
## along the towpath

**Phillippa & Martine**
**Some of the highlights of our epic canal walk from Cornwall to Scotland**

## Our favourite walks

Our epic walk along Britain's canals found its beginning and its end in Scotland's waterways. We always adore those humble canals in dear old England, but the canals of the Highlands sweep us off our feet every time. From the full-blown pleasure of walking the Caledonian coast-to-coast canal, to the simple joy of brushing the tiniest wild flora on the Crinan Canal - this is walking that makes your heart sing.

### A walk along the Caledonian Canal

From the start of this walk the scenery digs goose bumps out of your skin - holly, gorse, birch, fern and heather, the smell of pine trees and bright red berries of rowan trees. Celtic tree lore saw the yellow bloom of gorse as a sign of 'thanks to life' - and when spikes of yellow shower the towpath, the sentiment makes sense. The Caledonian Canal is a shockingly easy walk, off the beaten track, mingling with the wildest elements of the Highlands. Between the scuff of your boots on the towpath, you could swear you can hear the cries of clans and mournful bagpipes hugging this Highland landscape.

Ben Nevis, the highest mountain in Britain, looks down over the outskirts of Fort William at the start of the Caledonian Canal. Anywhere you've ever walked before, or are yet to walk, blanks from your mind as this place wills you to treasure the moment.

A giant sea lock followed by a double lock marks the start of the canal and then there's the spectacular Neptune's Staircase, a flight of locks that carries boats up into the Highlands.

Before the canal was built, boats had to navigate the ferocious sea of the north coast to travel from the west side of Scotland to the east, and there were no roads to make a Highland passage any easier either.

It was at the same time that the Napoleonic wars rampaged across the seas that Scotland's own Thomas Telford was busy engineering the Caledonian Canal. The canal was meant to provide a safe route for the navy, but Bonaparte was defeated before the canal was finished.

The Great Glen and its lochs and rivers gave the starting point for the canal. It took 19 years to build. They dug, and they dug, and they dug with just a shovel and bare hands. The Caledonian Canal began as a ditch 15 feet deep, (it had to be much deeper than most of the English canals to carry sea-going vessels.) and the endurance of the navvies is matched by the beauty of their canal. It was the time of the Highland clearances and many of the navvies were starving Highlanders with little choice in their labour. The canal opened in 1822, a route built on fiery Highland history.

An armchair walker's dream - and the reality is even better. The Caledonian talks to you with its own convincing spirit and leaves you with a wild inner peace that lurks within until you can come back again.

**CORPACH**
Neptune's Staircase
Sea lock & Double Lock
**GAIRLOCHY**

---

## Factfile

**Caledonian Canal**
Start: Corpach OS NN095766
Finish: Gairlochy OS NN176842
8 miles, 13 locks

### Highlights
Views of Ben Nevis
Neptune's Staircase
Loch Lochy

### Did you know?
The law is different in Scotland from the rest of the UK - wild camping is permitted along the Caledonian, so long as you are of course responsible, leaving no trace.

### Neptune's Staircase

The men who built the flight in the early 1800s gave the flight its name, Neptune, after the Roman God of the sea. If your timing's lucky, you might catch the morning or matinée performance of boats travelling through the locks with waterfalls thundering over the lock gates as they fill and empty in rhythmic logic.

### The Great Glen

Nature built the Great Glen around 400 million years ago when two land masses crashed together, causing mountains to erupt, giving the highlands and lowlands their relationship. It's Scotland's longest glen, over 60 miles linking west & east coasts. The Caledonian Canal was built in the 19th century to enable boats to avoid the risky sea journey around the north of Scotland, and the 77-mile Great Glen Way long distance trail opened in 2002. www.greatglenway.com

# ROUTES
boating

## Favourite boating routes

Scotland's canals are unique. The Forth & Clyde and Union Canals give holiday narrowboats the ride of a lifetime on the famous Falkirk Wheel. The Crinan Canal invites holidaymakers to crew its windswept sailing boats. And the coast-to-coast Caledonian Canal offers an unforgettable holiday steering a cruiser through spectacular Highland scenery.

### Boating holiday on the Caledonian Canal

It's impossible to pick any highlights along the Caledonian Canal, since the entire 60-mile route is one long breath-taking highlight - from Inverness, the capital of the Highlands, to Fort William sitting near the foot of Ben Nevis. Loch Ness, Loch Oich, Loch Lochy... the canal swells in and out of the natural waters of the Great Glen. Boats travel in the company of eagles, wild views and clean air, then moor overnight under the warmest hospitality of Scottish locals.

The magnificent Neptune's Staircase and the giant locks of this canal might look daunting to first-time boaters, but friendly lock-keepers are usually ready to hold your hand whenever you need.

Most holiday hireboat companies offer helpful suggestions for cruising itineraries, but you can plan your own route to suit. Some companies (such as Le Boat) offer one-way cruises that allow you to explore further without needing to turn around to return the boat to the same base that you picked it up from.

When you're plotting your route, it's easy to work out a schedule if you allow extra time for locks and expect to travel at around 4-5mph. A short break is enough time to explore a section of the canal from one of the hire bases at Laggan or Inverness. On a one-week holiday, you can cruise the full length of the canal on a return route, and two weeks gives plenty of time to linger and sightsee along the way.

## Factfile

**Caledonian Canal**
Start: Corpach OS NN095766
Finish: Inverness OS NN176842
60 miles, 29 locks

**Highlights**
Neptune's Staircase
Moy Swing Bridge
Loch Ness

**Did you know?**
The Caledonian (also the Crinan) Canal operates on a seasonal basis, so always check with the local canal office or by visiting www.scottishcanals.co.uk for exact operating times and dates.

| Moy Swing Bridge - Neptune's Staircase |

# ROUTES
boating

## Hotel boats cruising the Caledonian Canal

A cruise along the Caledonian in a hotel boat is the perfect way to pamper yourself. Let the crew of your hotel boat cook, wash up, entertain and guide you. But that doesn't mean you have to be sedentary. This is Scotland's great outdoors and the Highlands will tempt even committed couch-potatoes to walk, cycle, canoe, wind surf... the possibilities are endless.

### Fingal Cruising

When we were walking the towpath along the Caledonian Canal, we bumped into a holidaymaker who was enjoying a week on a barge with Fingal Cruising. "I'm walking the Great Glen and the barge is my Sherpa. So I don't have to carry a heavy rucksack all day, and the crew cook all my food too. It's a really chilled and sociable holiday, and the meals are a highlight!"

Fingal takes up to 12 guests and cruises the Great Glen. Whether you want to be energetic or beautifully lazy is up to you. The crew are always happy to help you plan your activities, and provide all the comforts you need at the end of each day.

### European Waterways

European Waterways offers a cruise from Inverness to Fort William aboard Scottish Highlander. They describe their barge as "having the atmosphere of a Scottish country house". Much attention is given to your every whim and good Scottish food is of course a high priority for your pleasure.

The boat takes 8 passengers and has a crew of 4. A week cruising the Great Glen can include a visit to Glencoe, a tour of Ben Nevis whisky distillery, ancient castles and cosy nights aboard chatting until bedtime. And 8 bikes are carried on board if you fancy feeling the wind in your wheels too.

## Factfile

**FINGAL OF CALEDONIA**
Converted barge. Sleeps 12
T:01397 772167 www.fingal-cruising.co.uk

**EUROPEAN WATERWAYS**
Luxury all-inclusive hotel-barges in the UK & Europe
T:01784 482439 www.gobarging.com

**FULL LISTINGS OF HOTEL BOATS IN THE UK**
Visit our website
www.greatwaterwaysoutdoors.com

### Did you know?

The Daily Mail was responsible for first publishing the notorious portrait of the Loch Ness Monster in 1934, and convoys of hopeful photographers have lurked over Loch Ness ever since. (The first mention of Nessie came in St Adamnan's 7th-century biography of St Columba, who reckoned he had fought off a monster who was trying to kill one of his monks).

# Boats
## in Scotland

**LE BOAT / WEST HIGHLAND SAILING**
Cruiser holiday hire.
Laggan Locks. T:01809 501234
www.westhighlandsailing.com
www.leboat.co.uk

**RHIW GOCH**
Canadian canoe and mountain bike hire. Bed & breakfast.
Banavie. T:01397 772373
www.rhiwgoch.co.uk

## Crinan Canal

**ARGYLL YACHT CHARTERS**
Skippered or 'bareboat' yacht charters.
Cairnbaan. T:01546 602436
www.argyll-yachtcharters.co.uk

## Forth & Clyde Canal

**BLACK PRINCE NARROWBOAT HOLIDAYS**
Narrowboat holiday hire.
Falkirk. T:01527 575115
www.black-prince.com

**CAPERCAILLIE CRUISERS**
Narrowboat holiday hire.
Falkirk. T:01324 627212
www.capercailliecruisers.co.uk

**FALKIRK WHEEL BOAT TRIPS**
(Days out)

**MARINE CRUISES**
Narrowboat holiday hire.
Falkirk. T:01244 373911
www.marinecruises.co.uk

**OUTDOORTRAX**
Canoe, kayak and bike hire. Also available at Linlithgow, the Falkirk Wheel, and Glasgow.
Auchinstarry. T:07828 008997
www.outdoortrax.co.uk

**UK BOAT HIRE**
Narrowboat holiday hire.
Falkirk. T:0845 1264098
www.ukboathire.com

## Union Canal

**BRIDGE INN**
Restaurant Boat trips. Private charter also available.
Ratho. T:0131 3331320
www.bridgeinn.com

**LINLITHGOW CANAL CENTRE**
Boat trips and day boat hire.
Linlithgow. T:01506 843194
www.lucs.org.uk

## Caledonian Canal

**BOOTS N PADDLES**
Canadian canoe and kayak hire, activities, courses, expeditions.
Nr Inverness. T:0845 612 5567
www.boots-n-paddles.co.uk

**CALEY CRUISERS**
Cruiser holiday hire.
Inverness. T:01463 236328
www.caleycruisers.com

**CRUISE LOCH NESS**
Explore Loch Ness with the Royal Scot's under-water imagery, or take a faster trip in a RIB.
Fort Augustus. T:01320 366277
www.cruiselochness.com

**EUROPEAN WATERWAYS**
Scottish Highlander, a luxury hotel barge. Sleeps 8.
T:01784 482439
www.gobarging.com

**FINGAL OF CALEDONIA**
Converted barge hotel. Sleeps 12.
Corpach. T:01397 772167
www.fingal-cruising.co.uk

**LADY KATHRYN**
Private charter on 1920s cruiser.
Loch Ness. T:07772 447735

### Did you know?

The Great Glen Canoe Trail, Scotland's first official canoe trail, is being developed and is due to open in spring 2012. It will run along the entire length of the Caledonian Canal, a Scheduled Ancient Monument. There will be a new series of 'Trailblazer Rests' - informal campsites with basic facilities.

www.canoescotland.org

British Canoe Union
www.bcu.org.uk

**British Waterways**

"When I look at the bustling Forth & Clyde Canal today, it's hard to believe I stood on the banks and said "it will never happen" when people talked about reopening the lowland canals and making it possible to sail between the east and west coast again for the first time since the early 1960s.

When I joined British Waterways as a Junior Canal Man at 17 years of age, over 25 years ago, the Forth & Clyde Canal was riddled with Duckweed, was unloved and neglected by the local community and much of my day was spent clearing rubbish. Then, little by little, we began to see some money invested in the canal, first by the former Strathclyde Regional Council who commissioned new lock gates from the Maritime Museum in Irvine.

Then the canal societies and waterway enthusiasts began lobbying to reopen the canal. By 1996, people started talking about this as a reality but I genuinely never thought it would happen. There had been too many changes since the canal closed. How could they get under the M80 motorway?

The three-day celebration when the Forth & Clyde Canal opened just five years later was amazing. A barrel of water from the Forth on the east coast had been ceremoniously poured into the Clyde on the west coast as part of the original opening ceremony two hundred years ago. This time, in homage, we did it in reverse.

Then they said to me, "you won't recognise the canal in ten years' time" and, again, I didn't believe them! Today, once more I'm eating my words. There has been a dramatic transformation. I can't believe how many people visit the canal each day – not just boaters but people walking, cycling, running, looking at the wildlife and the heritage. It's fantastic. Next time, I'll probably just keep quiet."

# WILDLIFE & NATURE

The canals in Scotland are bursting at the seams with a huge variety of animals, fish and plants. The lucky visitor might see buzzards, red squirrels, wild otters, pine martens or even a wild cat!

Many areas have been designated as Sites of Special Scientific Interest (SSSI) - there are 22 SSSIs on or within 500m of Scottish canals.

### Beaver Trial

European beavers were reintroduced to the Knapdale Forest (to the south of the Crinan Canal) in 2009 for the first time in 400 years. The beavers are being closely monitored for a trial period of 5 years to see what impact they may have and whether long-term reintroduction can be successful. The Cairnbaan Hotel can arrange beaver-spotting tours near the hotel.

www.scottishbeavers.org.uk
www.cairnbaan.com

### Moine Mhor National Nature Reserve

Alongside the Crinan Canal, Moine Mhor ('great moss') is one of Britain's best examples of an estuarine lowland raised bog. You'll see sphagnum moss, dwarf shrubs, dragonflies, butterflies, deer and curlews - and there's a raised wooden walkway on the Tileworks Trail extending out over the bog to allow you a closer look. Clay used to be taken from the bog to be made into bricks or tiles by a local tileworks, hence the name. Some of the best views of the bog are from the canal towpath around Bellanoch.

www.nnr-scotland.org.uk

# Waterways people

Alec Howie, Harbour Master
Crinan Canal, British Waterways Scotland

**British Waterways**

"Flying over the Crinan Canal in my ex-RAF Fawke Motorglider, it's easy to see the appeal of 'Britain's most beautiful short-cut' as it has been called. Stretching over nine miles from Loch Fyne at Ardrishaig to the Sound of Jura, the Crinan Canal boasts, to me, some of the country's most unspoiled and picturesque countryside. It offers a gentle pace of life, a restorative experience, a chance to slow down for those who take time to stop awhile, walk or cycle the towpaths or cruise the waterway.

And stop they do, time after time after time. Indeed, it's true to say we see our returning visitors not as customers but rather as visiting 'friends' taking this most beautiful 'short-cut' which flows into world-renowned sailing waters or enjoying the wildlife, perhaps spotting one of the newly introduced Beavers.

As I tell people at the winter series of talks I give at the Yacht Club, I've worked for British Waterways Scotland for over thirty years and I continue to be extremely proud of the fact that this 200-year-old Scheduled Monument, with

its 15 locks, is an engineering marvel but there are no 'hands off' signs. It's a fabulous working museum which visitors can see, touch and really get to enjoy and engage with.

With such a hectic job, it's funny to think that in my spare time, I love to glide over the Canal but maybe that's just a measure of this stunning waterway and its ability to rejuvenate and refresh after a hard day's work."

251

# DAYS OUT
in Scotland

## FALKIRK WHEEL

The amazing Falkirk Wheel is a modern wonder of the waterways that opened in 2002. It is the world's first & only rotating boat lift, raising boats from the Forth & Clyde Canal 115ft up to the Union Canal. An incredible engineering marvel.

## Factfile

**Forth & Clyde / Union Canals**
Falkirk OS NS852801

Open Summer Daily 0930-1730
Nov - Feb Wed-Sun 1100-1600 (Nov - no Boat Trips)

Café and gift shop.

Entry FREE to Visitor Centre, grounds, café & gift shop.
Boat Trips (charge). Wheelchair access.

T:08700 500208
www.thefalkirkwheel.co.uk

# Waterways people
Craig Sear, Team Leader
The Falkirk Wheel
British Waterways Scotland

"I'm here because this is where I want to be. I'd worked for British Waterways in England for many years but when the opportunity arose to work on the multi-million pound Millennium Link project to reopen the Lowland canals and build The Falkirk Wheel, I jumped at the chance. With as many as eighteen bankside teams working on the Forth & Clyde Canal alone, it was hectic but very rewarding. Then, when the crowning glory, The Falkirk Wheel, took shape, I became fascinated with it. It's a remarkable piece of engineering.

I took my two year old son to watch the Queen officially open The Falkirk Wheel in 2002. Two years later, I joined as Team Leader.

There have been lots of great times. I thought I'd seen everything but, in September 2010, 60 boats sailed from Edinburgh to The Falkirk Wheel in celebration of the tenth anniversary of the reopening of the Union Canal. It was stunning to see 35 boats moored at the top locks and crowds on the towpath. That day, we took 25 boats down through the Wheel in just over four hours – an amazing feat with one boat every eleven minutes.

Perhaps most satisfying of all has been watching The Falkirk Wheel evolve. We have more children than ever visiting and people are realizing that, as spectacular as a journey on The Wheel is, there are plenty of other activities here. Just today, we had fifty schoolchildren walking around the pathways in their wellies. That's priceless!"

# Days out
## in Scotland

## Caledonian Canal

### CALEDONIAN CANAL VISITOR CENTRE
Find out the history of the Caledonian Canal.

Fort Augustus. OS NH377092

Open daily Apr-Oct 0930-1730. FREE admission. Gift shop. Wheelchair access.

T:01320 366493

### WEST HIGHLAND MUSEUM
Renowned for its collection relating to Bonnie Prince Charlie and the Jacobites.

Fort William. OS NN102738

Open Jun-Sep Mon-Sat 1000-1700, Oct-May Mon-Sat 1000-1600. Jul-Aug also Sun 1000-1600. Admission charge. Gift shop. Wheelchair access to the ground floor only.

T:01397 702169 www.westhighlandmuseum.org.uk

### WEST HIGHLAND STEAM TRAIN
'The Jacobite' runs from Fort William to Mallaig (it crosses the canal at the foot of Neptune's Staircase), following the route of Hogwarts Express in the Harry Potter films.

T:0845 1284681 www.steamtrain.info

### GLEN NEVIS VISITOR CENTRE
Just outside Fort William at the foot of Ben Nevis, the UK's highest mountain. Visitor centre with exhibition and shop.

Glen Nevis. OS NN114742

Open daily all year 0900-1700. FREE admission.

T:01397 705922 www.highland.gov.uk/glennevisvc

### CLAN CAMERON MUSEUM
The 'Battle of the Shirts' in 1544 was a violent battle fought on ground now underwater at the head of Loch Lochy. So called because it took place on a hot summer's day, and the oposing sides threw off their plaids and fought just in their shirts! Reputedly it was the largest and bloodiest inter-clan battle ever fought, with almost 1000 men in hand-to-hand combat.

The Frasers' and Grants' clans opposed a larger force of Clan Cameron & Clan Ranald, and were almost wiped out.

Achnacarry. OS NN175877

Open Apr-mid Oct 1330-1700. Jul-Aug 1100-1700. Small admission charge. Gift shop.

T:01397 712480 www.clan-cameron.org

### NEPTUNE'S STAIRCASE
A flight of 8 locks built by Thomas Telford near the start of the Caledonian Canal.

Corpach. OS NN095766

### CALEDONIAN CANAL CEILIDH TRAIL
July/August. A 4-week extravaganza of music, song & dance at venues around Loch Ness and along the Caledonian Canal.

www.visitlochness.com

## Crinan Canal

### CRINAN CLASSIC BOAT FESTIVAL
Held at the beginning of July. Scotland at its rugged best. The fishing village of Crinan hosts a festival of fierce boat racing, haggis hurling, boat jumble, Ceilidhs and whisky swilling. Bring a boat with you if you have one. Sailing boats, motorboats and dinghies to fishing boats. Don't go expecting formalities, the fun is ferocious.

Crinan. OS NR790943

T:01546 830261 www.crinanclassic.com

## Forth & Clyde Canal

### FALKIRK WHEEL
(Days Out page 252-253)

### KIRKINTILLOCH CANAL FESTIVAL
Held at the end of August. Live music, classic cars, boat trips, heritage exhibitions, arts & crafts market, fun fair and a Farmers' Market.

Kirkintilloch. OS NS655735

www.kirkintillochcanalfestival.org.uk

## Union Canal

### LINLITHGOW CANAL CENTRE
Canal Museum with heritage exhibition. Boat trips and chartered cruises. Day boat hire also available.

Linlithgow. OS NT003769

Open Easter to end September. FREE admission (charge for boat trips). Tea room. Wheelchair access.

T:01506 843194 www.lucs.org.uk

### LINLITHGOW PALACE
Birthplace of Mary, Queen of Scots. Ruined palace set by a loch (SSSI due to high wildfowl population) near the canal.

Linlithgow. OS NT001773

Open daily all year 0930-1730 (Oct-Mar to 1630). Admission charge. Wheelchair access. www.historic-scotland.gov.uk

# FOOD & DRINK

## Pubs
in Scotland

### Caledonian Canal
**MOORINGS HOTEL**

Canalside by Neptune's Staircase. Bar
with views of Ben Nevis. Dog-friendly.
Banavie. T:01397 772797
www.moorings-fortwilliam.co.uk

### Forth & Clyde Canal
**THE BOATHOUSE**
Canalside at Auchinstarry Marina.
Large bar/restaurant with 4-star rooms.
Great views from the terraces.
Kilsyth. T:01236 829200
www.boathousekilsyth.com

**THE WHEELHOUSE**
Ultra-modern stylish bar/restaurant with
views of the Falkirk Wheel.
Falkirk. T:01324 673490
www.wheelhousefalkirk.com

### Union Canal
**BRIDGE INN**
Friendly pub with good range of
real ales and locally sourced meals.
Restaurant boat trips available.
Ratho. T:0131 3331320
www.bridgeinn.com

**PARK BISTRO & RESTAURANT**
Linlithgow. T:01506 846666
www.theparkbistro.co.uk

**THE STABLES**
Large traditional stone pub with real
ales and real fire. Originally built in
1812 as stables for the boat horses.
Kirkintilloch. T:01417 776088
www.vintageinn.co.uk/
thestableskirkintilloch/

# Teashops
in Scotland

### Crinan Canal

**CAIRNBAAN HOTEL**
The hotel is on the 'Seafood Trail'
(www.theseafoodtrail.com).
Cairnbaan. T:01546 603668
www.cairnbaan.com

**CRINAN COFFEE SHOP**
Part of Crinan Hotel in stunning
scenery overlooking the bay.
Crinan. T:01546 830261
www.crinanhotel.com

### Caledonian Canal

**TELFORD TEAROOM**

Canalside between Top Lock and Loch
Lochy. Former lock-keeper's house
dating from the time the first lock was
built. Telford used to stay here during
his visits to the canal.
Gairlochy. T:01397 713900

### Union Canal

**LINLITHGOW CANAL CENTRE**

Canal Tea Room in former stables and
cottage. Part of the canal museum.
Available for private hire.
Linlithgow. T:01506 843194
www.lucs.org.uk

For listings of waterside pubs & teashops
in the UK, visit our website:
www.greatwaterwaysoutdoors.com

# WATERWAYS LIFE
## Hidden history

Along the waterways, grand buildings and mighty monuments shout loud enough to thrill us, but sometimes it's the humble quiet nuggets of history that inspire us the most. The canals of Britain are riddled with sweet secrets carved into the landscape. This isn't second-hand history written in a book - this is the canal writing its own life in its landscape.

### Stone masons' signatures

A stonemason's work was his pride, and along aqueducts and bridges you might spot a signature carved into the stonework.

### Datestones

Behind every brick it's easy to imagine a romantic story of the canal building era - but carved date stones that mingle amongst the brickwork give more straightforward answers. You will often find them at the edge of lock chambers.

### Rope marks

Peer under bridges and you might see gouged rope marks in the stonework, from horses that once towed heavy boats. If you run your fingers through the gouges, you are touching the daily toil of yesteryear's working boat horses. Precious history.

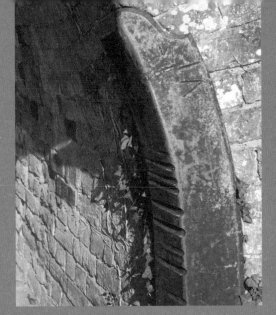

### Mileposts

Tucked amongst the ground foliage along almost every towpath you will spot mileposts scattered at regular intervals. Don't be fooled that these are merely dull iron or stone posts of no relevance to the leisure seeker - they are gems of history to the enquiring. Catch a glimpse of a milepost today and the Industrial Revolution is staring you in the eye. During the original working life of the canals, every canal company had its own style of mileposts. Canals were built under Acts of Parliament and mileposts were required to tell working boatmen the distances they had travelled and therefore how much toll would be due to canal companies who charged on a tonne and mile basis.

And the intrigue of the milepost's story doesn't stop with the Victorians - it rolls on into World War II, when it turned into a tale of national security. Many mileposts were removed to prevent Nazi invaders mapping the country. Some of those signs were lost or melted down for the war effort. When they were put back on the canal, to avoid confusion, new replica mileposts have usually been altered slightly from the originals.

(You don't need to wear an anorak to go milepost-spotting along the waterways!)

### Did you know?

Traditional canal pubs usually provided overnight stabling for the working boat horses that towed narrowboats. Sometimes the old stables have been integrated into today's pubs, and if you look closely tell-tale signs might remain.

Other pubs have retained great archways where horses once pulled their narrowboats to be loaded and unloaded.

### Traditional canal art

This was never art that was intended to hang cerebrally in galleries. Over 200 years ago, canal folk art was 'just' decoration, living colours daubed by the hands of ordinary boat people. A boatman's cabin was usually no more than a few feet long and 6 feet wide, yet crude roses and castles would have decorated almost every crevice and surface. Pots and pans, galley utensils galore, and even the boat horse's nosebag wouldn't have escaped the beautiful graffiti. Mania or magic, it's the art of the people, and a treasure of traditional culture that must be passed on for future generations.

No one knows why the original boat people chose the theme of roses and castles. Perhaps living in cramped quarters and economic hardship left them with dreams - and an English Rose might have been their garden and, as the saying goes, 'an Englishman's home is his castle'.

# THE BOOK
### Created in collaboration...
Britain's Great Waterways Outdoors

## coolcanals

The great British psyche makes us a nation of volunteers, ambassadors for good causes and entrepreneurs of charitable business. Great things have happened in the name of charity - RNLI, RSPCA, WRVS... and now our historic canals are set to be protected under the hat of a new British charity too. A new sort of national waterways trust.

Whilst the current political climate of our country makes much ado about 'The Big Society' and the pros and cons of chipping in without always asking to be paid for our labour - some might challenge why our nation's waterways heritage should be so underfunded from Government and left for the good deeds of volunteers. But Britain has a tradition of standing on its own feet with the legs of the great British volunteer. It's a spirit that gets things done when the cause is right.

So this nation has its sleeves rolled up and heads together for our great British waterways.

Once almost lost through neglect, canals are indebted to that stalwart bunch of volunteers, the IWA, who famously set out in 1946 to help British Waterways, and others, restore and save our waterways. Their's is a job done well, with modest magnificence, yet with plenty more still to be achieved.

2012 will bring the waterways into a new era with the launch of its official charitable status.

Canals are not only about boating - wildlife, heritage, green spaces, eco-tourism, car-free trails for bikes and boots and accessible linear parks in urban zones matter to many. And we asked some of the people who care about the inland waterways to contribute their specialist knowledge and experiences to this guidebook. In one voice, their different stories have offered a marvellously insightful picture of this destination. We thank them for their collaboration and for the vital work they all do.

# BW
## British Waterways

**British Waterways**

British Waterways (BW) cares for 2,200 miles of Britain's canals, rivers, docks and reservoirs, a network which is today more popular than ever with 13 million visitors every year and more boats than at the height of the Industrial Revolution.

Britain's waterway network represents one of the finest examples of working industrial heritage in the world and includes almost 3,000 protected heritage structures, such as locks, bridges and aqueducts, as well as five World Heritage Sites. BW cares for the UK's third largest collection of listed structures in the country and our heritage team ensure that these 250-year-old legacies of the Industrial Revolution can be enjoyed for generations to come.

BW's purpose is to maintain these historic waterways now and for future generations. Our engineers and canal bank staff carry out a diverse range of day-to-day activities from replacing lock gates and managing dangerous trees, to dredging the canal channel, repairing bridges and maintaining towpaths.

The waterways are also important wildlife habitats for a huge variety of animals and plants, providing vital green corridors connecting the countryside and the city. Our ecologists ensure that these biodiverse habitats are looked after and that rare and declining species are being conserved.

With more than 2,000 miles of towpaths to enjoy, cyclists, anglers, ramblers, commuters and joggers have a unique environment to enjoy. Combined with the thousands of boating enthusiasts that regularly use the canals, this adds up to an ever-growing supporter base. Volunteers are an important part of the work we do and volunteering activity has doubled since 2007. This includes a wide range of activities from graduate hydrologists seeking work experience to local business canal adoption schemes.

Of course, looking after a 250-year-old canal system isn't cheap. BW spends more than £100m every year on maintenance and repair alone and half of its budget comes from commercial income such as property, utilities and boat licensing. BW is working with Defra and other stakeholders on plans to transfer the canals and rivers in England and Wales into a new 'national trust' for the waterways in 2012. The move, which has been welcomed by a broad range of waterway stakeholders, will give the public and users a greater role in the running of their local waterway. It will enable the waterways to attract new sources of income from charitable sources, while protecting funding through a long-term funding contract from Government.

www.britishwaterways.co.uk
www.waterscape.com

*Created in collaboration...*
**Britain's Great Waterways Outdoors**

# IWA
## Inland Waterways Association

The Inland Waterways Association is a registered charity, founded in 1946, which advocates the conservation, use, maintenance, restoration and development of the inland waterways for public benefit.

IWA works closely with navigation authorities, national and local authorities, voluntary, private and public sector organisations. We campaign and lobby for support and encourage public participation in the inland waterways. IWA also manages the Chelmer & Blackwater Navigation for the public benefit, through its subsidiary Essex Waterways, having stepped in to prevent its closure in 2005 (www.essexwaterways.com).

IWA actively supports waterway restoration, and through its waterways restoration volunteering organisation, Waterway Recovery Group (see next page and www.wrg.org.uk), organises and subsidises over 20 week-long waterway restoration working holidays for volunteers of all ages throughout the UK each year, as well as conducting multiple work parties around the country on most weekends. This particularly enables young people to participate in the preservation and restoration of our heritage, and in doing so learn construction and heritage skills.

More than 500 miles of canals and navigable rivers have been re-opened to public use since the Association was founded in 1946. The Association is working to restore a further 500 miles of derelict inland waterways.

IWA is organised into 34 local branches covering geographical areas of the country, through which volunteers coordinate activities as diverse as policing planning applications through the waterway corridor, organising festivals and events to raise public awareness, providing engineering expertise, raising money for restoration schemes, and providing education on the value and benefits of their local waterways.

## Waterways people
**Liane Hunt**
**IWA 'Waterways' Art Editor**

Even offices working behind the scenes of the waterways leisure industry fall under the spell of the slow water road. A passion for water is contagious - and usually become an obsession.

Liane Hunt has been Art Editor on the IWA members's magazine 'Waterways' for several years, as well as working on a number of other IWA publications.

Partially inspired by her professional interest, Liane took her first narrowboat holiday last year - on the Grand Union Canal in Northamptonshire - and loved every moment of it. "Not only was it fun", she said, "but it increased my awareness of the issues surrounding the waterways. The canalside pubs were good too."

Liane lives by a canal with husband Dave and their King Charles spaniel Honey, and the couple chill out by walking the dog down by the marina... Boats, boats, boats!

> Find out more
> www.iwa.org.uk

*Created in collaboration...*
**Britain's Great Waterways Outdoors**

## Waterways people
**Ron and Mary - two people doing their bit to support Britain's canals**

Inland Waterway campaigners Ron and Mary Heritage cruised over 433 miles aboard their narrowboat Heron in 2010. Their trip retraced the famous journey Tom Rolt made on his crusading narrowboat Cressy in 1939. Tom's navigation was blighted by poor conditions and that was the reason he, and his friend Robert Aickman, formed the Inland Waterways Association (IWA) in 1946. Prior to Tom Rolt's vision, canals had been disregarded as old grimy trade routes, and so Rolt really is the father of canal leisure.

Ron and Mary and Heron set off from Banbury in April, travelling northwards through Middlewich and across to Chester before completing the route to Beale Park near Reading in time for the annual IWA Festival.

"We did the journey to draw attention to the potential problems for the waterways without funding and support." says Mary, "We can't just expect the waterways to be there. They'll go without support."

During the crowd-pulling celebrations along Heron's route, Mary met Tom's wife Sonia Rolt and asked her what she thought Tom would have made of the fuss. "He would have hated it!" said Sonia. Tom was a quiet man.

What was Mary's experience of the journey? "We took our time, had a natter. It was exhausting having to turn up at all the functions, but it was a lot of fun."

What was Mary's favourite canal on the route? "The Oxford Canal I think. And I loved the sunsets over the Weaver."

## Waterways people
**Colin Edmond - IWA Navigation Manager**

When, in 2005, the Inland Waterways Association took over the ailing Chelmer & Blackwater Navigation – under the auspices of subsidiary company Essex Waterways Ltd - they inherited Colin Edmond as the sole member of staff. Colin was taken on by the IWA as Navigation Manager, with day-to-day responsibility for the 14-mile waterway, as well as managing the Sea Lock at Heybridge Basin.

Colin wasn't always an inland waterways man. He started sailing on the Blackwater Estuary as a boy, and worked as a mate on a motorised sailing barge during the school holidays. After many years working as skipper of North Sea aggregate dredgers, he landed the job of lock-keeper at Heybridge Basin.

Colin describes working as Navigation Manager for IWA/Essex Waterways as a breath of fresh air. He now has a lock-keeper and full-time lengthsman to assist him, as well as part-time staff and local volunteers. Vast improvements have been made to the waterway over the past five years.

# WRG
## Waterway Recovery Group

waterway
recovery
group

Waterway Recovery Group had its origins in waterways restoration working during the 1960s, but formally came into being in 1970. The aim was to be the coordinating force, not centred upon any individual project but backing up and assisting local groups on any worthwhile restoration project. Since then considerable knowledge and experience of restorations methods have been built up. At present WRG owns a fleet of vans, and a range of plant including excavators, dumpers, pumps, mixers, winches, and other sundry equipment.

WRG has helped restore many derelict waterways throughout Britain - one of WRG's largest projects has been the complete rebuilding of the four Frankton Locks and the three Aston Locks on the Montgomery Canal, which passes through the spectacular Welsh Borders. Other projects include the construction of Over Basin on the Herefordshire and Gloucestershire Canal and more recently the restoration of Droitwich Barge Lock in the Midlands.

Thanks to the hard work of the volunteers, many canals have been reopened, while others are well on the way. Many more have not yet reached that stage - it is up to us, the volunteers, to demonstrate what can be done. We are not only doing useful work - and there is plenty left for us to do - we are also helping to convince those with the money (like the local authorities, and the National Lottery funds) that canals are worth restoring.

Created in collaboration...
**Britain's Great Waterways Outdoors**

## Go on a WRG CAMP

A holiday restoring canals! Go on a Canal Camp and become a modern day navvy. You don't need anything special... just a sleeping bag, pair of wellies, and a willingness to muck in. There's a job for everyone, no matter what skills you arrive with. WRG organisers say to first timers, "you are unlikely to feel a newcomer for long" - WRG camps are as legendary for sociability as they are for restoring the canals.

Expect mud, sweat and tears of laughter.

**Ju**
**WRG volunteer**

Age 42, Full-time Mum
"I went to a waterways festival several years ago and saw a lot of red WRG shirts around the site. I started by helping on the WRG North West stand and loved it, so progressed to camps. I really wish I had got into it a lot earlier. I have made so many great friends and trained on excavators and dumpers."

**Rowena**
**WRG volunteer**

Aged 29, Administrator
"I saw people in red shirts at an Inland Waterways Association National Festival and they seemed to be a great team. If they were having that much fun, I wanted to be a part of it too! I've now learnt how to drive an excavator and lay bricks."

**Adam**
**WRG volunteer**

Aged 27, Engineer
"I started WRG to find somewhere to put my skills to good use as I had been doing hands-on voluntary work for several years. I soon realised that I enjoyed it and I got on with the type of people that I met. It is a good sociable activity where you can have a laugh, good evening entertainment and see something that you have achieved - a load of bricks that have been laid, a section of canal dredged etc. I enjoy meeting up with the regulars once a month for the weekend digs/socials and it's given me a new circle of friends since leaving university."

GET INVOLVED!
www.wrg.org.uk

mud    sweat    and beers!

# RSPB CYMRU

RSPB Cymru is part of the RSPB, and speaks out for birds and wildlife, tackling the problems that threaten our environment. The conservation charity relies upon memberships and donations to fund its work.

RSPB Cymru recognises the importance of canals and rivers to the birdlife of the country. Not only do canals provide an important food source for many species, but the banks and verges also provide shelter and breeding areas which, after years of decline, are reviving and thriving.

Dr Sean Christian, RSPB Cymru's Head of Conservation says, "Our rivers and canals represent valuable wildlife corridors. They are nature's way of allowing the spread of species into new feeding and breeding grounds. The great thing for humans is that we can observe these natural events right in front of us, while enjoying all the benefits that our countryside offers."

**Reed Warbler (Acrocephalus scirpaceus)**

The reed warbler is a plain unstreaked warbler. It is warm brown above and buff coloured underneath. It is a summer visitor to breed in the UK, with the largest concentrations in East Anglia and along the south coast - there are relatively few breeding in Scotland and Ireland. It winters in Africa.

In the summer, can be looked for in reedbeds in lowland central and southern England and Wales - it is rarer elsewhere. Sings from within the reedbed rather than from a perch, so often heard rather than seen.

When to see them: Mid-April to early October.
What they eat: Insects; berries in autumn.

## How you can support us

Become a member or buy someone gift membership – annual membership includes free entry to over 100 nature reserves across the UK.

Make a donation – support the RSPB by making either a one-off donation, an on-going donation through payroll giving or funding a specific appeal.

Use our online shop - for bird supplies and other accessories.

Support our campaigns

Enjoy a great day out by visiting one of our nature reserves

Volunteer your time and skills

Visit www.rspb.org.uk

*Created in collaboration...*
**Britain's Great Waterways Outdoors**

### Kingfisher (Alcedo atthis)

Kingfishers are small unmistakable bright blue and orange birds of slow moving or still water. They fly rapidly, low over water, and hunt fish from riverside perches, occasionally hovering above the water's surface. They are vulnerable to hard winters and habitat degradation through pollution or unsympathetic management of watercourses. Kingfishers are amber listed because of their unfavourable conservation status in Europe.

They are widespread, especially in central and southern England, becoming less common further north but following some declines last century, they are currently increasing in their range in Scotland. Kingfishers are found by still or slow flowing water such as lakes, canals and rivers in lowland areas. In winter, some individuals move to estuaries and the coast. Occasionally they may visit garden ponds if of a suitable size.

When to see them: All year round.
What they eat: Fish and aquatic insects.

# WWT
## Wildfowl & Wetlands Trust

WWT is a leading wetland conservation organisation saving wetlands for wildlife and people across the world. It was founded in 1946 by the renowned naturalist and artist, the late Sir Peter Scott.

WWT's primary objective is to save wetlands and their wildlife by identifying and acting to counter the threats that affect their survival and, crucially, to enhance people's lives through learning about and being close to nature and inspiring them to take action.

From its humble beginnings at Slimbridge in Gloucestershire, sandwiched between the banks of the River Severn and the Gloucester Sharpness Canal, WWT now has a network of nine wetland visitor centres across the UK, including nationally and internationally important wetland habitats totalling 2,600 hectares. Our centres welcome over a million visitors each year, and over 200,000 members add their support to our cause.

*Created in collaboration...*
**Britain's Great Waterways Outdoors**

So why are wetlands so important?

Found from the poles to the tropics, from mountains down to the sea, wetlands are very diverse habitats including lakes, ponds, rivers and their floodplains, marshes, swamps, coastal waters and, of course, canals. Yet half the world's inland wetlands have been lost over the last century and with them their unique wildlife. Wetlands are being lost and degraded more rapidly than any other ecosystem.

Wetlands are essential for life on Earth. As well as storing and cleaning our water, they can help protect us from floods and storms. They also include some of the most productive and diverse living systems – they are the lifeblood of our planet.

Wetlands provide habitats for a wealth of animals and plants, from flamingos to swans, from marsh marigolds to mangroves, from water voles to dragonflies.

Millions of people depend directly upon wetlands for their livelihood and, in an increasingly urbanised and frenzied world, many millions more enjoy wetlands as places to walk, relax and get closer to nature.

Wetlands also play an important role in the regulation of greenhouse gases. They store large amounts of carbon, and can help protect against the effects of climate change by reducing flood risk, stabilising shorelines and controlling erosion. Climate change is a major threat likely to have significant impacts on freshwater systems with wide-ranging consequences for people and ecosystems.

Unfortunately, wetlands remain highly threatened. Reclaimed for building or agriculture, increasingly polluted and degraded, wetlands and their wildlife are among the first casualties of our drive for growth and development.

The wildlife that wetlands support is among the most threatened of all ecosystems: of inland wetland-dependent species, one third of all amphibians, 15% of wetland birds, over 40% of reptiles, 30% of mammals and 6% of fish species are globally threatened with extinction. Along with the wildlife, the many benefits that wetlands provide to people are also at risk.

# SUSTRANS
## Sustainable Transport

JOIN THE MOVEMENT

Sustrans is the UK's leading sustainable transport charity and is the organisation behind the award-winning National Cycle Network (NCN), Safe Routes to Schools, Bike It, TravelSmart, Active Travel, Connect2 and Liveable Neighbourhoods programmes - all projects that are changing our world one mile at a time. Our vision is a world in which people choose to travel in ways that benefit their health and the environment and to make this vision a reality we work on practical, innovative solutions to the transport challenges facing us all.

From the very beginning of its life 30 years ago, Sustrans recognised the enormous value the UK's waterways bring to the people of Britain. As well as being wonderful places to visit by boat or while away the hours with a fishing rod, our waterways attract millions of visits by walkers and cyclists every year because they provide enjoyable, safe, traffic-free journeys through some of Britain's most beautiful countryside, as well as into the hearts of our cities and communities.

Waterways have always played a crucial role in the ongoing success of the National Cycle Network and one of the earliest examples of this was the Kennet & Avon Canal between Reading and Newbury. The Kennet & Avon Cycle Route is now Britain's most popular long-distance waterside cycle, thanks to huge improvements made in partnership between Sustrans and British Waterways to long sections of the towpath, including the whole length from Bath to Devizes, around Newbury and between Thatcham and Reading. These kinds of projects continue to this day, the latest example being in Leeds where the Aire Valley Towpath has been completely resurfaced and new links created.

There are now over 650 miles of waterside routes that form part of the NCN, and there is more demand than ever from people to access the peaceful, pleasurable walking and cycling routes that waterways provide. If you want to find a route near you, simply go to www.sustrans.org.uk or take a look at some of our favourite routes in this brilliant book.

There's a wonderful world of waterways out there – we hope you enjoy them!

www.sustrans.org.uk

*Created in collaboration...*
**Britain's Great Waterways Outdoors**

4

NATIONAL
CYCLE
NETWORK

# USEFUL INFO
## WHO'S WHO

## The great engineers

**JAMES BRINDLEY (1716-1772)**
Pioneering genius responsible for the first canals and for developing the concept of canal networks.

**JOHN RENNIE (1761-1821)**
Famous for bridges and canal engineering, such as the Dundas Aqueduct on the Kennet & Avon Canal.

**JOHN SMEATON (1724-1792)**
The first person to call himself a 'civil engineer', differentiating between civilian and military projects so is the 'father' of civil engineering. Responsible for the Forth & Clyde, also renowned for his building of the third Eddystone Lighthouse (it survived over 120 years before being dismantled). 'Smeaton's tower' was rebuilt on Plymouth Hoe.

**THOMAS TELFORD (1757-1834)**
Prolific engineer responsible for marvels such as Pontcysyllte Aqueduct (now a World Heritage Site) and the second Harecastle Tunnel.

## The great entrepreneurs

**JOSIAH WEDGWOOD (1730-1795)**
Founder of Wedgwood pottery, he was quick to support canal development and collaborated with Brindley on the Trent & Mersey Canal. When complete, he was able to use the canal to transport clay to his factories & his finished goods to the ports.

**JOHN CADBURY (1801-1889)**
One of many Quaker social reformers and businessmen who supported the canals. Cocoa beans were carried by waterway from Bristol docks to Birmingham to the famous Cadbury's chocolate factories.

**SIR TITUS SALT (1803-1876)**
Wool baron who created Saltaire village (a World Heritage Site) for his mill workers on the Leeds & Liverpool Canal. Similar to Bournville village, built by John Cadbury's son for workers in Birmingham, Saltaire had a distinct absence of pubs due to his clean living idealistic influence, until a bar 'Don't Tell Titus' opened at Saltaire in 2007.

## Waterways

**BRITISH WATERWAYS (BW)**
(Page 264-265)

**WATERSCAPE**
BW's official leisure guide to canals, rivers and lakes.
www.waterscape.com

**INLAND WATERWAYS' ASSOCIATION**
(Page 266-267)

**WATERWAY RECOVERY GROUP**
(Page 268-269)

**THE CANAL TRUSTS AND SOCIETIES**
Tackling restoration and management of the inland waterways. Most canals have an active Trust or Society with regular events, meetings, talks and fundraising. Why not join your local canal society?

**THE WATERWAYS TRUST**
National charity promoting greater public enjoyment of the inland waterways.
www.thewaterwaystrust.co.uk

**ROYAL YACHTING ASSOCIATION**
The national body for all forms of boating, its work ranges from lobbying to training for professional qualifications.
www.rya.org.uk

**THE GREEN BLUE**
Helping boaters and waterside businesses reduce their impact on the environment.
www.thegreenblue.org.uk

## Art & Crafts

**WATERWAYS CRAFT GUILD**
Aims to maintain the high standards of traditional skills of waterways' arts and crafts. Membership for painters of narrowboats, giftware, roses & castles, also sign writers and makers of fenders, rope work, crochet work and cabin lace. They run courses in most traditional crafts at locations throughout the UK, with details on their website.
www.waterwayscraftguild.org.uk

**GUILD OF WATERWAY ARTISTS**
Formed to accredit and promote commercial art. Their website lists members of the Guild and exhibitions of their art around the country.
www.waterwayartists.org.uk

## Boating

**DRIFTERS BOATING HOLIDAYS**
Drifters is a consortium of boat hire operators on the canals. With 325 bases spread across the canals and rivers of England, Wales and Scotland, Drifters can get you anywhere you want to go on Britain's waterways. They offer a large choice of styles and layouts (nearly 500 boats - almost half the canal fleet) with quality gradings from 3-5 star, and different price levels.
www.drifters.co.uk

**HOSEASONS BOATING HOLIDAYS**
A large range of boating holidays in the UK, from narrowboats to cruisers.
www.hoseasons.co.uk

There are many small and family-run hireboat companies across Britain. We list them in the regions in this book, and you can find full listings on our website www.greatwaterwaysoutdoors.com

## Dogs

**HOW DOGS HAVING FUN WALKING THE CANALS CAN DO THEIR BIT TO HELP LESS FORTUNATE DOGS:**
Organise a fund-raising dog event, sponsored walk, canine towpath party... The possibilities are endless!
(Ask your local British Waterways staff for permissions)

- Support your local animal rescue centre

- Support the campaign against the obscene cruelty of organised torture in the dog meat trade www.wspa.org.uk

- Support www.dogstrust.org.uk

- Support www.rspca.org.uk

- Help stop UK puppy-trafficking trade www.rspca.org.uk/getinvolved/campaigns/puppytrafficking

## Horses

**HORSEBOATING**
The Horseboating Society's primary aim is to "preserve and promote horseboating". Membership is currently £10 per year & they're always keen for extra crew but, even if you're not able to get involved in any of their horseboating activities, your membership will help to ensure that the Society is able to continue with its aims.
www.horseboating.org.uk

**THE BROOKE**
On the canals today, working horses do their bit for eco-tourism, with good animal welfare demanded. But sadly,

less fortunate working horses, mules & donkeys in some of the poorest countries of the world can suffer violent hardship. The Brooke is a charity that aims to improve the lives of working animals - their work includes education, veterinary treatment and influencing governments to ensure animal welfare.
www.thebrooke.org

## Pubs

**PUB IS THE HUB**

Beer, cider, a packet of crisps, crackling in a bag, a Ploughman's or a plate of gourmet pub grub... Of all the things on offer in a pub, it's the space it provides for community that we probably value most. Many traditional and small pubs struggle to compete with bigger brands and chains, and tragically as many as 13 pubs a week are closing in the current climate. Pub is the Hub was initiated by HRH The Prince of Wales in 2001. It encourages rural pub owners, licensees & local communities to work together to help retain local services.
www.pubisthehub.org.uk

**CAMRA**
The Campaign for Real Ale campaigns for the appreciation of traditional beers, ciders and perries as part of our national heritage and culture. Also works to protect consumer rights and support the public house as a centre of community life.
www.camra.org.uk

## Waterways publications

**WATERWAYS WORLD**
www.waterwaysworld.com

**CANAL BOAT**
www.canalboat.co.uk

**TOWPATH TALK**
www.towpathtalk.co.uk

**CANALS & RIVERS**
www.canalsandrivers.co.uk

**NARROW BOAT**
www.narrowboatmagazine.com

## Tourist Boards

**VISIT BRITAIN**
www.visitbritain.com

**ENJOY ENGLAND**
www.enjoyengland.com

**VISIT SCOTLAND**
www.visitscotland.com

**VISIT WALES**
www.visitwales.com

## Travel

**BUSES:** Traveline
T:0871 2002233
www.traveline.org.uk

**TRAINS:** National Rail Enquiries
T:08457 484950
www.nationalrail.co.uk

## Walking, cycling & outdoors

**RAMBLERS' ASSOCIATION**
Walking information and canal walks
www.ramblers.org.uk

**DISABLED RAMBLERS ORGANISATION**
www.disabledramblers.co.uk

**SUSTRANS**
(Page 274-275)

**NATIONAL TRAILS**
www.nationaltrail.co.uk

**NATIONAL DISABLED ACCESS REG**
www.directenquiries.com

**GREAT WATERWAYS OUTDOORS**
www.greatwaterwaysoutdoors.com

## Wildlife

**RSPB**
(Page 270-271)

**WILDFOWL & WETLANDS TRUST**
(Page 272-273)

**THE WILDLIFE TRUSTS**
www.wildlifetrusts.org

**NATIONAL SWAN SANCTUARY**
www.theswansanctuary.org.uk

## Heritage

**NATIONAL WATERWAYS MUSEUM**
(Days Out page 180-181)

**GLOUCESTER WATERWAYS MUSEUM**
(Days Out page 54-55)

**STOKE BRUERNE WATERWAYS MUSEUM**
(Days Out page 97)

**LONDON CANAL MUSEUM**
(Days Out page 93)

**FOXTON INCLINED PLANE MUSEUM**
(Days Out page 138-139)

## Canal blogs & forums

**GRANNY BUTTONS**
www.grannybuttons.com

**COOL CANALS**
www.coolcanalsguides.com

**JUSTCANALS**
www.justcanals.com

# USEFUL INFO
## HOLIDAYS &
## SHORT BREAKS

### A waterways destination

The inland waterways are a destination to care about and use. A far-away place right on the doorstep, with new things to explore... and you don't even need a passport.

Thousands of us every year enjoy boating, but waterways holidays and short breaks don't always have to be afloat. The magic of the water can be savoured in countless ways. Be a towpath tourist and discover your own slow adventures.

There's accommodation to suit every taste. From cosy waterside inns to luxurious hotels, and from floating B&Bs to 5-star cruises.

### Cottages

Sleep in a historic lock-keeper's cottage with waterways heritage trickling through every nook and cranny. In the heyday of the canals, a lock keeper would be up before the ducks to look after his patch and make sure working boats travelled smoothly through the locks. It's a lazier affair today with lock cottages for holiday hire and relaxing weekends away from it all.

**5 WATERSIDE COTTAGES**
Whipcott Water Cottages 4-star, Grand Western Canal
Lock View Cottage 4-star, Kennet & Avon Canal
Lengthsman's Cottage, Stratford-on-Avon Canal
No. 3 Aqueduct Cottages, Llangollen Canal
Ness View Cottage, Caledonian Canal

For full listings of these & other waterside cottages in the UK, visit our website: www.greatwaterwaysoutdoors.com

### Camping & caravanning

A full day outdoors... then wind down watching the sun set over the water with a glass of wine in your hand. From the ducks stirring at dawn to the last clink of a mooring ring as boats moor up for the night - it's the sounds, smells and sights that make camping on the waterside so special.

**5 WATERSIDE CAMPSITES**
Pencelli Castle 5-star, Mon & Brec Canal
Barge Inn, Honeystreet, Kennet & Avon Canal
Wern Isaf Farm (short walk to the canal, Llangollen Canal
Eshton Road Caravan Park, Leeds & Liverpool Canal
Or why not go wild camping in Scotland?

For full listings of these & other waterside campsites in the UK, visit our website: www.greatwaterwaysoutdoors.com

### Walking & cycling holidays

All you need is on your back. Less is more. The adventure of travelling the towpaths, moving on every morning to discover what's round the next corner is thrilling. This isn't perilous orienteering, it's easy trail-blazing, peacefully off-grid with wildlife and nature, twinned with engineering wonders and heritage. The soft adventure of the great waterways outdoors.

How far you walk is up to you. Canal walking can be anything from slow sightseeing with dawdling over lunch in the pub - to the challenge of a full coast-to-coast walk along the towpaths.

The Kennet & Avon Canal is a good coast-to-coast link in the South. The Leeds & Liverpool Canal is a good coast-to-coast link in the North. And of course the Caledonian is Scotland's big coast-to-coast.

Full listings of all types of waterside accommodation, places to eat and everything you'll need to plan your holiday are on our website: www.greatwaterwaysoutdoors

And don't forget to tell us about your holidays - send stories, tips and snapshots to the website.

## Hotel boats

Be pampered. A holiday on a hotel boat is one you'll never forget. You can choose anything from a small friendly narrowboat hotel company such as Taurus and Snipe (Canal Voyagers) cruising the historic waterways of England, to a big converted barge cruising the Great Glen in the Highlands of Scotland.

### Factfile

**HOTEL BOATS**

Away4awhile: Single narrowboat. 3-star. Sleeps 6
T:0845 6445144 www.away4awhile.co.uk

Bywater Hotelboat Cruises: Traditional pair. Sleeps 8
T:07775 850098 www.bywaterhotelboats.co.uk

Canal Voyagers: Traditional boat pair. 4-star. Sleeps 9
T:07921 214414 www.canalvoyagers.com

Duke & Duchess: Traditional boat pair. 4-star. Sleeps 8
T:07711 836441 www.hotelboat-holidays.co.uk

English Holiday Cruises: Edward Elgar. Sleeps 22
T:0845 6017895 www.englishholidaycruises.co.uk

Fingal of Caledonia: Converted barge. Sleeps 12
T:01397 772167 www.fingal-cruising.co.uk

European Waterways: Luxury all-inclusive hotel-barges in the UK & Europe T:01784 482439 www.gobarging.com

LadyLine Hotel Boats: Two boats. 4-star. Sleep 8
T:07986 133122 www.ladylinehotelboats.co.uk

Periwinkle: Single narrowboat. 4-star. Sleeps 3
T:07747 017263 www.hotelboatperiwinkle.com

Reed Boats: Traditional hotelboat pair. 4-star. Sleeps 8
T:07977 229103 www.reedboats.co.uk

Takara: Single narrowboat. Sleeps 4
T:07981 798272 www.hotelboat.co.uk

Tranquil Rose: Widebeam barge. 4-star. Sleeps 9
T:07966 248079 www.tranquilrose.co.uk

Willow: Single narrowboat. Sleeps 2. Private charter only
T:07702 242100 www.hotelnarrowboat.com

For full listings of hotel boats in the UK, visit our website:
www.greatwaterwaysoutdoors.com

### Go canal bagging - by boat, bike or boot

There are people who scramble up and down the 283 Scottish 'Munros', ticking the peaks off a list, one by one. They are called Munro baggers. Munro-bagging wouldn't be our cup of tea – but we may be the first to officially declare a new craze of canal bagging.

Boaters have a tradition of displaying brass plaques on the doors of their boats, in an exhibition of their cruising credentials. (Each canal has its own plaque to collect). But a well-polished collection of plaques isn't just a display of pride, it's a reliable conversation starter for canal-camaraderie.

In our narrowboat, Bhaile, we've cruised many of the canals connected in the main networks... we've cycled a few further away... and we have walked the canals of Britain coast-to-coast and end-to-end from Cornwall to Scotland, following the water road through the Welsh mountains, over the Pennines, treading AONB, National Parks and brushing almost every National Trail. We've hiked across the Peak District, the Cotswolds, along the Great Glen Way, into the Lake District and even through London by the backdoor. But when we think we've ticked every canal in Britain off our list, we stumble on another hidden waterway to explore. The journey is addictive!

Canal bagging can be fun whether you travel by narrowboat, bike, boot, wheelchair, canoe.

Join the Canalbagging conversation...
www.canalbagging.com

# USEFUL INFO
## GLOSSARY

**AQUEDUCT:** structure carrying a canal over a road, railway or river

**ARM:** short stretch of canal branching off from the main canal

**BARGE:** cargo-carrying boat which is 16ft wide or more

**BEAM:** width of a boat

**BOW:** front of a boat

**BROAD CANAL:** over 7ft 6in wide

**BUTTY:** unpowered boat towed by another boat with an engine

**CANALIA:** gifts and crafts related to canals

**CRATCH:** triangular structure at bow of boat

**CRUISER:** pleasure boat usually made of wood or fibreglass

**CRUISER STERN:** extended external space at rear end of a narrowboat

**CUT:** slang for canal

**DOLLY:** post for mooring ropes

**FENDER:** external bumper, usually made of rope, to protect boat hull

**FLIGHT:** series of locks close together

**GONGOOZLER:** Boaters' lingo describing onlookers

**GUNWALES:** (pronounced 'gunnels') ridge to walk on along sides of a boat

**IDLE WOMEN:** the cheeky nickname given to the women who worked on canal boats during World War II to help the war effort. The name came from the initials 'IW' on the Inland Waterways badges they wore.

**IWA:** Inland Waterways' Association

**JUNCTION:** where two or more canals meet

**LEEDS & LIV:** popular nickname for the Leeds & Liverpool Canal

**LEGGING:** lying on top of boat and using legs on walls to push boat through tunnel

**LOCK:** a water-holding chamber with gates and paddles to lift boats up and down hills

**MILEPOST:** short posts informing boatmen about distances travelled

**MON & BREC:** popular nickname for the Monmouthshire & Brecon Canal

**MONTY:** popular nickname for the Montgomery Canal

**NARROWBOAT:** canal boats which are no wider than 7ft

**NARROW CANAL:** canals built for boats up to 70ft long and 7ft wide

**NAVVIES:** nickname for the navigators who dug the canals

**PORT:** left side of boat when facing the bow

**POUND:** stretch of level water between locks, whether a few feet or a few miles

**ROSES AND CASTLES:** traditional folk art

**SCUMBLE:** paint technique simulating the appearance of wood grain

**SILT:** mud that builds up at bottom of canal

**STAFFS & WORCS:** popular name for Staffordshire & Worcestershire Canal

**STARBOARD:** right side of the boat when facing the bow

**STAIRCASE LOCKS:** locks close together without pounds in between

**STERN:** the rear of a boat

**TILLER:** steering wheel of a boat, shaped like a pole

**TOWPATH:** path alongside canal built for working horses pulling boats

**TUG:** boat that pulls another boat

**TUPPERWARE:** irreverent name narrowboaters give fibreglass boats

**WIDE BEAM NARROWBOAT:** boat that looks like a narrowboat but is wider than 7ft 6in

**WINDLASS:** hand tool used to wind lock paddles up and down

# INDEX

# ABOUT COOLCANALS

## Phillippa & Martine
towpath tourists, waterways nomads...

Dressed in her bell-bottoms, Phillippa first went to the waterways in the 1970s, to help out on a family-run hotel narrowboat. She's been hooked ever since. Martine has lived in Ireland, Spain and countless land-locked parts of England - with incurable wanderlust, it made sense to live on a narrowboat so that her home could move with her.

Martine and Phillippa built their own narrowboat home and set off exploring the water roads with their four cats. The slow life suited them and the waterways have become the passion they share in their guides.

They've also walked the towpaths from Cornwall to Scotland, and continue to be amazed by the waterways.

## More of our books

### 'Cool canals Weekend Walks'

Some of our favourite canal walks from across Britain. With all the guide info you'll need and even places to stay if you decide to make a weekend of it.

### 'Cool canals Pub Days Out'

Soak up the charms of some special canalside pubs. Every pub is handpicked for its own virtues and its idyllic canal location - plenty for a full day out.

www.coolcanalsguides.com

**coolcanals**

## Visit our leisure website

Helping you plan your waterways leisure time, with full listings of everything you'll need - from waterside campsites and boating to dog-friendly pubs and teashops.

And be the first to hear about special offers, news and competitions - or join in with the canal-chat!

www.greatwaterwaysoutdoors.com

greatwaterwaysoutdoors●com